Praise for *Wyrdworking*

"Alaric has done it yet again. In *Wyrdworking*, he makes the magical wisdom of the Anglo-Saxons very accessible to today's practitioners. Without denying the modern world and other occult traditions, he remains true to the culture and practices of the Saxons and clearly demonstrates how we can follow this path of magick. His teachings make me appreciate the Anglo-Saxon practices found in modern Witchcraft and want to dive deeper into their heritage."

—Christopher Penczak, author of *The Mystic Foundation* and The Temple of Witchcraft series

Praise for *Travels Through Middle Earth*

"This book is a thorough and enjoyable voyage into the heart of modern Anglo-Saxon spirituality. With his breezy style and quick wit, the author displays a practical approach to this religion that is both fascinating and informative. I heartily recommend this book to everyone, particularly folks new to this path!"

—Reverend Kirk S. Thomas, ADF Vice-Archdruid

Joan Stewart

About the Author

Alaric Albertsson began his spiritual journey when he was introduced to the Anglo-Saxon gods and goddesses in 1971. Over the past four decades, his personal spiritual practice has developed as a synthesis of Anglo-Saxon tradition, country folklore, herbal studies, and rune lore. A native of Missouri and Arkansas, Alaric now resides in western Pennsylvania, where he is a founding member of Earendel Hearth, an Anglo-Saxon *inhíred*. For more information, visit www.alaricalbertsson.com.

wyrdworking

To Write to the Author

If you wish to contact the author or would like more information about this book, please write to the author in care of Llewellyn Worldwide and we will forward your request. Both the author and publisher appreciate hearing from you and learning of your enjoyment of this book and how it has helped you. Llewellyn Worldwide cannot guarantee that every letter written to the author can be answered, but all will be forwarded. Please write to:

Alaric Albertsson
c/o Llewellyn Worldwide
2143 Wooddale Drive
Woodbury, MN 55125-2989

Please enclose a self-addressed stamped envelope for reply,
or $1.00 to cover costs. If outside the U.S.A., enclose
an international postal reply coupon.

Many of Llewellyn's authors have websites with additional information and resources. For more information, please visit our website at:

www.llewellyn.com

wyrdworking

the path of a saxon sorcerer

ALARIC ALBERTSSON

Llewellyn Publications
Woodbury, Minnesota

FIRST EDITION, 2011
First Printing, 2011

Cover design by Kevin R. Brown
Cover images: background © Brand X Pictures;
    leaves © PhotoDisc;
    mortar and pestle © iStockphoto.com/Ales Veluscek
Editing by Nicole Edman
Interior illustrations by Llewellyn art department

Llewellyn is a registered trademark of Llewellyn Worldwide Ltd.

Library of Congress Cataloging-in-Publication Data
Albertsson, Alaric.
  Wyrdworking : the path of a Saxon sorcerer / by Alaric Albertsson. —
1st ed.
    p. cm.
  Includes bibliographical references and index.
  ISBN 978-0-7387-2133-0
  1. Magic, Anglo-Saxon. 2. Druids and druidism. I. Title.
  BF1622.A53A43 2011
  133.4'3—dc22
                    2010026992

Llewellyn Publications
A Division of Llewellyn Worldwide Ltd.
2143 Wooddale Drive
Woodbury, MN 55125-2989
www.llewellyn.com

Printed in the United States of America

Contents

MORE MAGIC TECHNIQUES

Acknowledgments

A book is much like a ship in that it requires more than the person at the helm if it is to reach its destination. Others are needed to row and help with the sails if the book is to carry its cargo of information successfully to its destination, the reader. So many people have contributed to *Wyrdworking: The Path of a Saxon Sorcerer* in one way or another that I do not even know how to begin to thank everyone.

Christopher Penczak has consistently supported my writing, and neither this book nor the preceding one would have come about were it not for his encouragement. I have to thank my acquisition editor, Elysia Gallo, who has helped give the book a more polished tone. Kevin R. Brown has once again created a striking and beautiful book cover. Bryan Chick's suggestions have shaped the style of the book; he reminded me that *Wyrdworking* will be, for most readers, a textbook on magic rather than an abstract study of the subject. Taren Martin kept me focused on the rune chapters. I want to thank Barbara Criswell, of Aquarius Books in Kansas City, whose support and belief in my work helps me keep believing in myself. Of course I need to thank those who contributed so generously to the content of this book, including but not limited to Jesse Garrison, Tina-Lisa Agresta, West Hardin, Deana Isendun, and Maria Stoy. I am grateful for the support and encouragement of ADF druid friends, such as the Reverend Kirk Thomas, Diane "Emerald" Bronowicz, Robb Lewis, and others. Judy DeRousse corrected endless grammatical errors for me and helped polish the manuscript with a smoother writing style. Perhaps more than anyone else, though, I need to thank Scott, who not only inspires me, but who also put up with my long absences and distraction as I crafted this book.

Finally, I want to thank Benjamin Brown, who left our Middle Earth twenty years ago. Although he is gone, he is never forgotten, for he helped shape and guide me in ways that I did not fully appreciate then, but so deeply appreciate now. It is to him, a great sorcerer, that *Wyrdworking* is dedicated.

Introduction

In my book *Travels Through Middle Earth: The Path of a Saxon Pagan*, I presented no more than a cursory look at magic. As I stated in my introduction then, "Spells and runes and charms have their place, of course, but this [book] is not that place."

Now, here in this new introduction, I can say that *this* book is the place to find the magic of Saxon sorcery.

Within these pages you will learn how to craft rune charms, brew potions, and cast effective spells. You will learn magical techniques to find love and prosperity. Whether you are merely curious, or if you seek to fully accept the responsibilities of a Saxon *drýmann* (druid), you will find a wealth of useful information here. *Wyrdworking* is a culmination of my own forty years' experience with magic. For me, magic is intriguing and fairly easy to master as a skill. Let me emphasize that this does not mean I am better or more enlightened than a Saxon Pagan who has no interest in the subject. In fact, there are days when I wish that I could trade magic in for a more dependable skill, like carpentry or perhaps tailoring. Unfortunately, I am hopeless with a hammer and sewing machines baffle me. If magic does not come naturally to you, rest assured that there is no reason you need to pursue these arts. There are many ways in which each of us can contribute to our continually evolving contemporary Pagan culture, and magic is just one possibility—just one potential path along your own journey through Middle Earth.

If you do have an interest in pursuing the arcane arts, then read on! We will begin this particular journey by defining precisely what we mean by *magic*, and by defining its nature. I feel that this is essential to any intelligent discussion of the subject. Modern English often has a fluid vocabulary, allowing me to say one thing and you to hear something entirely different. Take the word *love*, for example. You can "love" your husband or wife, and you can "love" beagles, yet these are (hopefully) two completely different kinds of love. The word *magic* is equally mutable. Some people use it for rituals and exercises intended solely to promote personal transformation. But this book is not about personal growth (which was addressed in *Travels Through Middle Earth*); this book will move past the fundamentals of personal growth and spirituality to explore old-fashioned, cauldron-stirring, spellcasting *wiccecræft*.

After we've identified our definition of magic, the next two chapters will take you through an inventory of what you will and will not need to develop a practice as a Saxon sorcerer. Your list of equipment—your tools and supplies—will vary according to your personal needs. A person who specializes in *wortcunning* will obviously want to have a fairly extensive selection of herbs on hand, whereas a *rúnwita* may only need a few or none at all.

We will then explore the Anglo-Saxon runes in depth. Runes are the characters of magical alphabets once used in northern Europe. My initial plan was to present the runes in a separate volume, but they are so fundamental to Saxon magic that I eventually decided to combine the rune book with a book covering other magical techniques. Fully half of *Wyrdworking: The Path of a Saxon Sorcerer* is devoted to the runes. I believe that I have made the runes, at least the Anglo-Saxon runes, more "user friendly" in this book. I take a different approach from that of authors who have traditionally presented the runes in an ABC order. Instead I present them in conceptual groupings, beginning with runes describing trees and plants, then animal runes, and so forth. I also encourage readers to divorce themselves from the idea that runes are primarily a tool for divination. They can be used for that purpose—and this book includes instructions for crafting your own set of divination runes—but the runes are also powerful tools for active magical workings.

The runes were also used for writing, and I know that many of you will want to make use of them in this way. In Appendix C you will find instructions for this, as the runes do not correspond exactly with the Roman alphabet we now use.

The chapters on runes are followed by a discussion of *galdor*, or incantations. This word, *galdor*, is related to the Old English verb *galan*, meaning "to sing or call out." The power of the spoken word is well attested to in Saxon lore, and we have many Old English charms to illustrate the basic techniques for producing effective "sound magic." We will look at some of these techniques and also explore how to combine galdor with other modalities.

After this we will look at wortcunning, the art of working magic with leaves, roots, and flowers. This is a favorite topic of mine. It is often called herbalism or herbology, but I feel that these words focus one's attention specifically on remedial (healing) herbs. Wortcunning includes this aspect, especially when the healing procedure falls into the definition we will establish for "magic," but it is also much more. Herbs are as versatile as runes and incantations when it comes to working magic. In the chapter on wortcunning, you will learn how to prepare herbal potions and ointments for a variety of purposes.

Although runes can be used for more than divination, a chapter devoted to *wiglung* (soothsaying) is essential for a book like this. An aspiring Saxon sorcerer will be much more effective at tackling a problem if he or she can discern potential forces shaping *wyrd* (destiny) as it unfolds. It is in this later chapter (rather than in the rune chapters) that we will explore runic wiglung, or divination, a topic that tends to dominate the numerous rune books available today. The primary difference between this book and many others is that the Saxon sorcerer will be using the Anglo-Saxon Futhorc runes, which have nine more characters than the Elder Futhark symbols commonly sold as "rune stones." We'll also look at a smaller but extremely effective set of symbols that I call wyrd stones. These are usually painted or engraved on small rocks. As an alternative to these symbol-oriented techniques, I will also discuss scrying, as well as methods of "world walking" that were briefly described in *Travels Through Middle Earth*.

After covering these modalities, we will explore how they can be combined to address common concerns relating to the human condition: health, love, and prosperity. The book then concludes by explaining how to incorporate all of this into your own life to develop a personal magic practice that reflects your own talents and interests.

Getting Started

The Nature of Magic

Before we can begin a reasonable dialogue about magic, we must first define what we mean by this term. *Magic* has come to mean many different things to people. There are some people who apply the word to almost any phenomenon—love, life, snow, rainbows, poetry—often to a point where it loses all meaning. Romantic applications of the word similar to these examples are beyond the definition of *magic* that we will be using in this book.

Conversely, pop culture often presents us with a dynamic vision of magic that is both fantastic and explosive. Whether it is the students of Hogwarts swishing and flicking their wands or Samantha Stevens twitching her nose, most of us have grown up exposed to these wondrous and exciting images of magic. However, these concepts too are beyond the definition we will be using. Fictional magic is great entertainment, but real magic is rarely so flashy or spectacular. Real magic does not create something impossible; it emphasizes possibilities. Real magic is, above all else, "real." It is *super*natural, but it is in no way *un*natural. Its effects can almost always be explained away or rationalized within the parameters of natural law.

The definition of *magic* that we'll be using is embedded in the title of this book, *Wyrdworking*. The Old English *wyrd* refers to the process in which the future unfolds from all of our past words and deeds. Wyrd is often interpreted as "fate" or "destiny," but that is a rough translation at best. Wyrd is similar to the ripples on a pond that move outward from a single action—perhaps from a fish breaking the surface, or a stone dropping into the water. Magic is the art of working with that process. It is the art of shaping the ripples as they emerge, and thus influencing future possibilities.

Real magic affects the world much as a smile can affect the world. There is no exact science to smiling, but most of us instinctively make use of this technique to shape our environment. A person—adult or child—who feels threatened will very often give an appeasing or apologetic smile. Another person hoping to make a strong impression will flash a confident smile. A mother coaxes her child by offering an encouraging smile. There's no certainty that the smile will be rewarded with its desired effect. The cynic will argue that a smile will not stop a bully, that it will not result in a promotion, and that a child may fail regardless of how often or how bravely a parent smiles. And yet we humans continue to smile, not only to express joy, but because we know in our hearts that a smile can and does shape the world around us.

Likewise, when you cast a spell or carry a charm in your pocket, there is no certainty that the magic will work. In fact, there is an excellent chance it will not, if that is all you do. I once knew a man who burned candles, chanted, and cast spells every single day to find employment. Weeks grew into months, but the man remained unemployed. Of course, if he had gone out and applied for a job somewhere—anywhere—his chance of success would have improved significantly. Magic does not shatter reality. Magic shapes reality to your advantage by subtly shaping your wyrd.

Magic and spirituality often overlap, but they are not the same thing. In Pagan religions especially, magic and spirituality often tend to be confused with one another. I think this is because magic is an inherent feature in Wicca, the religion largely responsible for the modern revival of Paganism. The religion of Wicca was envisioned, or created, primarily by Gerald Brousseau Gardner (1884–1964). Gardner claimed his religion to be a survival of a pre-Christian cult, but there is no question that his version of this "cult" (a word that has since taken on a negative connotation) was heavily influenced by his own interests in ceremonial magic and naturism. In fact, the very word *Wicca*—which Gardner himself spelled as Wica—is an Old English word that, in its original form, simply meant a man who works magic. A Saxon *wicca* may indeed be a very spiritual man, but the Old English word has no more to do with religion or spirituality than other Old English words like *hunticge* (a woman who hunts) or *gristra* (a man who grinds flour and bakes bread). Gardner's Wicca, because of his own interest in magic, was presented as an expression of spirituality that included a heavy dose of ceremonial magic. And because of Gardner's interest in naturism, nudity was the standard dress code for Wicca rituals.

Nudity has been largely abandoned outside of the Gardnerian Wicca tradition, but newer Wicca traditions as well as many Wicca-derived paths still consider magic to be an inherent aspect of spirituality. For many Pagans today, a religious ritual begins by casting a magic circle and balancing arcane energies. There is nothing inherently wrong with this. But in pre-Christian Saxon culture, and indeed all Indo-European societies, real magic was only incidentally related to spirituality. Only a minority of Saxons practiced wiccecræft, working magic for themselves and perhaps those closest to them. Most went to a professional—a Saxon druid (*drýmann* or *drýicge*)—when they needed magical assistance.

Admittedly, magic and spirituality often overlap. Both are tools for affecting change, and so it is not uncommon for a sorcerer's spirituality to intrude upon his magical practice, and vice versa. Jesse Garrison, a Pagan man from Arkansas whom I have known for a number of years, makes this distinction between his magic and his spirituality:

Some magick does involve asking the gods for things, but most of that is just as easily handled by prayer and sacrifice. The way I distinguish between the two is that prayer is asking the gods to intervene on your behalf, while magick is bending the universe itself to your Will, occasionally with the help of one or more gods. It's a passive/active thing. Either way, you decide where you want to go, but the difference is in who's driving and who gets to pick the road.

When we pray, we are speaking directly to our gods or to other spirits. Just as there are many reasons we speak to mortal friends and neighbors, there can be many reasons to pray. We may pray to give thanks. When confronted with a problem, we may pray for guidance. And it is not uncommon at all for people to pray when they need a favor. But a prayer for a boon or favor is nevertheless a prayer. It is not magic.

Jesse Garrison hits the nail on the head when he describes this distinction as a "passive/active thing." When we pray for a boon, we are asking someone else—some spirit, whether it is a god or the spirit of an ancestor or some local nature spirit—to affect a change. And there is nothing wrong with this, so long as you recognize that this is a request for a favor, and not a magical act. People who confuse magic with spirituality will sometimes ask me which god or goddess they should pray to for a specific need. If, for example, you were facing a civil trial, it might make sense to pray to the Saxon god Tiw, since he is sovereign over law and justice. But if you have no relationship with Tiw, if you have never prayed to him before or given any offering to honor him, then why should he care what happens to you? You would be approaching him like a beggar asking for spare change. He might help you out, but it is very likely that he will not. When you pray for a boon, the proper deity to pray to is whichever god or goddess you have a good relationship with.

And as Jesse points out, effecting change through prayer is a passive act. You are handing over the reins to somebody else. At times this can be beneficial and the best course of action. But while the outcome may please you, you are not the one shaping the ripples. This is how prayer differs from real magic. When you cast a spell or carve a runic charm or brew a potion, you are directly working to effect a change. It is you doing the work, not somebody else. The Saxon sorcerer actively reaches out to shape the ripples, to shape his or her wyrd.

This shaping is accomplished through a variety of techniques using sounds and symbols and natural substances. We will examine these techniques throughout the rest of this book. Some skills, or *cræftes*, may come easily for you, while you may decide to ignore others altogether. The important thing to keep in mind is that these skills are not directly related to spirituality. Working magic does not make you a "better" Pagan than the next person, and it does not mean you are more spiritual—although when done properly, magic can and should make your life run more smoothly.

Of course, as a Saxon sorcerer, you may indeed happen to be a very spiritual person. This is where the magic-versus-spirituality thing gets a little murky. It is not unusual to combine prayer and magic, which makes sense when you understand and appreciate the difference between the two. When confronted with a simple problem, the Saxon sorcerer may simply carve a bindrune to handle the situation himself. When confronted with a larger problem, the same person may carve a bindrune (active magic) and also ask for some help from a god or ancestor (prayer).

———

Now that I have said this, I have to add that although spirituality and magic are not the same thing, it is important to be grounded in the former if you want to be fully effective in the latter. Every culture has its own individual approach to magic. Græco-Egyptian magic bears little resemblance to traditional English folk magic, and both of these are different from the magic practiced in the

Caribbean. Within any given indigenous culture, religious and magical practices have evolved from that culture's world view. Thus, if you would understand Saxon magic, I encourage you to also develop an understanding and appreciation of Saxon spirituality. *Travels Through Middle Earth: The Path of a Saxon Pagan* is a good introduction if you are not already familiar with Saxon beliefs and customs.

In Saxon belief, to give one example, the "Self" consists of much more than just body + soul. The *lic* (physical body) is just one of nine parts of the Self, all of them bound together by the *æthem*, or breath of life. Practitioners of Saxon magic are aware of these nine parts of the Self and how these affect their work. Let us look at these nine parts before we go further.

The Lic (Physical Body)

The *lic* (pronounced like "leech") is as much a part of this equation as any other part of the Self. As Jan Fries asserts in his book *Helrunar*, the physical body is "our medium of interaction with the world" (p. 184). Your physical body is the part of you that interfaces directly with Middle Earth. When the æthem vanishes at the end of a person's days and the various parts of that person disperse, his or her lic literally returns to the earth. This process of returning to the earth actually occurs on a lesser scale throughout our lives, even though we are usually unaware of it. Every day, skin cells and hairs fall away from your body and return to the earth, eventually becoming part of the soil beneath your feet.

Conversely, the lic is continually sustained by the earth. The food that keeps us alive pushes up and out from the soil, and so this part of the Self is simultaneously a part of the earth. Your lic is constantly replenished by the soil, and is constantly returning to the soil.

The Saxon sorcerer recognizes that weakness and disease are hindrances to effective magic work. It is not impossible to work magic when your physical body is compromised, especially if you have developed an impressive degree of skill in one or more magical cræftes, but it is certainly more difficult. You do not need the physique of an athlete, but you should strive to maintain a reasonably healthy physical condition. When your lic—your interface with Middle Earth—is whole and sound, you can focus more effectively on your work.

The Hyge (Conscious Thought)

Ceremonial magicians often maintain that the four principles for effective magic are to Know, to Will, to Dare, and to Keep Silent. Three of these are, in Saxon belief, parts of the Self known respectively as the *hyge*, the *willa,* and the *wód*. Our faculty for conscious thought is called the *hyge* (pronounced HU-yeh). This is the part of you that objectively analyzes data and makes rational decisions.

This part of the Self is often underutilized by those who explore magic. When we engage the wód and other parts of the Self in our work, the hyge is set aside for a time. And this is as it should be. In trance work, for example, you should avoid the temptation to immediately analyze every impression that comes to you. During your trance you might see a wolf. It can be very easy to let the hyge step in and make a connection between the wolf and the god Woden, to whom wolves are sacred. But maybe the image you saw had nothing to do with Woden. Maybe it was just the spirit of a wolf. This is why it is important to keep the hyge in check during the work.

Nevertheless, this part of the Self is essential to your work; however, it must be utilized correctly. The Saxon sorcerer is constantly learning, engaging the hyge. To be effective, he should have a working knowledge of Saxon belief and symbols. *Rúncræft*, skill with the Anglo-Saxon runes, especially engages the hyge.

In the wake of any magic work, it is the hyge that keeps the Saxon sorcerer stable and balanced. You should always scrutinize your own work after the fact as objectively as possible. One thing to watch for is any hint of megalomania. If at any time you feel omnipotent, or somehow "better" than other people, if you believe nobody else can do what you do, or that other people cannot understand or perceive things you have seen, then it is probably time to set the wand and cauldron aside. For most people this is not a problem, but a very small number of would-be sorcerers fall prey to these delusions. Each of us feels that he or she is special and unique, and on some level this is true, but if you begin to believe that you are anything other than human, or that you possess gifts unknown to others, then your hyge is not functioning effectively.

It is also your hyge that recognizes whether your magic is having any positive effect on your life and the lives of those around you. A successful sorcerer is a successful human being. It is your hyge, your "analytical self," that objectively determines whether or not you are succeeding. Unfortunately many would-be sorcerers ignore their hyge. To develop effective magic techniques, you need to be cognizant of what works and what does not work for you.

The Willa (Willpower)

For the ceremonial magician, it is not enough just "to Know"—you must then exert your Will. The Old English *willa* can be translated as "willpower" or "determination." It is the part of you that keeps you motivated. For the Saxon sorcerer, it is the part of the self that "shapes the ripples."

Willa can also be translated as "joy" or "desire." The Old English verb *willian* means "to wish for." Your willa is the craving you have that causes you to forge ahead to attain your goals. To work magic effectively, the willa must be engaged in the process. Some purposes lend themselves to this more readily than others. Prosperity magic, for example, tends to be difficult because most people just do not get very sexed up about money. We all like the idea of having plenty of money, and nobody is going to turn down an unexpected inheritance, but it is not something most of us feel real passion for.

The various techniques of galdor (sound magic) help focus the sorcerer's willa on the work at hand. Alliteration, rhythm, and rhyme all engage the attention of the willa. Likewise, the scents of various herbs can engage the willa.

A weak willa is as much a hindrance to effective magic as a weak or diseased lic. Possibly more so. Without the push of the willa, any magic work is almost guaranteed to be fruitless. Like any other part of you, the condition of your willa is partially inherited and partially influenced by how you use it. Just as you can exercise your lic, for example, you can also exercise the willa.

To do this, find a time when you can be alone and undisturbed. Sit in a comfortable position and select one object within eyesight. It could be a doorknob or a light switch, or if outdoors it could be a flower or small plant. Fix your gaze on the object. Force your willa to remain directed on that object and nothing else. Hold this for as long as you can. In its natural state, your willa is drawn to its desires. It only remains focused in one place if you hold it there. While performing this exercise, you may feel your willa trying to pull away. By training your willa to remain focused on one object, you can gain a greater control over it. This exercise sounds simple enough, but for some people it is very difficult to focus attention on one object for even a minute or two. With practice you should eventually reach a point where you can remain focused for fifteen minutes or more.

The Wód (Inspiration)

You Know and you Will, now you must Dare. The part of the Self that corresponds to daring is called the *wód*. This is your passion. This is what inspires your willa. Pure wód, when undirected, erupts into madness and rage. But when guided by the willa, it becomes a powerful tool.

Wód is the inspiration that motivates both the poet and the warrior. When the classicist speaks of his "muse," he is speaking of something similar to what the Saxon would call his wód. The difference is that the Hellenic muse is perceived as another spirit, a daughter of Zeus, whereas the wód is an innate part of you. Furthermore, wód by itself is sheer undefined passion. It is madness. Wód only becomes a positive force when it is guided or directed by the willa.

Note that wód is not desire. Desire has direction and focus. However, your willa directs your wód, and so it can seem that wód itself is the manifestation of desire. But wód has no definition or direction of its own. Wód is a power that can be destructive as easily as it can be constructive. It was wód that drove the Germanic berserkers into their legendary frenzies in battle. It is wód, too, under the direction of the willa, that fuels the creativity of the poet, novelist, and songwriter.

The role of the wód in magic is self evident: wód is the inner fire—the power—that charges your work.

The Mód (Self-Identity)

In my opinion, it is the *mód* that we are usually thinking of when we speak of the "soul." Our modern word *mood* comes from this Old English term. Mód can be interpreted equally as heart, mind, or spirit. Your mód is what might be called self-awareness. It is your sense of identity.

The mód does not have an immediate, obvious connection with magic. With the hyge, willa, and wód, you have Known, you have Willed, and you have Dared. There is no part of the Self, in Saxon belief, that corresponds to the Keep Silent segment of the ceremonial magicians' equation, although that is indeed good advice for aspiring sorcerers of any discipline. Talking about your work dissipates the effect of your wód. This is true for writers as well as magicians. Many writers refuse to talk about their current projects because they find that it releases a lot of the inspiration—a lot of the wód—they would otherwise pour onto paper (or more likely, today, into their word processors). In the same way, sorcerers can lose much of the power behind their magic if they talk about it, either before or after the work.

Even though the mód does not fit in with the maxims of ceremonial magic, a healthy mód is as important as any other part of you for successful magic work. If your mód is unbalanced or unhealthy, it is going to show in your work. I won't say you need to be in a "good mood" for wyrdworking, but you do need to be in a *strong* mood. You need to identify with the work at hand in some way. You need to be fully present.

The Mægen (Spiritual Strength)

Mægen (MY-an) is an Old English word meaning "strength" or "vigor." When we say that someone has a lot of guts, we are speaking of that person's mægen.

This substance, your mægen, is a part of you that is easily replenished, but just as easily destroyed or used up. Mægen is used whenever we confront a significant challenge. Some of us have seemingly endless reserves, while others quickly expend their mægen. Since every work of magic is a challenge, at least some mægen is used whenever we concoct a magic ointment or chant a spell.

Mægen is also used up in other ways. It is quickly depleted by dishonorable acts. Whenever you break your word, some mægen is lost. If you betray a friend or family member in any way, some mægen is lost. Obviously anyone with a chronic habit of lying or cheating is not going to become an effective sorcerer.

Fortunately the reverse is true. Mægen is replenished by honorable acts. Whenever you are true to your word, whenever you are faithful to your folk, your mægen is replenished. How much you gain, of course, depends on how worthy your words and acts are. If you make a promise that is easy to keep, the reward in mægen will be minimal. Promises and deeds are more worthy when they require a degree of effort on your part.

In my opinion, your mægen is an underlying foundation for all of your magic work. No matter how sharp your hyge, no matter how strong your willa or how powerful your wód, your work is not going to be successful without a good foundation of mægen. At best your work will fizzle; at worst it will go awry. Your willa—your personal willpower—is seriously undermined when your words and deeds are not reliable. Strong reserves of mægen are essential for magic work.

All Saxon Pagans strive to build their mægen through honorable acts, but this is especially important for the Saxon who would be a wyrdworker.

The Hama (Astral Body)

I am going out on a limb here by describing the *hama* as your "aura," but that is the best way I know to express it. The word *aura* suggests an emanation, whereas the hama is an independent body. It is an astral or spiritual body that surrounds and protects you. The hama could be thought of as your spiritual shield. In Old English, *hama* literally means a "skin" or "covering." It is also the name of the god known to the Norse as Heimdall, who guards the path to Osgeard where the gods and goddesses live. The god Hama keeps watch to prevent any intrusion into that celestial realm.

Your own hama is the part of you that prevents the intrusion of forces that would harm or disrupt you. Like every other part of you, the hama is independent and intelligent. You do not have to tell your hama to ward off an intrusion any more than you have to tell your lic to keep your heart beating. Your hama is constantly protecting the rest of you.

Your hama ensures that you are not going to be possessed by another spirit. Again, the hama is an intelligent, independent part of your Self that can allow, if you wish, limited possession. But the chance of true, forced possession is very small. I will not say there is absolutely no danger at all, but then again, there is some element of danger involved every time you go to the grocery store. If your hama is healthy, the danger of forced possession is roughly equivalent to the danger of that grocery expedition. Thus a sorcerer who wants to connect with the Elves (natural spirits) and other entities will appreciate a strong and healthy hama.

Chronic use of drugs can compromise the hama. And by "drugs," I do not mean only illegal substances. Legal drugs such as alcohol and caffeine can also compromise the hama when indulged in to excess. Alcohol, in the form of mead (honey wine), is integral to Saxon spirituality, but no wyrdworker worth his or her salt is going to stumble around in a constant drunken state. Likewise, excessive caffeine in the form of coffee or caffeinated soft drinks can weaken the hama. If you must have a shot of vodka or a beer or a cup of coffee in order to function, the time has come to either cut back or, for some few of us, to emancipate yourself from the substance entirely. Stronger drugs can have a more harmful effects, and thus require even more caution.

When your hama is strong and whole, as it is for most of us, the dangers people speak of in reference to magic are negligible. This protective shell is constantly active and on guard.

The Myne (Memory and Emotions)

Your memories, all of them, good and bad, are the part of you known as your *myne* (pronounced MU-neh). I honestly do not think the myne comes directly into play in magic work except when the wyrdworker is memorizing a chant or the meanings of the runes, but it is one of the nine parts of the Self, so it needs to be mentioned here. At times your magic work may be directed to affect your own myne, just as you would use healing magic to affect your lic.

It may seem strange that the Saxons considered the memory and emotions to be the same thing, but they recognized that all of our emotional responses are indeed a function of the memory, or the myne. How often have you heard somebody say, "I wish I could forget about him," or, "I wish I could put that behind me"? Our emotions are our memories, both painful and pleasurable. Lovers once gave sprigs of rosemary to one another, because that herb strengthened the myne and thus helped ensure that they would be remembered.

The Fetch (Guardian Spirit)

The *fetch* is a part of your Self that is often encountered during "astral travel," or what the Saxon sorcerer is more likely to describe as *seething*. If that modality of Saxon magic appeals to you, your fetch may have a large role in your personal work. If not, and you have no interest in the art of seething, you might have only a passing acknowledgement of your fetch. In some ways the fetch can be similar to the hama, in that it can be a protective force. But unlike the hama, the fetch can and does travel beyond your other "selves" while simultaneously remaining connected to the rest of you by your æthem, or life breath.

The word *fetch* is related to the Old English *fetian*, meaning "to seek out or to obtain." Today it has this same meaning when used as a verb. In modern British English, the word used as a noun retains the meaning of a spirit or apparition, however this usage is no longer found in modern American English.

The fetch usually takes on the appearance of an animal. This is the "familiar" of traditional witchcraft. You might be approached and befriended by numerous animal spirits, but the fetch itself is a part of you. Just as you have only one hama and one lic, you have only one true fetch. Kveldulf Gundarsson asserts that the fetch will occasionally take the form of a woman (*Teutonic Magic*, p. 15). In my experience, however, a fetch manifestation in any human form is an exception rather than the rule.

You do not need to know just now what form your fetch takes; it will make itself known to you when the time is right. (To be more precise, it will make itself known to your hyge—to your conscious self—when the time is right. Obviously your fetch, which is itself a part of you, is already aware of the form it manifests.) Some people want to rush to find out what sort of animal they have as a fetch, but this can lead to self-delusion. Wait until your own experiences reveal, to your hyge, the form of your fetch. One of the best settings for this is in your dreams. Is there some animal that occasionally but repeatedly appears to you in dreams? It could be any kind of animal and is as likely to be something simple and unassuming—perhaps a toad, a songbird, or a butterfly—as something dangerous and romantic. It is amazing how many people claim to have fetches in the form of exciting, predatory animals. The wolves and raptors alone make up an inexplicable percentage of alleged fetch manifestations. I cannot help but wonder how many of these alleged manifestations are imaginary, and how many real familiar spirits manifesting as bluebirds or chipmunks or mice go completely unnoticed.

You need not restrict your exploration to the dreamscape to find your fetch. Go into the woods or walk through an open meadow and be mindful of any creatures that approach or follow you. And do not worry if nothing comes of this immediately. Your fetch will reveal itself to you in its own time.

———

These, then, are the nine parts of the Self: lic, hyge, willa, wód, mód, mægen, hama, myne, and fetch. Most of these will have a role in your magic work at some time or another.

At the beginning of this chapter we defined what is meant, in this book, by the word *magic*. I think it is equally important to also define what I mean by *Saxon* magic, since different people may view this concept in different ways.

There are some Saxon Pagans who restrict their activities—whether magical or spiritual—to practices that can be definitively documented as occurring in pre-Christian society, before Augustine became the first Archbishop of Canterbury in CE 598. The biggest problem with this approach is that the pre-Christian Saxons did not write anything down. All records pertaining to that era were written much later by Christian scribes. There are huge gaps in our objective knowledge of pre-Christian Saxon traditions, and nowhere is this more evident than in Saxon magic.

The other issue is that this approach ignores a wealth of lore that has been passed down through the years in the form of folk customs. I regard all English folklore as *potentially* Saxon unless it can be proven or demonstrated otherwise. What I look for is a sense of what I can only describe as "English-ness." If folklore includes a tradition of scrying into water—which it does—then I think we are reasonable in assuming the art of scrying to be an indigenous Saxon practice. *Scrying* is a means of divination in which a person gazes into a reflective surface, such as a bowl of water, or a mirror or crystal ball. Can I prove that the ancient Pagan Saxons utilized scrying? No, but I can prove that their descendants did, and there is certainly nothing overtly foreign about the practice.

On the other hand, ideas or customs derived from the study of chakras, classical astrology, or the Qabala are obviously foreign in origin and, I believe, should be acknowledged as such.

This does not mean I would never incorporate an idea or custom of non-Saxon origin in my magic work. I have seen Christians, especially young people, wearing woven bracelets with the letters *WWJD*, meaning "What Would Jesus Do?" This question becomes their guidepost for determining their own behavior. In both my own magic as well as my spirituality, I follow the principle of *WWSD*, meaning "What Would the Saxons Do?" In other words, if the Saxons had remained true to their gods, if they had not suffered the cultural genocide that swept across Europe, which innovations would they have adopted? This is always necessarily a matter of speculation, but it is unreasonable to presume that native Saxon traditions would have remained unchanged over the past fourteen centuries.

Later in this book, for example, I will touch upon Western elemental theory and its application in healing. This theory were formulated by the Greeks and was the foundation for the healing practices espoused by physicians such as Hippocrates and Galen. The Saxons converted to the new religion of Christianity before these healing practices became widespread in England, but there is no reason to suppose that this would not have happened anyway if the Saxons had remained Pagan. Elemental theory is not related to any particular religion. Hippocrates is still known as the "Father of Medicine" because his healing techniques, at the time, were more effective than any other. So What Would the Saxons Do? Would they reject elemental theory? Why?

On the other hand, it would be misleading for me to claim that elemental theory is an ancient Saxon tradition. Although this book is intended for wyrdworkers and not for scholars, I will attempt to be as clear as possible about the origins of the techniques described in the following chapters.

The art of wyrdworking is, in plain terms, witchcraft. In pre-Christian England, some Saxon wyrdworkers were acknowledged as druids (*drýmenn* or, if female, *drýicgan*) in recognition of their service to their respective villages or to a Saxon lord. Often, however, sorcerers served only their immediate friends and kinsmen.

Regardless of status, whether witches or druids, sorcerers practiced an art only peripherally related to their spirituality. Like the modern practitioner, the pre-Christian wyrdworker surely would have prayed for divine assistance from time to time. We have already discussed the distinction between magic and prayer, and have seen how these are often used simultaneously.

The recipient of such a prayer should always be a god or spirit with whom you have developed a relationship. The means of nurturing such a relationship is covered thoroughly in *Travels*

Through Middle Earth: The Path of a Saxon Pagan, so there is no need to repeat myself here. If you have good relationships with more than one spirit, the prayer should be directed to the god or spirit most likely to take an interest in your problem (e.g., Thunor for protection, Frige for household issues, etc.).

Also, Woden or Fréo are both good choices for wyrdworkers to pray to if they have developed relationships with one of these deities. The Saxon god Woden and the goddess Fréo are both sovereign over magic work. Thus it behooves the serious wyrdworker to build a positive relationship with one or the other. Fréo is the mistress of the arts of seething and scrying. If you find yourself drawn to shamanic practices, consider building a relationship with Fréo. I would recommend her also to the sorcerer who wants to focus on the art of wortcunning.

Woden, also known as Grim, is the god who revealed the runic mysteries. The Hávamál, a poem from the thirteenth century Icelandic *Poetic Edda*, tells us that Woden (known to the Norse as Odin) claimed the runes after hanging for nine days from the World Tree. He is obviously the choice for the sorcerer who enjoys working with the Anglo-Saxon runes. However, there is no hard and fast rule about this. If it is Fréo who speaks to you, then you might fare better with her, even if runes are your passion.

In fact it is Woden and Fréo—the latter addressed by her Norse name Freya—who are acknowledged as the "Lord and Lady" in the Seax Wica tradition. Wica (or Wicca) is a duotheistic religion in which the godhead is believed to be a divine pair, a Lord (masculine energy) and Lady (feminine energy). The Seax Wica tradition was formulated by Raymond Buckland and presented to the public in 1974 with the release of *The Tree: The Complete Book of Saxon Witchcraft*, which has since been republished as *Buckland's Book of Saxon Witchcraft*. Obviously Seax Wica is not traditional Germanic polytheism, nor has it ever been presented as such, but I find it interesting that Mr. Buckland chose Woden and Fréo (or Freya) as the images for the Lord and Lady.

The Saxon sorcerer, like other Saxon Pagans, does not believe that Woden and Fréo are the entirety of the Divine, but these are nevertheless the deities the practitioner is most likely to turn to for help in working magic. I do not know of any Saxon witch or druid who has not worked to develop a relationship with one or the other of these deities.

Review

1. What is the difference between magic and prayer?
2. What is the function of the hama?
3. Describe the connection between memory and emotion.
4. What distinguishes a Saxon druid (drýmann, drýicge) from a witch (wicca, wicce)?
5. What Saxon deity is associated with rune magic? Why?

Tools of the Trade

Almost every skill has its respective tools. The Saxon tailor or seamstress has a needle, shears, and, today, a sewing machine. The *scop* (Saxon musician) will often make use of a harp or perhaps a guitar.

The Saxon wyrdworker also has his or her own tools. These will vary depending on which magic techniques you favor. The *wiglere* will make use of different tools than the *rúnwita*. In this chapter we will explore some of the tools that most wyrdworkers will want to have on hand. Here again I am going to make use of the WWSD (What Would the Saxons Do?) principle. I do not always use the instruments and methods utilized fourteen centuries ago. I use tools appropriate for this time and place. You do not need to acquire all of the tools described here at once. Depending on your personal magic work, there are some that you may not want or need at all. If you focus exclusively on rune magic, for example, you may never need a mortar and pestle.

The Myse (Table)

The first thing to consider is where you are going to work your magic. Not for every little spell, of course, but for your more important work. This is where the *rúnwita* will carve runes, where the *wyrtwita* will infuse potions, where the *galdre* will sing spells. In *The Book of Seiðr*, shaman and author Runic John recommends at least a shelf or a flat stone placed on the floor as a focus for magic work (p. 60). This place, this surface, will eventually take on a power of its own, imprinted by the repetitious magic you have woven around and through it.

The Saxon sorcerer may refer to this object or location as the *myse*, an Old English word (pronounced MU-zeh) that simply means "table." The myse need not be an actual table; it can be as simple as Runic John's flat stone. Its defining qualities are that it provides a surface for your work, and that you perform the majority of your magic work on that surface.

The myse can be quite elaborate. I know a witch in southwestern Missouri who brews her potions and casts her spells on top of an ornate, beautifully preserved wood-burning stove. The large stove stands in her kitchen, where she also has a modern electric stove for everyday cooking. She acquired the wood burner specifically to serve as a location for her magic work. This myse is exceptional, of course, but it is an example of the effort some wyrdworkers will expend to create a special place for their magic.

Elaborate or not, there are obvious advantages to having your myse—your working surface—in or near the kitchen. In this room you have ready access to water, to waste disposal (usually down the sink), and to heat. This is especially advantageous for those who do a lot of work with herbs. There is no rule stating that your working surface needs to be in the kitchen, but it is a convenient location when you have to boil water or wash out a mortar.

Your household *wéofod* (altar) can also serve as a myse. I often make use of my own household altar in this way. If you are going to do this, it is a good idea to have at least one *wéoh* (statue or image) representing either Woden or Fréo, since these are the deities who take the most interest in magic. As a rule, I only work magic at my wéofod when I am also asking for help in my endeavor from

Woden or some other deity, so it is appropriate, I think, that I do this where I normally approach the Saxon gods and goddesses.

There are two opinions as to how the myse should be treated. Some people believe that the myse should be kept sacred, or separate, from mundane activities; other people feel the exact opposite, and that it should be integrated into all parts of your life. Both opinions have their merits, but you should pick one or the other and stick to that perspective.

If your myse is an ordinary surface where you also perform everyday activities, then I do not think you should use your wéofod in this way. The wéofod is, indeed, a sacred space, and you are approaching your magic as an ordinary activity. Let me emphasize here that there is nothing wrong with this. As we have seen, magic is not the same thing as spirituality, and more than a few wyrdworkers make no distinction between their magic work and other everyday activities.

The other point of view maintains that mundane activities dissipate the power that the myse would otherwise develop or acquire. From this perspective, magic is still not the same thing as spirituality, but neither is it "ordinary." If you wish to reserve your working surface as a separate space, then you cannot perform ordinary, non-magical activities on that surface. For most of us, this is impractical. Not everybody has an extra wood burner in the kitchen that can be reserved for magic work!

As an alternative option, you can use a board or cloth as your myse. Remember how Runic John suggested using a flat stone placed on the floor? This works on the same principle. The board or cloth serves as the myse, or actual working surface, even though it rests on something else. There is nothing radical or strange about this, as every myse rests on something. If you are using an oak table, the surface of the table is resting on its four legs. As I said previously, the defining qualities of the myse are that it provides a surface and that you perform most of your magic work on that surface. The myse board is simply a worktable without legs.

Before anyone accuses me of making something up here, let me clarify that there is no evidence of the early, pre-Christian Saxons having anything like a myse board. This is quite likely a modern innovation. But it is a very common innovation that many wyrd-workers today agree enhances their magic work. Runic John suggests a flat stone on the ground if a permanent working surface is not possible. And today's rune sorcerers very often lay out or cast their runes on special cloths used for no other purpose. A myse in some form or another has become a common tool for modern practitioners.

The cloth and the board each have their disadvantages. The disadvantage of the cloth is that it does not necessarily provide a flat surface, but this should not be a problem if you are always going to use it on a table or on level flooring. The disadvantage of the board is that you can't fold or roll it up, so storage can be more problematic. But most of us have space somewhere to store a myse board. Personally, I prefer the board.

A myse should be marked in some way to define it as sacred space. The board can be easily engraved with a wood burner. Inexpensive wood burners are sold at handicrafts stores, and are easy to use. The board itself can be a simple wood cutting board. A cloth, if you prefer this, is most easily decorated with embroidery. If you do not want the stitches to show through, a second lining can be sewn to the back.

How you decorate the myse board (or cloth) is a matter of personal taste. One obvious way is to engrave the Anglo-Saxon runes around the perimeter of the board. Whether you engrave twenty-nine or thirty-three runes is also a personal decision, depending on how you use these symbols in your magic work. We will examine the Anglo-Saxon runes in detail later on.

But maybe you want to focus on herb magic and galdor, and have no interest in runes whatsoever. If so—if you do not know the difference between *feoh* and *éoh*, and have no desire to know—then it does not make sense to engrave the entire Futhorc (the Anglo-Saxon runes) around your myse board. As an alternative, carve or paint this across the top of the board:

ᛁᚳ ᛋᚳᛖᛚᛚᛁᚷᛖ ᚾᚢ

These runes spell out the phrase, *ic spellige nu*, which means "I now proclaim" in Old English. The verb *spellian*, meaning "to utter or proclaim," is the origin of the modern English noun *spell*. When a witch casts a spell, he or she is casting or throwing down a proclamation. Your working space is now identified as such. This may seem trivial, but in Saxon magic, to name or identify something is to give it power. By engraving the words *ic spellige nu* across the top of your working surface, you are acknowledging its purpose and empowering it to fulfill that purpose.

If the myse board (or myse cloth) is intended to be a space set aside from your ordinary activities, it should always be put away when not in use. If, on the other hand, you have a permanent working surface, whether this is a shelf or a table, be sure to keep it clean and ready for use at all times.

The Telga (Wand)

The Saxon wand is a tool allowing the sorcerer to reach through the hama (astral body). Wands serve as conduits through which sorcerers can more effectively project their power.

The Germanic people valued and respected trees. European forests provided not only firewood, but also the raw material for crafting shelters, ships, tools, and weapons. The Anglo-Saxon Rune Poem tells us that the oak even provided "meat-animals' fodder" (*flæsces fódor*) in the acorns that swine fed on. In the *Prose Edda*, a thirteenth-century collection of Icelandic tales, the first man and woman are said to have been created from a pair of trees, an ash and an elm. And in Saxon cosmology, Middle Earth itself is connected to six other extradimensional planes through the branches of the World Tree.

The *telga*—the Saxon wand—is a small symbolic reflection of the World Tree. Just as the World Tree connects Middle Earth to six other realms, the telga connects the wyrdworker to the surrounding environment. It connects us to the greater Web of Wyrd that is constantly generated by all living things.

To craft your own telga, you will need a reasonably straight branch of wood. The length should be approximately one *fæðm*, an Old English measurement that reaches from your elbow to the tip of your index finger. This measurement is also known as a cubit, from a Latin word meaning "elbow." The exact length is not exceptionally important though. The only requirement is that the telga extend your psychic "reach" beyond your protective hama without being so long as to be unwieldy.

Ideally the branch should be something you find yourself. Any kind of wood can be used, but some people prefer wood from one of the trees of the Anglo-Saxon Rune Poem: oak, ash, hawthorn, elm, or birch. (Pine is also mentioned in the Rune Poem, but specifically as a source of firewood, which is not a *doom*—a fate—that you want to weave into your telga.)

It also does not matter if you find the branch among deadwood or if you cut it from a living tree. There are some who feel that the tree is being harmed in some way, and that this will imbue a negative energy into the wand. I disagree; it is a tree, not a person or an animal. Cutting a branch from a tree is nothing at all like cutting off one of your fingers, unless you have the extraordinary ability to grow new fingers. Trees lose their branches constantly due to various factors. I am not sure that I agree, either, with the idea that you need to give something back to the tree, although there are other wyrdworkers who believe this is important. The branch was not a gift from the tree; it is just something you took.

To call a branch that you have cut from a tree a "gift" seems, to me, like stealing a person's wallet and then claiming it was given to you. However, if giving back makes you feel better about cutting off the branch, then by all means pour a little ale or mead around the roots of the tree. It is important that you not have any pessimistic feelings about the branch you have cut.

Another approach is to do something beneficial for the tree. In Saxon belief, a gift's value is relative not only to the degree of sacrifice, but also to how much worth it is to the recipient. Watering the tree—if it would benefit from water—or trimming away unhealthy branches are ways to offer a gift in exchange for the branch.

If you find your branch lying on the ground, as deadwood, be sure that it is solid and whole. Deadwood is often subject to rot. Try to bend the branch in your hands and see if it snaps in two. The branch should feel sturdy in your grip.

Strip the bark from the branch and sand away any irregularities. Your telga does not have to be perfectly smooth, but you do not want projections that may catch on your clothing or other objects. Some people like to embellish the telga by affixing a small thunderstone (quartz crystal) or semiprecious stone at the tip, but this is personal taste.

After you have shaped the telga and added any embellishment, carve the following along its length:

ᛗᛗᛗᛗᛗᛗᛗ

This rune is *os*, repeated here seven times, once for each of the Seven Worlds. *Os* is the rune of the god Woden, who is described in the Anglo-Saxon Rune Poem as the creator of all language or speech (*ordfruma ælere spræce*). As I mentioned earlier in this chapter, when a Saxon sorcerer casts a "spell," he literally speaks or proclaims his will. As the creator of speech, Woden can be thought of as the creator of magic, at least as it is practiced by us mortals. The *os* rune is carved seven times into the telga to invoke this magic throughout the Seven Worlds.

After carving the runes, the final step in crafting your telga is to rub it down with oil. This can be linseed oil, any commercial furniture oil, or even an essential oil that is pleasing to you.

The Staff

The Old English word for staff is just *stæf*, which is nothing more than an older spelling for the same word with the same pronunciation.

In function the staff is a larger, longer version of the telga. The only real difference is the physical form of the tool; however, that is a very big difference. Because of its size, the staff can be used in a very practical way as a walking staff, which is especially useful at night. The staff can test the ground to ensure that the sorcerer is not stepping into a puddle, a deep pool of mud, or worse. Brambles are easily swept aside. But the staff is more unwieldy than a wand. If you want to mark runes in the air, the staff tends to be awkward.

I have known sorcerers to clutch a staff during trance work. The symbolism is quite obvious. Like Woden, traversing the Seven Worlds along the length of the World Tree, the wyrdworker is using the staff to help journey beyond the confines of his or her lic (physical body).

Your staff should be no longer than you are tall. As with the telga, this is an approximate guideline, but anything much larger may be unmanageable. Also as with the telga, the staff can be shaped from deadwood or cut from a living tree. In this case, if the wood is freshly cut, you should let it age for at least a few months before trying to shape it. This will lessen the chance of the wood splitting. You can carve the *os* rune into the staff seven times or, if you prefer (since there is much more room), carve all of the Anglo-Saxon runes along its length. This second approach imbues the staff with all of the mysteries described in the Anglo-Saxon Rune Poem. A few years ago, I had the pleasure of sitting with a talented wiglere (soothsayer) in the Colorado mountains as she journeyed through a seething. The wiglere held a strong wooden staff throughout her journey, with all of the Anglo-Saxon runes carved into its length.

The Mortar

If you are going to explore wortcunning (herb magic) at all, you will want a mortar for mixing and crushing herbs. Plant materials—usually seeds or leaves—are placed in the mortar and crushed with a blunt tool called a pestle. These two items, the mortar and pestle, are almost always sold as a set.

You can find mortar and pestle sets at gift shops, herb shops, and New Age shops or in the kitchenware departments of discount stores. The problem is not where to find them, but what to look for. Mortar and pestle sets are made from almost every material imaginable, including some you should avoid. You need to be able to thoroughly clean these tools, so porous materials are out. It can be difficult or impossible to get all the residue out of a wooden mortar.

Very often you can find mortar and pestle sets made of solid marble. In my opinion, this is your best choice. The marble is non-porous, can be scrubbed, and is difficult to break—difficult, but not impossible. I once managed to break a marble pestle, but it took some work on my part.

Your second choice—and these are almost as good as marble— are porcelain mortar and pestle sets. They are as easy to clean as marble and, although easier to break, they are surprisingly durable. I would not hesitate to purchase a porcelain mortar if I could not find one made of marble.

The Cauldron

It would not be wiccecræft if we did not have a cauldron to stir! Nevertheless I feel compelled to invoke my What Would the Saxons Do principle here. The cauldron is nothing more or less than a vessel for heating liquids. The early Saxons might have called this vessel a *citel*; a modern Saxon sorcerer is more likely to call it a "pot."

You can, of course, still purchase old-fashioned iron cauldrons. I own one myself, and occasionally use it in my spiritual work as a symbolic representation of the Well of Wyrd. The Well of Wyrd lies at the roots of the World Tree. In Saxon belief, all of our words and deeds fall into this Well, which in turn affects all that is to come. The shape and design of my cauldron is perfect as a representation of this concept, but the same design is impractical, at best, for any magic work today. This is because, in its time, the cauldron was a state-of-the-art culinary implement; in the twenty-first century, it is archaic and outmoded for its intended purpose. We no longer cook over an open fire in the hearth. A practical, modern cauldron must be an implement adapted to a gas or electric range. So we ask ourselves, What Would the Saxons Do? They would probably do now as they did then, and use a contemporary vessel for heating liquids.

Your mód (self-identity) may want to connect with the ambience of an older, simpler time, and this is understandable. You do not need to use a plain, long-handled pot if you can find something more to your liking. The only requirement is that the vessel have a flat bottom that can rest easily on a stove burner. A small stock pot, for example, can serve as a suitable contemporary cauldron. Whatever you use should also be easy to clean. I favor stainless steel, which I readily admit is not a material the early Saxon sorcerers had at their disposal. But it is lighter in weight and easier to clean than cast iron, and thus a very suitable material for twenty-first-century Saxons.

If you follow the philosophy that your magic is an ordinary activity in your life, you do not need to reserve a special cauldron at all. The average modern kitchen will have a variety of pots and pans to use. But just as some practitioners prefer a separate, special working surface for their magic, there is an argument to be made for having a cauldron that is used only for that purpose. Since this cauldron serves no other use, it becomes "trained" over time as a magical implement. It will gradually acquire a power of its own. Some would argue that the change occurs within you and not with the cauldron, but the distinction is moot. The important thing is that the cauldron, for many of us, can become a more effective tool if it is used only for magic work.

You may want more than one cauldron, especially if you do a lot of work with herbs. In fact a dedicated herb sorcerer will eventually have an entire arsenal of equipment: cauldrons, kettles, cups, measures, and so on. For most of us it would be impractical to collect enough implements to stock an alchemical laboratory, but it is not unreasonable to reserve a couple of cauldrons and perhaps a kettle for your magic work.

The Seax (Knife)

The *seax* (SAY-ax) was an indispensable tool for the pre-Christian Saxon. The traditional seax was larger than a knife but smaller than a sword, its blade sharpened along only one side. It is most often thought of as a weapon, but the seax would have been used in this way only when a fight joined too closely for the spear. It was an all-purpose cutting tool. The blade was occasionally decorated with engravings of snakes or braids or simple lines.

I honestly think there is too much emphasis today on the seax as a magical tool. It is sometimes used to help project a wyrdworker's power, but this is more properly the function of the telga. I rarely employ a seax in my own magic work and, when I do, I use it to challenge or redirect *external* forces. The seax is the more effective tool for this purpose due to the ferrous metal in its blade. (We will discuss the magic properties of iron in the next chapter.)

For the early Saxon, the seax was a personal tool with a spirit of its own. To empower your seax, you can give it a name and engrave this into the hilt. Alternately, you can engrave your own name into the hilt, identifying the seax as an extension of yourself. Here again I must emphasize that magic is an intensely personal pursuit. Whether you give your seax a name or share your own name with it depends on which approach gives this tool a sense of force and power.

You may not want to engrave the seax at all. If this is your choice, you can still empower it with a name (your own or another) through the process of Weland's Transfer. Weland is an elf, or spirit, who attained the status of a Saxon god. Known for his ability as a smith, Weland was captured and imprisoned on an island. There he was forced to craft jewelry and other items for his captor. But eventually Weland escaped the island using a pair of wings he had made for himself. It was Weland who crafted the chainmail shirt worn by the hero Beowulf.

To empower a blade with Weland's Transfer, the name is clearly marked on a piece of paper. Carefully burn this paper in a flame. It is easiest to do this with a candle flame, using a pair of tweezers to hold the paper. It does not matter if the corner held by the tweezers does not burn so long as the name itself is reduced to ashes. The ashes are then carefully rubbed along the length of the blade, thus transferring the power of the name into the metal.

I cannot attest that Weland's Transfer is an ancient Saxon magical practice. I first heard of it in 1977, from an American wyrdworker who had learned of the procedure from an English wicca. Weland's Transfer seems to work, though, and that is what really matters.

———

Once you have acquired some of your magical tools, you will want to prepare them for their intended purpose. All things are subject to a universal magical principle often known as the Law of Contagion. This law states that an object (or person) remains connected to anything else that it touches. The Law of Contagion is why sorcerers will often obtain and use personal items, such as clothing or a comb, belonging to whomever they are working magic for. The items in question provide connections with these people. The Law of Contagion is also the principle behind the technique of Weland's Transfer. The name for the seax, reduced to ashes, is rubbed into the blade and thus becomes connected with the blade.

Whether it is your mortar or your seax or some other object, you cannot know for certain what objects or people came into contact with any given magical tool before you had it. Therefore it is always a good idea to use a simple spell to cleanse or wash away any previous connections clinging to the tool. This spell should even be cast over your myse before you use it for the first time if you are using a portable version, such as a board or cloth.

To work the spell you will be using the powers of water (cold) and fire (heat). In a later chapter we will examine European elemental theory, but for the purpose of this spell, all we require are the opposite forces that engendered the raw materials formed into the Seven Worlds. This primal event, the Germanic "big bang," took place at the beginning of time, when frost coming from the north poured into the raging fires coming from out of the south.

You will need the tool you are preparing, plus a small bowl of water and an open flame. A candle flame will suffice. If using a candle, it should be made of either pure beeswax or red paraffin. Red, as we will discuss later, is the color of blood, and thus the color of life and strength.

Using your fingers, sprinkle your new magic tool with water as you say:

Waters of wisdom, work my will
With wód and wyrd my words fulfill
Banish any bane or blight
And wash away the wayward wight.

Here you are using galdor (magic of sound) to work your will. You are proclaiming what will occur, stating firmly that the water will remove any previous connections that will impair the tool's ability to function. This particular galdor utilizes the techniques of rhyme and alliteration to lend further power to your words. A *wight* is any entity, living or dead, although in this context it usually references a spirit being.

After this, pass the tool over the open flame, holding it firmly in both hands as you say:

Flames of fortune from afar
Favor me with force and fire
Burn away all blight and bane
Let frith and fréot e'er remain.

The same galdor style is used here. The alliteration has changed, but the third line uses the same "b" sound alliteration to bind fire (the second galdor) to water (the first galdor). *Frith* and *fréot* are two Old English words that roughly translate as "peace" and "freedom." You are charging the flame to render the tool free of any contrary influences.

Remember, though, what I have said about magic being intensely personal. If you feel silly speaking in rhyme, dispense with that and come up with similar, non-rhyming verse. Truly adept sorcerers always develop their own style.

Once you have passed your new magic tool through water and fire, it is ready for use. In the next chapter we will look at some of the components you may wish to collect for your spells.

Review

1. What is the purpose of the myse?

2. Which rune is carved repeatedly into the telga, and why?

3. Describe the difference between the use of the telga and the use of the seax.

4. What is the function or purpose of the cauldron?

5. What is the Law of Contagion?

The Alchemy of Magic

We have discussed the tools that a practitioner might need for his or her magical work. Now let us turn our attention to the components or ingredients used in Saxon sorcery.

Before we begin, I recommend that you start thinking about where you will store these various items. Think of it as your "sorcerer's cabinet," although it need not be a literal cabinet. It is a good idea to keep everything together in one place, where you can find whatever you need easily. This may seem like common sense, but if it is, common sense is something that a lot of us occasionally lack. I cannot begin to describe how frustrating it is when your work is disrupted because you forgot where you stashed your powdered orris root.

Your sorcerer's cabinet should be a place reserved exclusively for your magic items. You may want to keep your telga (wand) and mortar with your herbs, but this is not the place to put store coupons, paper clips, restaurant menus, and spare change. Only the tools and ingredients intended specifically for magic work should be kept in the sorcerer's cabinet. Again, I am using the word *cabinet* loosely—what I mean is any storage space. Depending on your preference and needs, this storage space can take many forms. It could be a leather satchel or a large covered wicker basket, a desk drawer or a closet shelf. It could even be an actual cabinet.

Ideally your sorcerer's cabinet should be a storage space that can be covered or otherwise protected. Remember the Law of Contagion mentioned in the last chapter? Covering your supplies will help shield them from potentially contrary outside influences. We are speaking of reasonable precautions. There is no need to worry excessively about outside influences, but it should be obvious that items kept by themselves will be "cleaner," psychically, than if they are tossed carelessly among a stack of late bills, sales flyers, and old newspapers.

Jars

You will almost surely need jars or similar containers for the various ingredients used in your work. I say "almost" because I do not know what magic techniques and practices you will focus on. If most of your magic is worked through trance, bolstered perhaps with some galdorcræft (sound magic), you may not need many physical implements or ingredients. The majority of sorcerers, however, will have a variety of substances at their disposal.

There is absolutely no mundane, physical reason why you cannot keep these substances in a collection of old mayonnaise jars. But atmosphere is important for magic work. It is more difficult to focus when you are surrounded by symbols sending a message that the work at hand is worthless or in any way unimportant. I recommend new jars, purchased specifically for your work.

You can often find attractive, decorative jars at gift or import shops. I am using the word *jar* much as I used the word *cabinet* earlier. The container need not be an actual jar. A small box can serve equally well as a suitable container for salt, amber, or any powdered resin. I use a variety of containers, including a beautiful little metal box set with lapis lazuli that was given to me as a

Yule gift. However, any container made of wood or metal should be used only for solid substances. Liquids can soak into wood and can leach metal.

Jars themselves can be either earthenware or glass. You may find glass preferable, as it is easier to clean thoroughly. When selecting glass jars, your best choice is colored glass. Many magical ingredients—herbs, especially—break down when exposed to heat and light. Colored glass will help filter any light reaching these ingredients, thus extending their longevity.

Purchase the smallest size jars suitable for your needs. If you use a lot of wormwood, then a larger jar is warranted, but keep in mind that oversized jars are more difficult to store and move about. Also, any containers for liquids *must* have tight, waterproof seals!

Labels

As important as the jars themselves are the labels that you will put on those jars. A lot of new practitioners think they do not need labels, that they will remember what the crushed dried sage looks like, and if you are one of these people, you are probably going to ignore me here. But I know from personal experience. I had to dump out more than a few mystery jars before I learned to label everything.

Trust me when I say that most herbs look like nothing more than little bits of grass after they have been dried and ground up. It can be very easy to take a pinch of southernwood when you meant to use a pinch of shepherd's purse, especially if you are in a hurry. Errors like this are minimized when all of your jars and boxes have proper labels.

Your labels should be as attractive and inspiring as your jars. If you have lousy handwriting, consider printing your labels on a computer using a decorative font.

———

Now that we have discussed how to store and organize your ingredients, we will explore the substances you are likely to need
at some time or another. You will not need all of these at first, and
some you may never need. It is a good idea, though, to consider
what magical techniques you intend to pursue, and to have the
appropriate ingredients at hand.

Alliums

Herbs are considered collectively later in this chapter, but the alliums are important enough to have an entry of their own. Alliums
are a family of bulbous, stalked plants notable for their protective
properties. From a northern European perspective, all alliums are
variations of the leek (*Allium porrum*). Leeks have been a source of
nourishment for civilizations all over the world. They were a staple for the Sumerians, along with grains and beans. Our modern
word for the leek comes from the Old English *léac*. The leek is notable for its thick, edible stalk. Young leeks are typically planted
in trenches. These trenches are slowly filled with dirt as the leeks
grow to cover and blanch the stalks (bleach by excluding light).
It is this thick, white stalk that is valued in both culinary and
arcane arts. Like all of the alliums, the leek has mild antibiotic
properties. The leek was so prevalent in Saxon culture that the
Old English word *léactún*, literally "leek-enclosure," was used for
any herb garden. It was assumed that leeks would be among the
assortment of herbs grown.

Even if you decide not to pursue the lore of wortcunning to any
extent, you would still do well to familiarize yourself with the leek
and other alliums. The leek is protective. We can talk about its healing ability, but this is a book about magic, not medicine, and the
early Saxons did not make a significant distinction between these
anyway. From the Saxon perspective, the leek has healing properties because it protects the physical body—the lic—by driving
away malevolent forces. More than this, the leek can protect against

any spiritual malevolent forces. If you believe that somebody is psychically attacking you, hang leeks over your doorway and in your windows.

The common culinary onion (*A. cepa*) is a close relative to the leek, and was known to the Saxons as the *ynneléac*. This allium is cultivated all over the world as a vegetable but can be used exactly like the leek in herb magic. The difference is that the power of the onion is in the large, familiar bulb rather than in the stalk. You can cut an onion in half, or quarter it, and set the pieces in a room for its protective influence if you are ill or if you are concerned about a potential malign influence of any kind. For a longer term but lower level of protection, whole onions can be set out uncut. I set out whole onions at the start of the influenza season. Do I believe the onion is a cure for the flu? No, but I believe it can help ward off negative or malign forces that can leave me more susceptible to sicknesses.

The Old English word for garlic (*A. sativum*) is *gárléac*, and means "spear-leek." This is an appropriate name for an especially pungent relative of the leek. Garlic is a very strong herb, both in terms of flavor and magical efficacy. Vampire legends and stories remind us of garlic's exceptional ability to fend off hostile forces. A garlic bulb can be worn in a charm bag to ward off any kind of negativity.

Notice that all of the alliums are interchangeable with respect to their magic properties. The choice of which allium to use is primarily related to the physical form of the plant. Garlic, the most potent of the alliums listed here, is best for small charms, or braided into protective wall hangings. Leeks are best if you want a dramatic visual representation. The onion falls between these two and, from a magical perspective, it does not matter whether the bulb is white or yellow. For myself, the larger alliums are something that I usually acquire as needed, but I think it is a good idea to keep a few cloves of garlic on hand in your sorcerer's cabinet.

Amber

Amber is considered a gemstone even though it is not a true mineral. It is a resin, a semi-solid substance produced by certain trees and hardened over time. Amber deposits are found all over the world, and amber is sacred to the goddess Fréo. It is said that her tears turn to gold when they fall on land, and turn to amber when they fall into the sea. Fréo's magical necklace, Brísingamen, was crafted of gold and amber. As you might expect, this organic gem is favored by many Saxon women, who wear it in strands around their necks or set into rings. It is listed here because of its magical properties.

It may be that amber is a magic gem because it is sacred to Fréo, who is, of course, the mistress of magic. Or it may be that Fréo favors the stone because of its innate magical qualities. Whatever your opinion about this chicken or egg debate, amber is another substance that many wyrdworkers use. The early Saxons called it *glær*, which was a reference to amber's vitreous or glassy appearance.

Amber can be included in any spell or charm to boost its efficacy. I think of it as a stone "for what ails you," magically speaking. It is especially good for prosperity and love spells. Amber is also a good healing stone and was traditionally worn in charms to promote health.

Artemisias

The artemisias, like the alliums, are another genus of herbs that I believe are worth mentioning independent of the herb section. The modern, scientific word for this genus is the name of Artemisia, a Greek queen who was married to King Mausolus. After Mausolus' death in 353 CE, Queen Artemisia built a tomb called the Mausoleum, which became one of the seven classic wonders of the world. In addition to her other achievements, Artemisia was a notable herbalist. (Of course this has absolutely nothing to do with the early Saxons or their magic, but I thought you should know why we call these herbs "artemisias" and why the stone buildings in cemeteries are called "mausoleums.")

For the Saxon sorcerer, the artemisias are useful for driving away evil influences. One of these herbs, mugwort (*Artemisia vulgaris*) is addressed directly in the Nine Herbs Charm. This charm was recorded in a tenth-century Anglo-Saxon manuscript called the *Lacnunga*. In the Nine Herbs Charm, mugwort is told:

> *Una you are called, oldest of worts,*
> *You are mighty against the three and thirty,*
> *You are mighty against venom and against infection,*
> *You are mighty against the harmful things that move through*
>   *the land.*

Carrying a sprig of mugwort in the mouth is said to ward off tiredness. Because of its defensive qualities, the herb was often woven into protective wreaths. Trance workers often burn mugwort, however this is as much spiritual in purpose as it is magical. Mugwort, like all of the artemisias, is sacred to the god Woden.

The more aromatic wormwood (*A. absinthium*), as its common name suggests, was once valued for its ability to expel internal worms. Do not try this at home! Wormwood is toxic and should not be taken internally. However, an infusion of wormwood leaves is an excellent wash for repelling negative forces. The dried leaves can be set out, much like a potpourri, for the same purpose. As a side benefit, this can help repel fleas, moths, and flies.

Southernwood (*A. abrotanum*) is also effective at repelling insects and lice. It can be used in the same way as wormwood. Although this is not strictly a magical use, I often burn southernwood as an offering to Woden before beginning a significant magic work. There is no mystic significance for choosing southernwood over the other artemisias, it just happens to be what grows in my garden. Any artemisia is a suitable offering for Woden.

Blood

Blood is the fluid of life. It is our physical essence, the force that animates and empowers the physical body. We know this in our gut when we see the life force flowing from a wound. Young boys know this when they swear pacts of blood brotherhood. Sorcerers know this as they weave their spells. Blood is power, and no blood is more powerful than your own. Your own blood is imbued with your wód (inspiration).

Unless you are a medical professional, do not attempt to draw your own blood. Doing so could result in infection or even permanent injury. I was hesitant to mention blood at all here, but it is so very important, so primal and essential to the alchemy of magic, that I would be remiss to omit it. But there is *never* any need to jeopardize your health and safety.

Like many *rúnwitan* (rune workers), I have "blooded" a set of Anglo-Saxon runes that I use regularly. This is one very common use of blood in Saxon magic. This particular set of runes was carved from horse bone. By marking each of the runes with my own blood, I have bonded myself to them, and them to me. I have a permanent psychic connection to those runes; however, I drew the blood for this in a medically safe way, with the approval of a physician. Otherwise I would not have blooded the runes at all. As we will discuss in the next chapter, it is not necessary to mark your runes with blood.

Blood is used when sorcerers want to instill their own essence into something. We see this concept in the idea of blood brotherhood, where the two parties involved mingle their life essences. This is a central feature in many Pagan marriages in which the fleshy part of the palm at the base of the thumb, known as the "mound of Venus," is pricked on both the wedding partners and their hands are then bound together to let their blood mingle.

When blood is used, however, the connection is always a two-way street. You are bound to whatever you have marked with your blood as surely as it is bound to you. Blood magic, even when practiced safely, should only be used when you want a two-way connection like this. There are other ways for sorcerers to mark something as their own, as we will discuss shortly.

Fat/Oil

In Old English charms, we very often see the use of fats and oils. The Æcerbot, an eleventh-century charm with both Pagan and Christian elements, instructs the sorcerer to mix salt, fennel, and frankincense with "hallowed soap" (*gehalgode sapan*). This *sapan* was a semi-solid fatty unguent. Another charm recorded during the same century required three herbs—feverfew, red nettle, and plantain—to be boiled in butter. Magical ointments were also made with lanolin, a fatty substance secreted by sheep.

The value of a fat or oil is usually as a carrier for whatever other ingredients—very often herbs—are mixed with it. Fats and oils repel water and thus prevent the active ingredients in a magical preparation from washing away.

Different fats and oils have different properties. Lanolin and natural vegetable oils absorb into the skin, which make them more useful for transferring the benefits of herbal preparations. Their disadvantage is that they eventually become rancid. Animal fats will become rancid very quickly without refrigeration, and they should be avoided unless the preparation will be used immediately.

Petroleum jelly, or soft paraffin, does not become rancid. Developed in the nineteenth century, this substance was unknown to the early Saxons, but it is a very effective base for some ointments. Petroleum-based ointments should only be used over small areas of the skin, as the soft paraffin blocks the skin's pores.

One jar of petroleum jelly and one of cold pressed almond oil should cover most of your needs. An experienced practitioner, of course, may have a variety of prepared oils and ointments at hand. There are good reasons to have your magic ointments and potions prepared in advance when you can. We will discuss this further in the chapter on wortcunning.

Essential oils are an exception to what I have said here. Essential oils are not used as carriers, although they may be mixed with a carrier oil. An essential oil is "essential" in that the oil itself is the extracted essence of a plant; thus, an essential oil can be considered an active agent in a preparation. *Wyrtwitan* (herb sorcerers) are especially likely to utilize a number of essential oils in their work.

An essential oil is usually produced by distillation, cold pressing, or solvent extraction. Cold pressing and solvent extraction require professional work. Home distillation is possible for some herbs, but the process is far more trouble than it is worth. Essential oils are readily available and are priced less than it would cost for you to distill them yourself.

When working with essential oils, it is important that you read labels carefully. Very often fragrance oils and essential oils are marketed together, their jars side by side in the same sales display. But a fragrance oil is *not* an essential oil. Fragrance oils are synthetic chemical preparations that simulate the scents (fragrances) of various herbs. Due to the Law of Sympathy, these synthetic oils do have some value, but you should be aware of whether you are working with the essence of an herb or with a sensory simulation.

Herbs

Almost all Saxon sorcerers use a few herbs, even if wortcunning is not their primary interest. Some herbs, such as the alliums and artemisias, are so prevalent in Saxon magic that I have listed them individually in this chapter. Herbs are not just sipped as infusions ("teas"). In your magical work they may be burned, used as the active reagents in magical ointments or tinctures, woven into garlands, or crushed and blended into powders. The use of essential oils discussed previously is one aspect of herb magic.

The best herbs to use are those you have either grown or gathered, rather than purchased. Homegrown herbs have a very strong connection with you, since it was you who nurtured and cared for them. And many herbs are easy to grow even if you do not have a green thumb.

Wild, natural herbs that you gather yourself have been nurtured and cared for by the local Elves. More importantly, perhaps, they are part of your immediate world, and thus are connected with you. You should not attempt to gather any wild herb unless you know exactly what it looks like. Many plant species with completely different properties bear a remarkable resemblance to one another. You could accidentally take a poisonous herb if you try to gather wild plants without expert knowledge.

You also should not gather any wild plants—even if you know what you are doing—from land that does not belong to you, unless you have permission from the owner to do so. This is theft, pure and simple, even if in your mind you are sure the owner "would not mind." Public land also falls into the category of land that does not belong to you. It belongs to the public, most of which is not you.

We will, of course, examine herbs in depth in the chapter on wortcunning. Some of the herbs in your sorcerer's cabinet will be dried, crushed, and kept in jars. Others may be prepared as ointments, potions, or in specially blended powders.

One thing I would like to recommend here is that you not collect or acquire herbs unless you know that you will actually be needing them. It is very easy to get caught up in the mystique of magical herbalism to a point where you find that you have stuffed your closet full of rue, St. John's wort, henbane, and dozens of other herbs that you may never use. Before purchasing or planting an herb, ask yourself exactly what you will do with it; set it aside and select another species if you cannot think of at least two good, solid answers.

Iron

In traditional Saxon magic, iron has the power to disrupt or redirect psychic energies. It is often used as a protective metal. This is, at least in part, the reasoning behind the lucky horseshoe. The horseshoe is traditionally hung over a doorway with its two ends up to "hold" luck. But this idea is debatable, and sometimes the horseshoe is hung with its two ends down. In England, at the great hall of Oakham Castle in Rutland County (now merged with Leicestershire), countless horseshoes hang on the interior walls with their points down. For the past five hundred years, it has been a custom for English royalty to donate or "forfeit" a horseshoe at the great hall when visiting the town of Oakham.

Points up or down, folklore attests that the horseshoe has a magical effect on its environment. But any piece of iron can be utilized to disrupt or redirect psychic energy. Even scrap iron has been used in counterspells and defensive magic. There are some who believe that just touching iron will cancel or help dispel bad luck brought on by breaking a taboo.

Sharp iron—anything that can cut or perforate—is even more effective. Hooks and shears were once hung in stables to protect livestock. Hammering an iron nail into the headboard over a bed is one method of repelling the *mare* (pronounced MAR-eh), a spirit that torments mortals in their sleep. These night-mares (Old English, *niht maran*) disrupt their victims' sleep and weaken the spirit. Iron horseshoes have also been used to repel the mare.

If you have acquired a seax among your magical tools, this implement can be used to disrupt any negative forces directed at you. Note the difference between the telga (wand) and the seax (knife). The former is used to help your own force flow through your hama (astral body) and connect this power with the outer world, whereas the seax is used to disrupt or redirect outside forces. This tool can be very effective when used in protective spells.

In addition to having a seax, you may also want to keep some iron in your sorcerer's cabinet in the form of pins, small nails, or even iron filings. All iron possesses the same disruptive quality, so your own personal style should determine the form of iron you keep at hand.

Lead

Lead is believed to be an "impure" or even an evil metal. Of course, today we know its reputation is not unfounded. Lead is a neurotoxin that can build up in the body over long periods of exposure. But lead's reputation is not an entirely new development. When the Romans came to Britain, they brought with them the custom of using lead plates or tablets for curses. The aggrieved Roman would engrave into the soft metal a curse against a specific person or group of people. The plate or tablet was then left in a temple or dropped into a sacred pool. The tradition didn't leave Britain when the Romans departed; lead cursing tablets were engraved as late as the 1600s.

Using lead for cursing has fallen out of favor, largely because cursing itself is avoided by most people today, but the fact is that in the real world we are sometimes attacked or otherwise treated unjustly and left with no ordinary means of retaliating. I do not actively condone cursing another person, not because I believe it is innately "immoral," but because it usually is not your best option. If you feel that you need to resort to a curse, I would encourage you to read the fourth chapter of *Travels Through Middle Earth: The Path of a Saxon Pagan*. If you have already read that chapter about wyrd (destiny) and honorable actions, and still think you need to curse someone, please read it again. Everything you do throughout your life, no matter how justified you believe your actions to be, will affect your future destiny.

Once in a very great while you may, being fully cognizant of the cost, nevertheless still feel the need to curse, if for no other reason than to gain a personal sense of closure. If this becomes a frequent practice for you, know that your work will ultimately harm you much more than it will harm your perceived "enemies."

The reason I mention lead at all here is because there are also other, less sinister ways of cursing. There are many influences in our lives that can be safely cursed and wished away. Nicotine addicts, for example, might wish to curse their addiction. Overweight people could curse their emotional dependency on food, if this is the cause of their condition. Heartache is something a person might want to curse in the wake of a loved one's death or a difficult breakup.

This last example also shows how a dangerous and malevolent curse can be turned around into a positive, safe curse. Everyone hurts after a breakup with another person, and when we hurt we often instinctively want to lash out. Instead of doing something that you will surely regret later, why not curse the pain itself? Hate the heartache. If you can acquire a reasonably thin, small sheet of lead, carve your curse directly into the metal. For heartache, the wording could be something like:

Hate and hurt held in my heart
I banish now! Be gone! Depart!

Take the engraved metal to a lake or, if you live near the ocean, the coast and throw it into the water at sunset. Sunset is the eve or beginning of a new day, so it is a good time to set aside things that will impair our future endeavors.

Lead can often be purchased at hardware or plumbing stores. It is also sold to fishing enthusiasts, who use it for molding sinkers and lures. If you cannot find lead in a sheet suitable for engraving, write your curse on paper and tie it securely around a small piece of lead. The ideal, traditional technique, however, is to engrave the curse directly into the metal.

Mead

Mead is a drink made of fermented honey, similar to wine. It was a gift to mankind from the gods, and its importance to the early Saxons cannot be overemphasized. They had nearly twenty words related to this beverage and its consumption. Mead was served to the Saxon in a mead-cup (*meduscenc*), as he or she sat on the bench for drinking mead (*medubenc*) in the hall where mead was served (*meduheall*). There was a word for the field where the mead-hall stood (*meduwang*), which was easy enough to find if you followed the path that led to the mead-hall (*medustig*).

It is not difficult to brew your own mead. I describe the process in an entire chapter devoted to the drink in *Travels Through Middle Earth*, but you can also purchase commercially bottled mead in many wine stores today. The advantage of brewing your own is not only the cost, but also your ability to brew a wide and interesting variety of meads. The advantage of purchasing a commercial mead is, of course, the convenience.

Saxons and other Germanic Pagans often offer mead as a libation to our gods, and the Saxon sorcerer is no exception. Rune sorcerers, especially, like to give offerings of mead to Woden before beginning any important work. From a purely magical perspective, mead is most often used in the preparation of potions known as *metheglins*. We will discuss these in the chapter on wortcunning.

Red Paint

Red paint may seem like a strange thing to keep in your cabinet, but red pigment—typically paint—plays a significant role in Saxon sorcery because of another important magical principle known as the Law of Sympathy. This law asserts that two things that resemble each other have an innate magical connection. The Law of Sympathy is the reasoning behind the poppet or "voodoo doll," formed in the image of the person it is intended to affect, and it is often supplemented by the Law of Contagion by incorporating hair, fingernails, or other intimate items belonging to that person.

The Law of Sympathy connects red pigment with blood. Blood is power. Blood is red. Ergo, anything red has some innate power. Rune sorcerers will often color their runes with red pigment when crafting charms. I do not think anyone would claim that red pigment is as powerful as blood, but it is usually more practical than blood.

My *inhíred* (Saxon tribe) has used red paint effectively for runic healing. Using a safe, water-based red paint, runes were marked over the appropriate area of the body as part of the healing work. Of course, other techniques, notably chanting, were employed at the same time the runes were painted. These runes were then left overnight, and showered or bathed off the following morning. We did this for one of my fellow híredmenn when he needed back surgery. His wife painted runes down his spine to the accompaniment of drumming and chanting; after the surgery, he was released from the hospital much earlier than expected.

I had a bindrune painted in red across my throat the night before I had part of my thyroid removed. Passages from the Anglo-Saxon Rune Poem were read aloud as each part of the bindrune was applied. Other people were chanting, and those voices blended with the readings to build a cacophony of power. It was an intense experience. More importantly, though, the medical procedure went smoothly.

I also keep both red cloth and red thread on hand for magic work. It is the color that connects these to blood, and therefore connects them to power. Red cloth is the best color to use for charm bags, all other things being equal. If you have a reason to use cloth of some other color, bind the charm up with red thread. Can you make an effective charm bag with another color cloth and thread? Of course, you can, but the color red gives your magic a boost because it is a symbolic link with the power of blood.

When you apply the color personally, do not eschew modern advances. A red felt tip marker is often more practical and useful than a brush and bottle of paint. Avoid using markers on your skin, though—the ink often does not wash away readily and may leave a stain for days.

Salt

Salt is one substance I believe is essential for every sorcerer to have on hand. From a magical perspective, due to the Law of Sympathy, salt has a connection to blood because of its taste. Blood tastes salty, and blood is the life fluid. Ergo, salt is linked to life force. This connection is even more apparent to us than it was to the early Saxons, now that we know life began in and emerged from the salty oceans. Saltwater truly is the life blood of Mother Earth.

The magical properties of salt are also related to its power to preserve food. This was especially important before refrigeration. Salting meats and fish was one method to keep them from spoiling. That there is a natural explanation for this is irrelevant. As I said earlier, magic is *super*natural, not *un*natural. The fact remains that salt preserves and protects. This is how it is used in magic. Salt has been used as a magical protection throughout England, Scotland, and Wales. It is one of the magical ingredients prescribed in the Æcerbot charm.

If you feel that you are being magically attacked, throw a handful of salt into a fire. (This is easier to accomplish if you have an actual fireplace.) I have also known witches to protect their homes by pouring a defensive symbol, often runic, in salt just inside the entry door. I do not know of any historic documentation for this latter technique, but it seems to be effective. The rune *eolh* would be a good choice for the defensive symbol, although the salt itself is an important active ingredient in this process.

The idea that spilling salt brings bad luck dates back to at least the 1500s, and possibly much further. The remedy, of course, is to immediately throw a pinch of the spilled salt over your left shoulder.

Because of its preservative property, salt is sometimes used to "set" a magic work, especially when the spell will continue over several days or more. After the physical components of the spell—candles, runes, or other symbols—have been laid out, a circle of salt is poured around them to preserve and contain the work at hand.

I have also seen salt used, and have used it myself, to purify or cleanse a tool as a first step in preparing that tool for magic work. Usually the fire and water spell given in the previous chapter is sufficient for this purpose, but if the object has a questionable past, especially if it was used extensively by another wyrdworker, it can be buried in salt for a fortnight (two weeks) to expel any contrary spirit the tool may harbor.

Spittle

The next two substances I want to mention may seem unusual and perhaps even a little disgusting. The one nice thing I can say about spit is that you will not need to keep any in your sorcerer's cabinet—we each carry around our own supply.

Spit is used to seal and protect. In traditional Saxon magic, the sorcerer's spit (*spatl*) was sometimes mixed with herbs (Griffiths, 187). The very act of spitting brings luck and repels evil influences. Due to the Law of Sympathy, simply pretending to spit has a similar if slightly lesser effect. Spittle has been applied to the skin to dispel warts and rashes, and to seal and protect cuts.

I cannot prove this, but I suspect the power of spittle was originally observed in the behavior of animals licking their wounds. Saliva, including human saliva, does contain several antibacterial compounds that provide a physical rationale for the perceived healing properties, but the significance of spittle is deeper than this. Like blood, spittle has traditionally been used to seal oaths.

At one time two people shaking hands to bind themselves to an agreement would first spit into their palms. Both the similarity and difference between this and an oath of blood brotherhood are readily apparent. Both involve an exchange of body fluids, but the exchange of blood is more penetrating and more permanently binding.

Urine

As with spittle, the only pleasant thing I can say about urine is that you do not have to pack away a supply of it in your sorcerer's cabinet. If at any time you do not have a generous supply, drink a tall glass of water and wait thirty minutes.

From a magic perspective, the power of urine is to claim ownership. Here again, I suspect this to be another concept originally observed in the behavior of animals, especially males. Dogs routinely mark their territories with urine, and male cats are notorious for spraying. These behaviors leave scent markers to let other animals know that the object or immediate area has been claimed. We humans have a relatively weak sense of smell, but traditional sorcerers use magic in much the same way to lay claim to an object or area.

An example of this is found in the classic charm known as a witch bottle. The purpose of this charm is to protect the homestead. To make a witch bottle, fill a small jar or bottle with pins and nails. Note that you are using iron—the pins and nails—to disrupt any negative forces directed at your home. You do not need to use a combination of both, either all pins or all nails work equally well. After this, fill the bottle or jar with your own urine. In doing this you are essentially marking your territory. The bottle should then be sealed tightly and buried somewhere on your property near the home.

Witch bottles can be made for somebody else by using their urine rather than your own. For the obvious reason that most of us do not care to handle another person's urine, the witch bottle is a charm that you usually make for yourself.

There is another tradition in which the witch bottle is not buried, but is cast into a fire. I do not recommend this, as it results in a terrible mess to clean up.

Wax

I do not know of any inherent magical properties of beeswax or paraffin wax, but both of these can be useful in your magic work. Of course, the early Saxons would have only used beeswax. Paraffin wax is less expensive and more readily available for the modern practitioner and is usually just as suitable.

Both beeswax and paraffin wax are malleable at fairly low temperatures. Holding a small piece of wax in your hand will warm it enough to where you can carefully mold and shape it. You can easily mold a piece of wax into the shape of a human being. We have already seen how a figure like this can be used, thanks to the Law of Sympathy, as a magical link. In the same way, wax can be molded into almost any shape you desire. The only limit is your ability to conceive a symbol or image appropriate for your work.

The use of wax overlaps and includes the practice of candle magic. A candle, after all, is simply a lump of wax imbedded with a wick. It is unlikely that the pre-Christian Saxons made much use of candle magic, primarily because they did not often use candles at all. Candle magic became more common as candles became more accessible to the average person. In Buckinghamshire women would thrust two pins through a candle, each pin passing through its wick, while chanting a simple spell. This was done to attract a lover, but candles have been used for almost every purpose imaginable.

In 1970, Raymond Buckland published an excellent book about candle magic. *Practical Candleburning Rituals* has since been reprinted and is available at this time for those who are interested in pursuing the practice. The spells given in his book are also excellent examples of galdor, which will be discussed later.

You will not need all of the items described here, but now you have some idea of how they are used. Hopefully this also gives you some idea as to which ingredients you will be more likely to need.

One other thing I would like to mention before moving on is magical timing. What you do can be more effective if you know when to do it. For the Saxon sorcerer, two things to consider are the day of the week and the phase of the moon. These are only considerations, however, and should not become an impediment to your work. Frequently there will be times when you need to cast a spell even though it is not the best day of the week, or the moon is waning rather than waxing. This does not mean that your spell will have no effect, it only means you will have to work a little harder.

The day of the week is the lesser of these two considerations. There are some who ignore this entirely, arguing that the seven-day week is a Roman contrivance and not integral to Anglo-Saxon tradition. The counterpoint is that the Roman week was adopted and Anglicized early on, certainly before the English kings converted to Christianity, and does significantly reflect an Anglo-Saxon perspective. Both points of view have their merit. As for myself, if I am going to work some magic affecting my home, I will do it on the day sacred to the goddess Frige if it is at all convenient, since she is sovereign over the household. There is certainly no harm in it, and there may be some benefit.

One significant difference between the Roman week days and Saxon week days is that the latter begin at sunset. For example, the Saxon "Monday" begins at sunset on Sunday and ends at sunset the following day.

Another difference is found in the names of the week days. In languages which have evolved from Latin, the days of the week are named after Roman gods; Mars, Mercurius, Iupiter, and so on.

By contrast, the English days of the week are, for the most part, named after Saxon gods who were perceived to embody similar qualities and interests. This is where timing comes into play. If you are working magic to ensure a fair trial it makes sense to do this, when convenient, on Tiw's Day (Tuesday) since the god Tiw takes a special interest in order and justice.

The glaring exception in the Anglicized week is Saturday, which retains the name of the Roman god Saturnus. It is unlikely that we will ever learn why *Dies Saturni* kept its Roman name, but my personal belief is that the early Saxons did not think any of their own deities reflected the same qualities and interests as Saturnus. He was an important agricultural god of seeds and sowing. As a god of the earth and its fertility, Saturnus shares something in common with the Saxon tribe of Wanic gods and goddesses, but apparently not enough with any one deity to forfeit his rulership of the seventh day of the week. The Wanic powers were not worshipped as widely among the Anglo-Saxons as they later were among the Scandinavian peoples. Only brief references to these earth-centered deities survive in works such as *Beowulf* and the Anglo-Saxon Rune Poem. The last day of the week, *Sæterdæg*, may have been a day honoring all of the Wanic powers collectively under the name of a foreign agrarian god.

Because of this agrarian connection, the hours between sunset on Friday and sunset on Saturday are especially conducive to earth-focused magic. This is a good time to work magic for the fertility of the land, for farms or gardens, and also for prosperity.

Sunday is, of course, named for the sun, or for the goddess Sunne, as the Saxons knew her. Unlike the Greeks and Romans, who perceived the sun as a masculine body, northern Europeans saw the sun as feminine. Sunne was a positive figure, and her physical body, the sun, was greatly valued for its use in navigation. For this reason, the hours between sunset on Saturday and sunset on Sunday are conducive to magic intended to promote guidance and understanding.

The following day of the week is named for the moon god, Mona. Here again we see a reversal of gender in contrast to the feminine moon of the southern Europeans. Mona governs the cycles of life. The hours between sunset on Sunday and sunset on Monday are conducive to magic workings to nurture growth, and to any magic related to water or creatures that live in the water.

After this comes Tiw's day. Tiw is the Saxon "sky father" and ruler of the North Star. He is a god of order, stability, and justice. Tiw is sometimes referred to as a war god, but that description could be applied to almost any northern deity. The hours between sunset on Monday and sunset on Tuesday are conducive to magic bolstering the stability of the community, or for a fair judgment in a trial.

Woden's day is named, of course, for the god Woden, the chief god of the Saxons. Woden is a god of inspiration. In this respect he is another deity who can easily be described as a war god, because it helps to be psyched up or inspired when marching into battle with nothing more than a spear and a seax. Woden's inspiration is shared equally with the poet and the musician, as well as the warrior. Woden is also the master magician who discovered the runic mysteries. The hours between sunset on Tuesday and sunset on Wednesday are conducive to runic magic, as well as any magic intended to stimulate and foster creativity.

The following day is named for the Saxon god Thunor. His name means "thunder," and he is the strongest of the gods. Thunor is a protector of Middle Earth (the physical plane). Wielding a mighty hammer, he defends our realm of existence from the depredation of hostile, chaotic forces. For this reason, the hours between sunset on Wednesday and sunset on Thursday are especially conducive to protective magic.

Frige's day is named for Woden's consort, the goddess Frige. She is sovereign over household arts, which in the context of today's society includes almost every industry other than farming, fishing, and fighting. Frige also concerns herself with marriage.

The hours between sunset on Thursday and sunset on Friday are conducive to love magic, magic to protect or stimulate business, and any magic for the benefit of children or the home.

———————

The god Mona gives his name to Monday, but his physical manifestation, the moon, governs all cycles of life and of magic. It is the moon that summons the tides. For centuries on end people have consulted the phase of the moon before planting or cultivating or harvesting their crops. The wyrdworker too considers the moon when planning any spell or charm.

When people today speak of planting or doing anything else "by the moon," they are often referring to the moon's position in the zodiac of classic astrology. This was not a practice among the early Saxons for two reasons: The first is that astrology as we know it is a science based on the constellations of southern Europe. Eventually astrology was accepted in England as it was everywhere else throughout Europe. Would the Saxons have accepted images of Castor and Pollux (Gemini), or Zeus' lover Ganymede (Aquarius) if they had not abandoned their own traditions? We may never know. I would like to think that, just as there is a Chinese astrology, we may someday evolve an astrology based on the constellations of northern Europe.

The second reason classic astrology played no role in the lives of the early Saxons is because they were largely an illiterate people. They had no almanacs or calendars to tell them when the moon entered or left the sign of Cancer. The zodiac consists of twelve imaginary, equal zones across the path of the sun. These only loosely correspond with the southern European constellations for which they are named. Determining the moon's sign on any given evening is not a simple matter of glancing up at the sky.

Of course today we *do* have almanacs and calendars that tell us precisely where Mona is traveling along the zodiac. I do not advocate an eclectic method of magic because I believe it distracts the practitioner from mastering any specific approach. It is natural, though, for a practitioner to occasionally explore and even adopt a procedure or system from a different discipline. Classic astrology has become an integral part of our contemporary culture, and it would be unreasonable to rebuke a fellow drýmann or drýicge for integrating astrological moon signs into his or her work.

For the Saxons, though, it was the moon's phases that mattered. Moon phases *are* visible to the naked eye. With only a little practice, you can quickly learn to distinguish the full moon from a moon that is a day early or later than full.

What the traditional Saxon sorcerer looks for is whether the moon is waxing or waning. By *waxing* we mean the moon is growing larger, from new to full. The waxing moon is conducive to magic intended to nurture and cause things to expand or grow. Any time you want to increase something, plan your work during the waxing moon.

A *waning* moon is diminishing from full to dark. This is the time for magic intended to eliminate or weaken things. Some people shy away from working magic during the waning moon because they do not understand its nature. To weaken or diminish something is not necessarily "evil."

The trick to working with the moon is learning how to phrase your magic in such a way that you ride the prevailing lunar influence. Almost any magic work can be conducted with equal efficiency under both a waxing or waning moon, assuming the work is designed appropriately. Let us assume you want to help a friend who is battling a chronic viral infection. If the moon is waxing, or growing larger, design a spell to strengthen your friend and bolster his or her health. If the moon is waning, your spell should target and attempt to banish the virus. These are two entirely different approaches, but the result, should your magic succeed, will be the same.

Review

1. What is amber used for?

2. Why are petroleum-based ointments only used over small areas of the skin?

3. Describe the magical properties of iron.

4. What is the Law of Sympathy?

5. What is the best time to work a spell intended to expand your creative skills?

Runes and Rúncræft

The Futhorc:
The Runes of England

What exactly are runes?

The answer to this seemingly simple question is surprisingly complex. Superficially, runes are northern European alphabets that were in use before the coming of Christianity and during its early years in England and Scandinavia. The idea of using rune "stones" for divination is a modern contrivance. Historically, stones with runic engravings were not little pebbles, they were boulders. And the stone surface did not have a solitary rune engraved on it, but entire sentences inscribed in a runic statement. Rune stones were often erected as grave markers or monuments, and the inscriptions on them described the people or events to be remembered. The runes engraved on the huge stones consisted of the straight, angular strokes favorable for inscribing on hard surfaces.

Before we go any further, let me say here that you do not need to master the runes to succeed as a Saxon druid or witch. If you feel no affinity for these ancient symbols, you can skip ahead to More Magic Techniques and continue on from there to explore galdor, wortcunning, and wiglung. But rúncræft can be a rewarding study and can enhance any other techniques you may favor. Just as the rune sorcerer benefits from knowledge of magical herbs, the wyrtwita (herb sorcerer) and the galdre (song sorcerer) can benefit from knowledge of the runes.

The use of these northern symbols continued for some years into the Christian era before they were eventually replaced by the Roman alphabet. Scandinavian runes, in fact, were used well into the fifteenth century CE. In England, the runic alphabet was abandoned much earlier. The Roman-based alphabet used for recording Old English made some concessions to the old style, retaining runic-based letters, such as *thorn* (Þ), which have since disappeared.

The runes meant more to our ancestors than the modern ABC's mean to us today. The word *rune* (Old English, *rún*) means a "mystery." Each runic character represents a sound, much like the letters of our alphabet, yet each simultaneously embodies a sacred mystery. These mysteries were recorded in Iceland, Norway, and England in three separate Rune Poems and are further alluded to in an Icelandic text known as the Hávamál. Each poem describes the sacred mysteries of its respective culture. Just as these cultures— Icelandic, Norwegian, and English—bore some resemblance to each other, so too do their indigenous mysteries.

The three Rune Poems described the characters found in different rune scripts; the Elder Futhark (Proto-Germanic), the Younger Futhark (Scandinavian), and the Anglo-Saxon Futhorc (English). Most published material today focuses on the Elder Futhark, whereas this book will focus on the Anglo-Saxon Futhorc. The point I wish to emphasize just now is that there is no one single set of runes. While there are similarities between the various runic alphabets, there are also very distinct differences.

One commonality shared by all three rune sets is that the runes themselves are symbols. Often today the runes of the Elder Futhark are etched or painted on small stones and marketed for divination or fortune-telling. This has led to a common misperception that the stones themselves are the "runes." A rune is a symbol of a mystery.

If you do not have a symbol, you do not have a rune. A stone without a symbol is just a rock.

Small divinatory sets of runes—whether in the form of pebbles, baked clay, or antlers—may be a modern innovation, but this does not make them any less valid or useful for the contemporary Pagan. We make use of many tools that our ancestors did not have: personal computers, automatic dishwashers, propane camping gear, telephones. For example, a book like this one that you are reading, printed rather than hand copied, was unknown to the pre-Christian world. Modern sets of runes are a legitimate manifestation of an old and traditional method of divination. The Roman historian Tacitus described a procedure the Germanic people used for "casting lots." The characters described by Tacitus were marked on slips of wood rather than more permanent stones or bone, so we see that divinatory rune stones are traditional in spirit if not in exact form. The important point to keep in mind is that the rune is the symbol, not the medium it is inscribed or painted on.

In the past, runes were often etched into weapons and armor to make use of their mystic essence. The appearance of runes on weaponry is well documented because iron holds up well over the centuries. Runes were prominent, however, not only on weapons but throughout the Anglo-Saxon world. Less militant objects, such as household pottery, have often been found with runic inscriptions. Evidence indicates that runes, in fact, were used far more often for charms and blessings than for divining the future. There were different techniques for using runes as charms, as we will discuss in a later chapter, Rúncræft.

In England, at least, runic symbols beyond those of the Futhorc are often found on pottery and other artifacts. Some scholars have suggested that these rune-like symbols may have been purely decorative. But just because we do not know the significance of a symbol today does not mean it had no specific significance fifteen centuries ago. These "decorative" symbols may have been personal glyphs or devices used to identify a family's possessions. This would not be a surprising practice in a society that was largely illiterate. A symbol used in this way, however, is not truly a rune because there is no sacred mystery embodied in its form.

One commonality of the Elder Futhark, the Younger Futhark, and the Old English Futhorc is that they are all inseparably wedded to Germanic thought. The rune is a symbol representing a sacred mystery specific to the cultures of the northern European people. If you divorce the runes from these concepts, they are no longer runes, they are only Germanic symbols being utilized in another context. I am not suggesting anything horrible will happen when they are used in this way. Nobody is going to blow up because he or she used a rune without understanding the Germanic mystery it embodies. But just as it is not a rune if there is no symbol, it is not a rune if there is no sacred mystery.

Many people who use runes today use them for *sortilege*, the practice of foretelling the future by drawing random symbols or images. It is an ancient and time-honored system of divination. Admittedly runes can be used in this way quite successfully, but if this is the *only* use you intend, why bother with these odd and inscrutable European hen-scratches? The Tarot, with an illustration on each card conveying its meaning, is a much easier tool to master for the purpose of sortilege. I am not suggesting that the Tarot is in any way shallow. However, the cards of a modern Tarot deck are thoroughly illustrated, a convenience that runes lack. For that matter, you can make up your own set of symbols for sortilege; perhaps a heart for "love," a dollar sign for "money," a smiley face for "good fortune," and so forth.

When people use the runes only for sortilege, the inherent mysteries represented by these symbols are typically reduced to simple concepts, one rune meaning "prosperity," another meaning "fertility," and so on. The depth and complexity of the mysteries are lost. None of the runes have one meaning. Each is a complex concept that can be interpreted in many ways depending on who and what and where you are at that moment in time. To connect with these sacred mysteries, with these elements of northern European spirituality, is the real value of runic study. I again refer students of the Futhorc to *Travels Through Middle Earth: The Path of the Saxon Pagan* for a deeper understanding of Saxon spirituality. Likewise for the student of the Younger Futhark, I would recommend any similar book on the spirituality of Forn Sed or Ásatrú. It is important to be spiritually centered in the cultural context of the runes to fully appreciate them.

The runes not only represent sacred northern European mysteries; each set represents specifically the mysteries of its respective culture. Since these northern people held similar world views, those mysteries often coincided, but not always. For example, there is a vast difference between the mystery embodied in the Anglo-Saxon *cen* and the corresponding Norwegian rune. In the Anglo-Saxon Rune Poem, *cen* refers to a fire; the corresponding Norwegian rune, *kaun*, describes an ulcer or sore that causes the death of children. Furthermore, these rune scripts vary in number, with the Futhorc having approximately twice as many characters as the Younger Futhark.

The divinatory rune sets sold today are almost always sets of the Elder Futhark. Unfortunately there is no lore to shed light on what meanings early Germanic tribes ascribed to them. The meanings given are usually derived from the much later Anglo-Saxon Rune Poem. These same meanings may or may not have been ascribed to the equivalent runes of the Elder Futhark. Runic meanings certainly differ dramatically between some characters shared by the Futhorc and the Younger Futhark. The Elder Futhark is so called, obviously, because it is the oldest of the rune scripts. Its exact age depends on whom you talk to and whom you want to believe. Scandinavian myth asserts that Odin (whom the Saxon Pagan knows as Woden) claimed the mysteries of the runes during a ritual of self-sacrifice where he hanged himself on the World

Tree for nine days and nights. This event presumably occurred around 250 BCE.

Those who do not believe in the gods naturally dispute this origin, and instead look for similarities between the Elder Futhark and the Roman alphabet. The similarities in appearance are unquestionably present, especially with runes such as *rád* (R), *hagol* (H), *is* (I), *sigil* (S), *tir* (T) and *beorc* (B). The non-theist theories presume that these Germanic characters were copied from Mediterranean alphabets, thus pushing the origin of the Elder Futhark as much as four centuries (or more) forward on history's time line.

As a Pagan, I do not see any inherent contradiction between these ideas. Obviously the mysteries would have to be discovered or codified before they could be passed on to humankind, and in "god time," four centuries is no more than a blink of a divine eye. I care not a whit about the similarities between the various Futharks and the Roman alphabet. I will readily concede that the letter *R* may have inspired the form of *rád*, mostly because it does not matter. So what? The shape of a rune is its physical expression, not its divine essence. It may be true that the Roman alphabet inspired the shape and design of some of the runes, and it may at the same time be equally true that the runes themselves—the mysteries—were initially identified by Woden. These arguments are not mutually exclusive.

The oldest of the rune scripts, the Elder Futhark, consists of twenty-four characters. Today they are referred to by reconstructed Proto-Germanic names. The Elder Futhark is what people are usually talking about when they speak of "the" runes, and it is probably what you have been exposed to if you have read or studied anything about the runes before now. The good news is that all of your prior work will apply to some extent to a study of the Anglo-Saxon runes.

The Younger Futhark is the youngest of the rune scripts. These Scandinavian runes evolved as a distinct script around CE 800, around the same time that the Elder Futhark was disappearing from use. It was a tighter, more concise script with only sixteen characters. The Younger Futhark is rarely explored these days, which seems odd in light of the fact that Ásatrú, or Icelandic Paganism, is currently the most popular form of northern European spirituality in North America.

The Medoburg Kindred is a respected group of Ásatrúar with kinsmen in several eastern states. A few years ago they invited me to one of their *blóts*—a religious service—that a kinsman in Maryland hosted. Ann Gróa Sheffield and Richard Ambrose picked me up early on the morning of the blót, and we all took turns driving to the gathering. Once we arrived, I found their kinsman, our host, to be a man deeply devoted to his Icelandic spiritual heritage. He enlisted my help in cooking some lamb from Iceland. Icelandic sheep are a distinct breed, and this man was determined that the feast following the blót would have a connection with the island where his spirituality evolved.

Our host's dedication to Iceland did not end at the feast table. He offered to consult the runes for some of his guests and, as an Ásatrúar, the runes he used were those of the Younger Futhark. He had carved his runes on wooden staves, or flat sticks. It was clear that this was no simple game of fortune telling. The first thing he did was take up the rune staves in his hands and pray to Odin. He stepped into the role of a *gothi*, an Icelandic chieftain-priest. Medoburg is an egalitarian kindred with no official chief as such, but at that moment, this man was our authority.

After praying for Odin's guidance, the man drew three rune staves and interpreted them. Although the Younger Futhark consists of only sixteen symbols, there was nothing simplistic about these divinations. Indeed, the merging of Icelandic spirituality with Icelandic runes was, for me, a profound experience. Ann has since told me that she too uses the Younger Futhark exclusively now.

The mysteries of the Younger Futhark are described in two Rune Poems: the Icelandic Rune Poem and the Norse Rune Poem. The most obvious difference between the Younger and Elder Futharks is that the former lacks eight of the latter's characters. But the Younger Futhark is not a runic alphabet with pieces missing. It reflects the unique mysteries of the Icelandic and Norwegian cultures. Some runes, while retaining the identical form, have very different meanings in these poems. For example, the fourth rune in the Younger Futhark means "the mouth of a river" in a Norwegian context. In an Icelandic context, however, this same rune means the All-Father, the god Odin. Some other runes of the Younger Futhark have equally distinct interpretations depending on whether they are viewed from a Norwegian or Icelandic perspective.

How can one rune have two different meanings? One might as well ask why the word *bum* means one thing to Americans and quite another to the British. Language changes from one culture to another, and the runes are, essentially, sacred languages. Some of the symbols for these cultural mysteries changed meaning on the voyage to Iceland. Each became a distinct voice describing the mysteries of its respective culture.

The focus of this book, however, is yet another runic alphabet, neither the youngest nor the eldest, but in between these two. The Futhorc, the runes of the Anglo-Saxons, consists of thirty-three characters. Of these, twenty-nine are described in the Anglo-Saxon Rune Poem. Our understanding of the Anglo-Saxon runes comes from two sources. The first source is the Rune Poem; the second is personal revelation.

Personal revelation can be entirely valid so long as we recognize it for what it is. Everyone who has ever written anything about the runes has included at least some of his or her personal revelations, or repeated those shared previously by other authors. Diana Paxson, writing about the Elder Futhark in her book *Taking Up the Runes*, does an unusual and exceptionally admirable job of distinguishing "Ancient Meanings"—interpretations based on the three Rune Poems—and "Modern Meanings." But she is the exception rather than the rule.

The modern meanings of the runes—those meanings not found directly in the Rune Poems—are all derived from personal revelations. Often one's personal revelations can be confirmed through consensus, but equally often a consensus coalesces simply because many people have heard the same interpretation. Even this does not invalidate the interpretation, but it is important to distinguish between these personal revelations and the lore passed down to us in the Rune Poems. For a study of the Futhorc, we must look specifically to the Anglo-Saxon Rune Poem as the source of this lore.

The origins of the Anglo-Saxon runes have been dated back as far as 400 CE, well into the Pagan era, but the Rune Poem itself was not composed for several more centuries and was preserved in a tenth-century manuscript. Thus we are looking at a poem composed and recorded by Christian scribes. For the most part, those scribes had no incentive or interest in preserving the earlier beliefs of the Pagan Saxons, so we must often read between the lines and search for clues to enlighten us as to those earlier beliefs. Here too I believe it is important to clearly distinguish, as far as possible, our own speculation from the actual words that have been passed down to us.

If you would pursue the study of the Futhorc, I urge you to keep these distinctions in mind. Always remember that the Rune Poem and the runes themselves are the ultimate source of all the revelation and speculation you will find espoused anywhere. Do not accept without question any other person's speculations, including my own speculations in this book. What I have found in the runes and what others have found may help you on your own journey, but it is *your* journey. Look to the source—the runes themselves and to the poem that hints at their meaning—and form your own speculations. Meditate on a rune and find your own personal revelation. Explore the ideas and inspirations of others, but never lose sight of the source.

As mentioned above, the Futhorc has more runes than either the Elder or Younger Futhark. If you are already familiar with the Elder Futhark, you will see many similarities, because the meanings now associated with the Elder script have largely been extrapolated from the Anglo-Saxon Rune Poem. The Rune Poem also describes five additional runes not found in the Elder Futhark. Furthermore, the fourth rune of the Elder Futhark, the rune known as *ansuz*, becomes the twenty-sixth rune of the Anglo-Saxon Futhorc, where it is known as *æsc* and has an entirely different meaning. It is replaced in the Futhorc by the rune *os*.

I cannot overemphasize the importance of centering yourself spiritually as a Saxon Pagan if you would reap the maximum benefit of working with the Futhorc. Again, I recommend *Travels Through Middle Earth* if you do not know where to start in this regard. You will find that book has very little information about runes, which was intentional. An understanding of the runes is not a requirement for exploring Anglo-Saxon spirituality; however, an understanding of Anglo-Saxon spirituality is indeed essential for those who wish to fully explore the runes of the Futhorc.

Making a Divinatory Rune Set

Sets of the Elder Futhark are sold everywhere as "the runes," but the entire Futhorc is much more difficult to find commercially. You will probably need to make your own set. This is easier than it sounds, and there is some benefit to making your own runes for divination. By making them yourself, you put a part of yourself into your runes.

The first thing to consider is the medium you will use. As we have seen, runes do not have to be painted on or carved into small stones. It is my personal opinion that stones are less desirable than other materials. Stone can be difficult to engrave, and paint is likely to chip away with use. That said, small, smooth river rocks are a good choice if you want to work with stone. A rune is carefully marked into each stone with a rotary engraving tool. Dremel is the best known brand, and these power rotary tools are often referred to generically as "dremel tools." Obviously the pre-Christian Saxons did not make use of power tools, but they also did not carve runes on little pebbles, so the point is moot.

Runes can also be painted on river rocks, with or without the engraving. I have also seen stones marked with permanent marker pens. Whether using a pen or paint, the color is less likely to chip away if applied to an engraved indentation. As for what color to use, red is the obvious choice, as discussed in the previous chapter.

Antler and bone are two other durable materials that can be used for divinatory rune sets. Antler disks are sometimes sold by craft suppliers as "buttons." Be sure to purchase buttons without holes drilled into them. Larger disks, at least one inch in diameter, are preferred. Antler is easily engraved with a power rotary tool, and it takes color readily. Bone is also an easy material to work with if you can find it in a usable size and shape.

In the first century of the Christian Era, the Roman historian Tacitus described a Pagan practice of carving lots onto slips of wood, and for this reason wood is a popular material for those who make their own sets of divinatory runes. As with the telga (Saxon wand), trees from the Anglo-Saxon Rune Poem are often favored: oak, ash, hawthorn, yew, or birch. But this is personal preference. Any wood can be used. Cut disks of wood from a sturdy branch at least one inch in diameter. If you do not want to cut your own wood disks, some craft supply shops sell buttons or disks of wood. Flat craft sticks can also be used for this purpose. If you do not care for the Popsicle stick appearance, clip off the rounded ends to give each stick a sharper, more rectangular shape. Craft sticks work especially well if you intend to cast or throw your runes for divination. When engraving wood, I recommend an electric wood burner. These are inexpensive and easy to use.

Perhaps the simplest medium for a set of divination runes, and the medium I recommend for beginners, is cardstock. Did the pre-Christian Saxons use cardstock? No. But ask yourself why not. Because they did not have cardstock to work with. There is no reason to suppose they would not have used it if it were available to them. To make a simple set of divination runes, buy a pack of blank, unlined index cards and use a bold red marker to draw your runes.

After you have decided what medium to use, you will need to decide how many runes you are going to make. There are twenty-nine runes described in the Anglo-Saxon Rune Poem, but there are four other runes that have no extant lore. I work with the twenty-nine, using the others only in writing, but you may decide to work with all thirty-three symbols, relying on your intuition to understand the four runes we have no historical understanding of.

Some rune sorcerers insist that the runes must be "blooded," that is, marked with your own blood. This belief comes from the Hávamál, a poem from the *Poetic Edda*. But the poem is referring to using runes in active magic work, not in divination. Staining your runes with your blood creates a bond because of the Law of Contagion. On the other hand, many people—probably the majority—who practice runic wiglung (divination) do not mark their runes with blood, and this does not impede their ability in any measurable way.

You may be fortunate enough to find a set of Anglo-Saxon runes for sale at your local alternative spirituality shop, or perhaps at a Pagan festival. You do not have to make your own set if you can acquire one in some other way. The two sets of divinatory runes I use most often were gifts from my híredmenn (members of my tribal family), and both sets work quite well. I also have sets of runes made by other people in every medium that we have discussed: stone, antler, bone, wood, and even cardstock.

I need to include a word of caution here concerning commercially produced rune cards. As with other sets of runes, most of these are usually decks featuring the Elder Futhark, but occasionally decks of Anglo-Saxon runes (Futhorc) are published. Whether Elder Futhark or Futhorc, these decks are illustrated with images intended to convey each rune's meaning or mystery, much as the Tarot is illustrated for the same purpose. I have been extremely disappointed with the rune decks that I have seen over the years. The artist almost invariably embellishes his or her illustrations with personal and fanciful images that are not supported by the Anglo-Saxon Rune Poem. The only deck I can recommend is the Martin Rune Deck, published by Wolfden Designs (http://www.wolfden-designs.com). The cards in this deck are attractively illustrated with images that are faithful to the lore.

This section of the book has been designed to help the reader grasp and claim the mysteries inherent in the Futhorc. It is a good idea to have a set of runes—whether these are stone or bone, antler or wood, or cards—to use for study and meditation. As you examine the runes, explore them one chapter at a time. This will be more effective than leaping around from one chapter to another. Unlike most books, which describe the runes in "alphabetical order," the runes are presented here in conceptual groupings. I have known quite a few people who diligently studied the runes and then later could not remember the distinction between *sigel* (sun) and *dæg* (day). By grouping these two runes together—along with others—in an earthly runes category, the contrast should be more readily understood.

Working through the following chapters, we will begin by looking at the trees and plants of the Rune Poem. From there we will go on to the animal runes, then the aforementioned "earthly" (natural) runes followed by a grouping of runes describing human activity and interactions, and finally runes that I define as belonging to the "outer world." This last category is different from the earthly runes in that the symbols represent mankind's own interactions with the world.

Each rune section begins with the rune itself, its name, and its English meaning. The next item in parentheses is a rough guide for pronouncing the name of the rune. After this, I give the appropriate section of the Rune Poem in Old English, followed by my own Modern English translation.

I recommend keeping a study journal. As you read about each rune, write down any passage or phrase that seems to stand out. Add to this any personal revelation that may come to you as you meditate on the rune. Do not worry about what that revelation may or may not mean as you record it. Later, as you progress in your studies, you may find deeper meaning in your vision.

Meditation is important to your understanding of the runes. You can read what I have to say about them and what other authors have said about them, but what are the runes saying to you? These are powerful symbols. They can speak to you, but in order for them to do so, you must take time to listen.

As you work your way through the next five chapters, spend some time with each rune before moving on to the next. Read the translation of the respective passage of the Rune Poem. Look at the rune itself and try to connect with it. For each rune, I give a description of its form and how I personally relate to this. There is nothing traditional, historical, or official about my commentaries concerning the shapes of these symbols. You may relate to the rune in an entirely different way, and that is perfectly all right so long as you relate to it in *some* way. Remember that the runes themselves embody mysteries.

Meditate on each rune before going on to the next. Close your eyes and focus on your breathing until you reach a calm, relaxed state. Visualize the rune itself. Let it speak to you.

You may want to begin your meditation with a brief prayer to Woden for guidance. In Germanic belief, the god Woden is the master of rune magic. He appears as an old man, often hooded or wearing a floppy brimmed cap. Your prayer need not be lengthy or complex. It can be something as simple as, "Woden, wise one, I ask for understanding of (name of rune)." An offering of beer or mead is a nice gesture too. After all, if you are going to ask for something, it is only polite to offer something in exchange.

Let me hasten to add that there is nothing wrong if you are not receiving a flood of personal revelations during these meditations. You are merely listening to the runes, giving these symbols an opportunity to speak to you; you are not demanding explanations. If you do not get any impressions, it may be because you already have a sufficient understanding of that mystery. And by sufficient, I mean sufficient at this time. The study of runes is an ongoing, lifelong process.

Do not rush the first steps of this process. There is no reason you should attempt to comprehend more than one rune each day. If you work at this daily, you will have examined all of the Futhorc in about one month. You cannot devote ample attention to each rune if you go any faster than this.

Remember to keep a record of your progress in your journal. It is a good idea to devote a full page or two to each rune. Even if this leaves a lot of blank space, you may have more notes to add later.

———

While it is essential to develop your own relationship with the Futhorc, the perspective of another person can be of considerable help. At the back of this book is a bibliography that includes rune books written by a variety of authors. As you study the runes, do not hesitate to seek out the opinions of others. Just keep in mind that their views are indeed opinions, speculations, and personal insights. The only historical knowledge we have concerning the mysteries of the Futhorc is what we can discern from the Anglo-Saxon Rune Poem.

You will find, too, that almost all of the books in the bibliography devote themselves to the Elder Futhark. This does not negate the value of these books for those who would study the lost runes of England. As mentioned earlier, the meanings assigned today to the Elder Futhark are primarily taken from the passages of the Anglo-Saxon Rune Poem. Likewise, the modern commentaries and insights concerning the Elder Futhark are often rooted in those same Old English verses, so do not accept what I have to say in this book as your one and only truth. Other books will give you a broader perspective. When you see a strong conflict between what I say and what someone else says, return to the Rune Poem and consider its words carefully. These verses or passages are the only extant lore preserving the mysteries of the Futhorc.

In your studies, do not hesitate to supplement your reading with your own personal revelations. During your meditations, a rune might speak to you in some way that is inconsistent with the Rune Poem. This does not mean that your revelation is invalid. The runes hold very deep mysteries, and how one of these ancient symbols speaks to you may be entirely different from how it speaks to me. You will probably notice after a time that you have a closer affinity for or understanding of some runes than of others. There are a great number of factors—lifestyle, career, affectional orientation, age—that can influence how the runes speak to you. In the third chapter, I discuss the rune *feoh*, a rune meaning "cattle," and I explain that it rarely indicates a cow for those of us who use the runes today, but if you happen to raise cattle, whether for a hobby or for a living, that is very likely the meaning this rune will have for you.

If you wish to work with the final four runes of the Futhorc—*cweorth*, *gár*, *calc*, and *stán*—you will have to rely entirely on personal revelation. As we will discuss later, there is no surviving lore to give us any insight as to the mysteries inherent in these runes.

To make the most effective use of this book, I recommend you follow these steps for each rune:

- Read the section of this book pertinent to the rune, paying particular attention to the Modern English translation of that passage of the Rune Poem.

- Look at the rune itself, at the shape of the symbol. Refer back to my commentary on the shape of that rune. If this does not make sense to you, study the shape of the rune and see if there is something else you can relate it to.

- Ask Woden for guidance, and then meditate on the rune. Sit in a quiet place with your eyes closed and concentrate on your breathing until your mind is calm and relaxed. Visualize the shape of the rune and try to keep that shape focused in your mind. Let the rune speak to you, if it will.

- Record any insights you may have concerning the rune in your personal journal, even if those insights make no sense to you at this time. I also think it is a good idea to record the relevant passage of the Rune Poem, so you can readily compare this with your insights.

After this, the next step in mastering the runes is practical experience. I was going to say the "final step," but there never will be a final step; you can work with the Futhorc for decades and continue to discover more about these symbols.

In the next chapters, we will discuss and explore the twenty-nine runes described in the Anglo-Saxon Rune Poem, but for now, as an easy reference, here is my translation of the poem itself:

The Anglo-Saxon Rune Poem

FEOH (Cattle) are compensation for everyone,
   though each man shall greatly share his
if he will be awarded honors from his lord.

UR (Aurochs) is brave and has horns above,
   this very fierce animal fights with its horns,
a great wanderer of the moors, it is a proud creature.

THORN (Hawthorn) is exceedingly sharp for every servant,
   seizing it is evil, and it is extremely harsh
to each man who rests among it.

OS (The God) is the creator of all language,
   wisdom's foundation and consolation of sages
and every man's joy and trust.

RÁD (The Ride) up to every man's hall is
   comfortable and very fast for he who sits high on
a mighty horse over the miles.

CEN (Pine) is a tree known by all for its flame,
   shining and brilliant it often burns
where the people relax inside.

GYFU (A Gift) from others is an honor and praise,
   a help and of worth, and for sojourners everywhere
a benefit and presence that is otherwise missing.

WYNN (Joy) possesses him who knows little want,
   illnesses and sorrows, and himself has
prosperity and happiness and also a sufficient dwelling.

N HAGOL (Hail) is the whitest of seeds, its circling comes
 from the lofty sky,
it tosses in the wind's shower,
it then becomes water afterwards.

✝ NÍED (Need) is oppressive on the heart,
 although it often befalls this affliction of men
to help and to heal somewhat,
if it is heard beforehand.

| IS (Ice) is extremely cold, very slippery,
 it glistens clear, like precious gems,
a floor wrought by frost, fair thing seen.

◈ GEAR (The Year) is mankind's joy, when the god bequeaths,
 ruler of the sacred sky, the earth offers
splendid crops for the well-born and the poor.

↓ ÉOH (Yew) is a rough tree on the outside,
 hard and secured in the earth, keeper of the fires,
sustained by deep roots, it is a pleasure to have on one's land.

⟨ PEORTH (Gaming) is always sport and laughter,
 where boastful they sit to make war
in the banquet hall cheerfully together.

Y EOLH (Elk-Sedge) is native to the marsh,
 it grows in the water, it can wound cruelly,
the blood of any man burns who in any way dares to seize it.

ᛋ SIGEL (The Sun) for sailors is always hoped for,
 when they depart over the fishes' bath,
until their ship carries them to land.

ᛏ TIR (The North Star) is one signal, it holds faith well
  with nobles, it is always on track,
throughout night's darkness it never deceives.

ᛒ BEORC (Birch) is without fruit, it bears even so,
  it bears shoots instead of fruit, its branches are beautiful,
high in the tree tops decorated attractively,
laden with foliage, lofty pressing.

ᛖ EH (The Horse) is for lords the joy of the aristocracy,
  horse hooves boastful, where around the hero,
prosperous in respect to horses, it exchanges discourse,
and its restlessness is ever a help.

ᛗ MANN (Person) with joy is beloved of his kin,
  even though each one depart away,
for moreover the lord wills his fate,
the destitute flesh be delivered to the earth.

ᛚ LAGU (Water) seems of endless length to people,
  if they must venture on unstable ships,
and the sea waves terrify them exceedingly,
and the ship does not heed its reins.

ᛝ ING (Lord Ing) was first seen among the East Danes
  it is said,
until he later went back over the sea, his chariot following after,
thus the brave men named that hero.

ᛞ DÆG (Day) is the god's ambassador, beloved of men,
  the great god's light, mirth and also hope,
prosperous and poor, all enjoy it.

ETHEL (Home) is very dear to all people,
if there they have the opportunity for justice and honesty while
enjoying prosperity in the dwelling most often.

ÁC (The Oak) is on Earth for the children of men,
meat-animal's fodder, it travels often over the gannet's bath,
the sea tests whether the oak possesses noble truth.

ÆSC (Ash Tree) is lofty, glorified by men,
stiff in its trunk, it holds its position exactly,
although it fights against many men.

YR (Bow) is for noblemen and warriors everywhere
joy and a mark of distinction, upon a fair horse,
steadfast on its course, a part of the war-gear.

IOR (Beaver) is a river fish, and though he resides there,
he forages on land, he has a fair dwelling,
water surrounding, that place he joyfully holds dear.

EAR (The Ground) is loathsome to all men,
yet certainly the body will be set upon there,
the corpse grows cold, the soil accepts its pale bedfellow;
leaves fall, pleasures depart, men cease to be.

Following the chapters describing the runes is a chapter on rúncræft, or rune magic, and later a chapter on wiglung, including runic divination. Both of these arts will give you practical experience to deepen your understanding of the runic mysteries. In the chapters describing each rune, I have also included possible rune combinations to use for crafting charms and runic helms.

Whether we use runes for magic or divination, the value of these lost runes of England is directly proportionate to the degree in which we incorporate them in our daily lives.

Review

1. What does the word *rune* mean?
2. Which is the oldest of the rune scripts? The youngest?
3. What is sortilege?
4. Why are woods such as oak and birch often favored by rune workers?
5. What do the runes *cweorth, gár, calc,* and *stán* have in common?

Runes of Leaf and Root

Many of us today are so divorced from the world around us that the entire plant kingdom is perceived as little more than a green backdrop for the activities of humankind and animals. But at the time the Rune Poem was composed, and in the centuries preceding this one, people were more directly dependent on and aware of the herbs and roots and trees that grew around them.

Trees provided firewood, fodder for livestock, and the raw material for constructing shelter, tools, weapons, and ships. Some trees, living through generations of men and women, became geographical markers. A tree such as this was often a symbol of the continuity of the local community, and it would be accompanied by a claim of being the largest or oldest of its kind. The people of northern Europe felt a kinship with the trees around them. The *Poetic Edda*, written in the thirteenth century, claims that the first man and woman were created from an ash tree and an elm tree. For the Anglo-Saxons, trees were also a habitat for Elves, wood-woses, moss-wives, and other spirit creatures. The Anglo-Saxons occasionally built temples of worship, especially in Kent, but they more often honored their gods in sacred groves (Hutton, 270).

Five trees—the oak, ash, hawthorn, birch, and yew—are represented by the runes of the Futhorc. (Six, if you want to count the pine, but the relevant passage in the Rune Poem focuses on pine wood rather than the pine tree itself. The "pine" rune—*cen*—is often translated as "fire" so as not to mislead the student of rune lore.) Each of these five trees is a living incarnation of a Germanic mystery, and each has lessons to share with those who would listen and observe.

At the same time the runic alphabets were evolving, the Celtic tribes were developing another form of writing known as the Beith-luis-nin. Also known both as Ogham writing and as the Celtic Tree Alphabet, every symbol in this Celtic script was associated with either a tree or some other form of plant life. All of the sacred trees of the Futhorc are also represented in the Beith-luis-nin:

Tree	Futhorc	Beith-Luis-Nin
Oak	Ác	Dair
Ash	Æsc	Nin
Hawthorn	Thorn	Uath
Birch	Beorc	Beith
Yew	Éoh	Idad

The pine was also represented in the Beith-luis-nin by the symbol *ailm*. But here the similarity ends. Each of the symbols of the Beith-luis-nin is associated with a tree or plant, while most of the Futhorc runes are not. And when the Futhorc and the Beith-luis-nin share an image such as the oak or the ash, the symbolic language is as distinct as Old English is from Gaelic. Nevertheless, the Futhorc and the Beith-luis-nin both reflect an awareness and appreciation of trees that few of us have today.

What kinds of trees grow in your immediate vicinity? Do you know? This knowledge is not essential to progress in your study of runes, but I believe you will have a deeper appreciation for the differences between oak and ash and thorn if you take the time to go outside and discover the distinct and interesting species of trees that you live among. Many bookstores carry inexpensive tree identification books. One of the better online resources is provided by the Arbor Day Foundation at http://www.arborday.org/trees/whattree/. You will find it much easier to identify deciduous (non-evergreen) trees in the summer when their leaves are on full display.

I also recommend learning to recognize plant life other than trees. Many of the "weeds" that grow underfoot are useful herbs. Plantain (*Plantago major*) will help wounds heal and can soothe a bee or wasp sting. Mugwort (*Artemisia vulgaris*) is a protective herb sacred to Woden. These species have two things in common. First, they are both today considered to be invasive weeds in parts of North America. Second, they are both named in the Nine Herbs Charm recorded in the *Lacnunga*, a tenth-century Anglo-Saxon manuscript. Eleven centuries ago, plantain and mugwort were sacred herbs used for healing. In the Nine Herbs Charm, these plants are assisted by the god Woden and his nine "glory-twigs" (*wuldortanas*). These twigs may have been wooden staves carved with healing runes. This is, of course, speculation, but it is not an unreasonable supposition. Would you recognize plantain or mugwort if you saw either of these growing wild? What about shepherd's purse (*Capsella bursa-pastoris*) or wild thyme (*Thymus serpyllum*) or cleavers (*Galium aparine*)?

Just as you do not need to recognize trees, you do not need to recognize herbs in order to pursue a study of runes. However wortcunning (knowledge of herbs) and rúncræft (skill with runes) complement each other very well. My only caution is that you not ingest any herbs unless you know exactly what they are and how their properties will affect you. It can be very difficult to accurately identify herbs in the wild with only photographs and descriptions as guides.

Representations of plant species other than trees are almost entirely absent from the Futhorc. The only exception is the elk-sedge. This variety of sawgrass is mentioned in the Rune Poem not because of any healing properties, but because of its sharp, serrated leaves.

If you have your personal rune journal ready, let us begin our exploration by looking at the plant life found in the Futhorc.

ᚪ

ÁC: Oak
(OCK)

PHONETIC VALUE: a, as in father

Ác biþ on eorþan ielda bearnum
flæsces fódor, féreþ gelóme ofer ganotes bæþ,
gársecg fandaþ hwæþer ác hæbbe æþele tréowe.

The oak is on Earth for the children of men,
meat-animal's fodder, it travels often over the gannet's bath,
the sea tests whether the oak possesses noble truth.

The oak tree is a symbol of strength and courage. Sacred to the god Thunor, this sturdy tree can live for centuries. Many oak trees throughout England enjoy local fame even today. The Parliament Oak in Nottinghamshire is supposedly where King John convened a Parliament in the early thirteenth century. A tree known as Son of Royal Oak, in Boscobel Wood, is the descendant of the oak tree that provided refuge for King Charles II near the end of the English Civil War. But the most venerable of these noble trees may be the Major Oak found in Sherwood Forest. Legend says that Robin Hood and his men convened beneath the limbs of this tree. Whether or not the legend is true, the Major Oak is old enough and large enough to support the rumor. Simply standing in the presence of this vast, enormous tree can be an overwhelming spiritual experience. The Major Oak is estimated to be one thousand years old and has a trunk circumference of 35 feet. Its mighty limbs are as thick as the trunks of ordinary oak trees. The heavier limbs are today bolstered with wooden poles installed by dedicated caretakers to prevent the limbs from collapsing from their own weight.

The value of the oak for the Anglo-Saxons cannot be overstated. The Rune Poem tells us that the oak is here on Earth for the "children of men" (*ielda bearnum*). It is a gift from the gods. The Rune Poem goes on to remind us that the oak provides meat-animal's fodder (*flæsces fódor*) in the form of acorns. The word *acorn* means the corn or seed of the oak. Acorns are a valuable food for many animals, including deer, mice, squirrels, jays, pigeons, and woodpeckers. They can even be consumed by humans if boiled first to remove the bitter tannin. But the Anglo-Saxons valued these oakcorns primarily as feed for their pigs and sheep. Oak bark was used for tanning leather. The natural tannin in oak barrels used for brewing improved the taste and quality of mead, the honey wine favored by the early English.

Oak was also the favored wood for ship building. This is what is meant in the Rune Poem when it says that the oak "travels often over the gannet's bath." The gannet is one of the largest sea-birds in the North Atlantic, and "gannet's bath" was a common Anglo-Saxon reference to the sea. Oak was the primary wood used for ship building by the Anglo-Saxons, and it continued to be used extensively for this purpose throughout Europe until the 1800s.

Ác is one of four runes that I think of collectively as the four *F* runes. This is because of their shape, not because of the sound they represent (although one of these, *feoh*, does indeed represent that sound). All four of these *F* runes—*ác*, *æsc*, *feoh*, and *os*—consist of two cross-strokes extending from a longer upright stroke. There are three different kinds of cross-stroke. Downward strokes indicate stability. Upward strokes indicate mobility. The third cross-stroke, in form, is a marriage of the other two, extending down and then back up to make a *v*. This may be thought of as a representation of divinity.

Let me hasten to add here that these are my own personal interpretations of these cross-strokes. I have no evidence to prove (or disprove) that the Anglo-Saxons believed the cross-strokes to represent stability, mobility, and divinity. But these interpretations may help the reader recognize the four *F* runes and distinguish them from one another.

Ác is the only one of the four *F* runes to feature two different cross-strokes. The bottom stroke extends down, representing stability, which is certainly a suitable feature for this rune. The top stroke, however, extends down and then up, indicating divinity. This is also suitable, since, as the Rune Poem clearly suggests, the oak is no ordinary tree. It is a gift, placed here on Earth for the children of men. The two different cross-strokes show us that the oak is both stable and divine.

It is reassuring for *ác* to appear in a divination. The rune is a reminder or message that the querent has adequate resources to address whatever concern he or she may have. Those resources can take any form, and they need not be tangible. The querent's resource could be patience or ambition. Or it could be a reference to a talent or skill. *Ác* tells the querent that he has what he needs. But the rune also indicates the presence or potential for some kind of challenge: "The sea tests whether the oak possesses noble truth." The querent has what he or she needs, but there is no guarantee of success. The querent will be tested. Overall, however, this is a good rune to have in a reading.

Likewise, in magic, *ác* can be a useful rune for many positive purposes, especially if the rúnwita knows from the start that he is going to be "tested." Combine *ác* with *eolh* as a bindrune to create a protective charm (you can also incorporate *wynn*, which has protective properties of its own). Use it with *tir* and *gear* to win a fair decision in a trial. Used alone, *ác* is a good rune to use for a charm to promote personal fortitude.

With your mind's eye, see an oak tree standing in a pastoral setting. Beneath the boughs of the tree, a hog forages on acorns. As the Rune Poem tells us, forage is just one of the resources provided by the mighty oak. In the background, beyond the foraging hog, we see a ship built of oak wood sailing across an inlet. The ship will be tested on the sea, but it appears to be steady and sure.

When you look at the rune itself, meditate on its shape. See the stability and divinity of this mighty tree revealed in the two cross-strokes. The oak represents blessings.

ᚫ

ÆSC: Ash Tree
(ASH)

PHONETIC VALUE: a, as in ash

Æsc biþ oferhéah, ieldum déore,
stiþ on staþole, stede rihte hielt,
þéah him feohtan on fíras manige.

The ash is lofty, glorified by men,
stiff in its trunk, it holds its position exactly,
although it fights against many men.

The ash in this passage of the Rune Poem refers both to a weapon (the spear) and the tree from which it is constructed. That the Old English word *ash* had this double meaning should not be a great surprise. We use our language in the same way today. For example, we say that we "iron" clothing, even though the device used for this purpose is no longer constructed of cast iron. The authors of the Rune Poem may even have been poking fun at this quirk in their language by using both definitions in the same passage.

The ash tree is noted in the poem as being exceptionally tall. The European ash has been known to grow up to 150 feet in height. We are told also that the ash is "glorified by" or "dearest to" men (*ieldum déore*). Why? Because it is "stiff in its trunk." Ash has a hard wood that resists splitting. It was used not only for spears, but also for making bows and various tools. Even today, ash is the favored wood for crafting the handles of everything from hammers to tennis rackets. The Anglo-Saxons also used ash wood for making buckets, cups, and other vessels. The first part of the Rune Poem is describing this tall, sturdy tree, highly valued by men, which "holds its position exactly."

With nothing more than the briefest pause, we then find that the poem is no longer talking about a tree, but is instead describing a spear fighting "against many men" (*on fíras manige*). Ash is indeed a versatile wood, but the Rune Poem wants us to focus specifically on its use as a spear. The primary weapons of the Anglo-Saxon warrior were the seax and the spear. The former was—depending on your point of view—either an extremely large knife or an extremely small sword. It was fast and deadly but had little reach. To use a seax, the warrior had to move in close to his opponent. For defense, he relied upon his spear. This larger weapon wasn't as maneuverable as the seax, but it had a longer reach than most bladed weapons. The spear afforded protection against hand-to-hand attacks, keeping an opponent at a distance.

In folklore, the ash tree is believed to have curative properties. It is also said that snakes are repelled by the ash. These two ideas may have a common origin—the Nine Herbs Charm. The Nine Herbs Charm is a magical formula recorded in the *Lacnunga*, the tenth-century collection of healing spells mentioned earlier in this chapter. The formula utilizes the narrative technique common to many Old English charms. In this narrative, the disease is described or envisioned as a snake. The god Woden strikes the snake with nine "glory twigs," causing it to shatter.

Æsc is another symbol that I refer to as an *F* rune because of its shape. In this rune, both of the cross-strokes extend downward, indicating stability. This form is a key to the mystery inherent in *æsc*. If I could describe that mystery in one word, the word I would use is *stasis*. This concept is often ascribed by others to the rune *is*, but, as we shall see in the chapter on earthly runes, there is nothing in that passage of the Rune Poem to suggest such a meaning.

Protection is one of the first concepts that comes to mind as an interpretation for this rune. But many of the runes are protective, and *eolh* (elk-sedge) is the quintessential protection rune. To understand *æsc*, we need to dig a little deeper. What is the Rune Poem saying? The ash is described as stiff, holding its position and—as a spear—fighting off others.

When *æsc* comes up in a reading, it may be telling the querent to stand by his or her principles. However, depending on the situation and the runes that fall around it, *æsc* could mean the exact opposite, indicating a need to "loosen up." This rune expresses unyielding stability. It is up to the interpreter, the wiglere, to determine how this relates to the querent.

In healing magic, *æsc* can be effectively utilized as a general tonic to fortify the body. It lends itself well to charms intended to bolster immunity, especially when used with the rune *ur*. Combine *æsc* with *ing* in a bindrune to help alleviate erectile dysfunction. Use it in combination with *lagu* for kidney or urinary issues. But always remember that rúncræft is not a substitute for medical treatment. You should consult with your physician about any serious or unusual physical malady.

Æsc certainly can be incorporated into a protection charm, so long as the magic is intended to help "take a stand." This rune protects the status quo. It is not a good choice to protect a project or situation that you want to move forward with. Use it with *ethel* and *éoh* to protect the home. Combine *æsc* and *wynn* in a bindrune for a nice, general charm to protect or sustain your good fortune. Again, this assumes the magic is not intended to procure good fortune, but rather to stabilize what you already have. However it is used, *æsc* always promotes stability, stasis, and immobility. Use it when you want to create an unyielding, unmovable force.

With your mind's eye, see a resolute warrior, male or female, standing before an ash tree. The warrior holds a sturdy spear. All three—tree, warrior, and spear—stand upright, proud, and un-yielding. And yet there is nothing overtly hostile in this stance. The vision is almost peaceful. The warrior's intention is not to at-tack, but neither will she yield.

Þ

THORN: Hawthorn Tree
(THORN)

PHONETIC VALUE: th, as in thin or them

Þorn biþ ðearle scearp ðegna gehwylcum,
anfeng is yfel, ungemetum reþe,
manna gehwelcum ðe him mid resteð.

Thorn is exceedingly sharp for every servant,
seizing it is evil, and it is extremely harsh
to each man who rests among it.

From the wording of this passage and the general tone of the Rune Poem, it seems clear that the thorn referenced here is a thorn tree rather than an individual barb. Common hawthorn, also known as mayblossom or whitethorn, is a small tree with a large body of folk-lore surrounding it. As with the oak, some thorn trees in England gain their own names and notoriety: Beggar's Bush, Doble's Thorn, the Glastonbury Thorn, and so on. Boughs of hawthorn were tra-ditionally hung over doors on May Day. In Herefordshire, the branches were burned in fields on New Year's Day to protect the coming year's harvest.

The lore associated with the hawthorn doesn't always exude praise and adoration. Hawthorn blossoms are often considered unlucky. Uprooting a hawthorn is said to bring bad luck. Jesus' crown of thorns is sometimes said to have been made from haw-thorn branches, although I don't see how anyone can blame the poor tree for that. But whether the lore is good or ill, the thorn tree is without question a plant with an extraordinary reputation.

Growing no more than 45 feet in height, the common haw-thorn protects itself with thorns extending up to more than half an inch in length. This may not seem very long, but the thorns are sharper than the fangs of any predator and can tear into the flesh of an unwary person who grasps or brushes against one of the tree's branches.

The berries produced each year by this tree, called haws, pro-vide food for birds and other wildlife. Haws can also be consumed by humans, but are most often employed this way in the mak-ing of jellies, wines, and liqueurs. But the most ingenious use of the thorn tree is found in English hedgerows. Hedge laying is a complex, skilled practice of encouraging horizontal growth and weaving this growth into an impenetrable barrier to contain live-stock. Used in this way, the thorn tree is an earlier, natural ver-sion of barbed wire and it is still found extensively throughout the English countryside. The strength and durability of these hedgerows is nothing short of amazing. When I was in Lancashire a few years ago, I came across a family of American tourists who were distraught because they had accidentally driven their rental car into a hedgerow. The hedgerow itself was fine, but its sturdy branches had pulled the bumper completely off their car!

The Anglo-Saxons were obviously aware of the inherent haz-ards of this natural barbed wire. The Rune Poem describes the barbs as evil (*yfel*) and harsh (*reþe*). At the time the Anglo-Saxon Rune Poem was written, many men were farmers or herders and spent the majority of their waking hours outdoors. These men would take their rest, more often than not, in the shade offered by a grove of trees. And so the Rune Poem reminds us that not all trees are equally welcoming. Resting among thorn trees could prove to be quite an unpleasant experience.

The form of the rune depicts an upright branch with a thorn protruding from it. This would seem intuitively obvious, but I feel compelled to mention here that both the Icelandic and Norwegian Rune Poems attribute an entirely different meaning to this rune. These other poems describe this particular rune form as the symbol for a "giant," meaning a powerful and often antagonistic entity. We do not know the reason behind this change in meaning. Paxson suggests that the Christian scribe who recorded the Anglo-Saxon Rune Poem may have altered the passage to avoid referencing Pagan mythology (*Taking Up the Runes*, p. 49). She also postulates that the scribe may have been attempting to explain a term that no longer had significant meaning in the evolving English language. When I look at the rune passages for *thorn* and *os*, this latter hypothesis seems the more likely.

By the ninth century, words like *thyrs* (giant) and *os* (deity, god) were becoming obsolete in the English language, either changing in meaning or disappearing from the language altogether. Some of this was undoubtedly due to the spread of Christianity, but in the case of *thyrs*, at least, there may be a more natural explanation. A *thyrs* (or *thurs*, to use the Scandinavian cognate) is an extradimensional, primal force that may occasionally enter our physical plane. As a Pagan, I accept these forces as real and not unrelated to the physical landscape. The nature of these giants is reflected in disruptive climatic conditions. A *thurs* in the northern, Scandinavian environment can be a terrible and volatile presence. By contrast, the *thyrses* of England, with its much milder climate, are relatively benign.

Changing the name from *thyrs* to *thorn* and using the poetic imagery of the thorn tree may have presented a clearer vision of the mystery embodied by this rune. It certainly needs little clarification today. The Rune Poem focuses on the harsh, painful barbs of the thorn tree. But it also tells us that the "evil" described is not an inescapable doom. It is something easily avoidable. In fact we need to almost deliberately walk into it, or grasp it (*anfeng*), for there to be any threat.

Thorn is a warning when it appears in a divination. It is saying, "Don't touch!" There may be a temptation to gather haws or to rest in the shade, but to do so is to risk pain. The querent may choose to move forward anyway—to enter the hawthorn grove—but he should proceed with caution. Keep in mind always that *thorn* represents a potential hazard, not an unavoidable hazard. The thorn tree is not going to chase you down and tackle you. For example, if you consult the runes before an important meeting and the *thorn* rune comes up, this does not mean that you need to cancel your meeting. What it is saying is that you should be well prepared, because something unexpected is likely to come up. A thorn, after all, is only unpleasant if you prick yourself on it.

In rúncræft, *thorn* is most useful for warding an object, person, or place. This may seem similar to a protection charm, but there's a distinct difference. I may have something private or personal that I am not trying to protect from any perceived threat, I just do not want other people messing with it. Use *thorn* when you want to enclose something with what you might think of as a "runic hedgerow."

In your mind's eye, envision a hawthorn tree. At first glance it appears no more threatening than any other arboreal species. But look closer. See the harsh barbs along the branch. They cannot harm you if you are mindful of their presence, but caution is called for if you would avoid their sting.

ÉOH: Yew

(EH-och, ending with a glottal stop, as in *loch*)

PHONETIC VALUE: i, as in pine

Éoh biþ útan unsméþe tréowe,
heard hrúsan fæst, hierde fyres,
wyrtruman underwreþed, wynn on éþle.

On the outside, the yew is a rough tree,
hard and secured in the earth, keeper of fires,
sustained by deep roots, it is a pleasure to have on one's land.

There are at least fifteen different species of evergreen plants and trees referred to as "yew." The species described in this passage of the Rune Poem is the European yew. This slow-growing tree can live for two thousand years or longer. Its leaves are extremely toxic.

The oldest yew trees in England are most often found growing in churchyards. There have been attempts to connect this in some way with Pagan spirituality, but evidence indicates that it was early Christians who introduced the practice of planting yews in cemeteries in both England and Ireland. The northern yew resembled the cypress and laurel that adorned the Mediterranean cemeteries of southern Europe, where the Christian missionaries had come from.

Churchyards aside, the yew was greatly valued by the Anglo-Saxons for a number of reasons. The best known of these was its use in the construction of the English longbow. The natural properties of yew make its wood ideally suited for longbows. Because the yew was in such demand for this purpose, coupled with its slow growth, the species was eventually depleted across the English countryside. This could be another reason why the yew tree is associated with churchyards—it was chopped down everywhere else.

However, the *éoh* rune doesn't concern itself with the longbow. (That iconic English weapon is addressed by the *yr* rune.) The *éoh* rune, or rather its passage in the Rune Poem, wants us to look at the tree itself. We are told immediately that the tree is outwardly "rough," and this is true. The European yew has a scaly bark that easily flakes off. But what is the Rune Poem trying to convey here? A rough bark is not unique to the yew. The oak has rough bark, and yet the Anglo-Saxon Rune Poem makes no mention of this when describing the *ác* rune. We are being told from the start that the mystery of *éoh* is that of a "diamond in the rough." The mystery does not shine or sparkle. We may not even recognize its value unless we look very closely.

The yew tree, we are told, is hard. It is securely rooted in the earth (*hrúsan fæst*). On one level, this rune can be expressed as "reliability." In the story of the tortoise and the hare, *éoh* is the tortoise. What the rune represents may not be flashy, but it is solid and stable. Furthermore, it is useful. Yew is a "keeper of flames." This refers to its value as firewood, which was considerably more important before the advent of natural gas furnaces and electric stoves.

In the final line we are told that the yew is sustained by *wyrtruman*, an Old English word that means both roots (in the sense of a plant's roots) and origins. This concept has not changed so very much in our language. We still speak of a person's origins as his "roots." This word—wyrtruman—indicates that the blessings of *éoh* are connected in some way with the past. And then we are told, finally, that *éoh* is indeed a blessing or source of joy (*wynn*). But *éoh* is not joy itself. (*Wynn* is another rune that we will examine in the chapter Runes Within the Hall.)

The form of the runic character suggests balance. *Éoh* is one of ten runes—fully a third of the Futhorc—that appear exactly the same whether upright or inverted. This particular rune has a sort of hook at each end, connecting it to the earth below and also to the sky above.

There is something very warm and comforting about this rune. When *éoh* appears in a divination, it is usually a reminder of some resource that the querent either is not aware of or does not fully appreciate. The resource is very often a person, perhaps a loved one the querent has taken for granted. But the resource can as easily be a place or an object. Your home is a resource. Your job or career is a resource. Each of your friends and family members is a resource. Whatever resource is referenced, it is both reliable and well rooted. By "well rooted" I mean that it (or he or she) has been around for a while.

Use *éoh* in rúncræft with *ethel* for a charm to bless the home, or with *beorc* and *ur* for good health. With the rune *gyfu*, it can help build a stable marriage, but only attempt this if you are sure it is what you want. *Éoh* is not a rune of excitement and romance. (If you want romance, there are better ways to use *gyfu*, as we will discuss later.) By itself, *éoh* can help you remain balanced and grounded in a healthy way.

In your mind's eye, envision the sturdy trunk and boughs of the yew. See how strong and grounded the tree is. You may notice a homestead in the distance, a secure but welcoming structure. The vision is one of balance and strength.

BEORC: Bírch
(BEH-orch)

PHONETIC VALUE: b, as in bib

Beorc biþ bléda léas, bereþ efne swá þéah
tánas bútan túdor, biþ on telgum wlitig,
héah on helme hrysted fægere,
gehlóden léafum, lyfte getenge.

The birch is without fruit, it bears even so,
it bears shoots instead of fruit, its branches are beautiful,
high in the treetops decorated attractively,
laden with foliage, lofty pressing.

This rune is often said to represent "fertility," but that interpretation is, at best, coincidental. The passage describing *beorc* begins by saying that the tree does not bear fruit. This is an odd way to begin the narrative if fertility is the rune's primary or essential meaning! Given the right circumstances, the *beorc* rune could indeed be speaking of fertility; however, this same meaning could be equally ascribed to runes such as *gear* or *ing*, which we will explore in coming chapters. We are told in the Rune Poem that the birch, without bearing any fruit or seed, reproduces "even so." And so we have reproduction, but it is an asexual reproduction, not the union of female and male, stamen and pollen, ova and sperm usually associated with the idea of fertility.

In real life, the birch tree does reproduce in the conventional manner and is easily grown from seed. In their book *Rune Games*, Osborn and Longland present the compelling argument that this passage of the Rune Poem is actually referencing the black poplar, not the birch tree (45–46). The Old English word *beorc* is translated as "birch," but we cannot know for certain if the Anglo-Saxons were speaking of the same tree that we know by that name today. It is possible, too, that the word *beorc* was used to identify both the birch and the poplar. Like the birch, the poplar tree can also produce seed, but it is notable for the ease in which it reproduces from cuttings. Even small twigs and branches that break away naturally from the tree can form roots and become new trees.

While it might be intriguing to speculate on the exact species of tree described, that is not the emphasis of the passage in the Rune Poem. We are being told of a tree—whether a birch or a poplar—that reproduces in an unusual way. The tree is in no way crippled or hindered by this unconventional reproduction. It is described as beautiful and attractive. Its branches are laden with foliage (*gehlóden léafum*). We are given a vision of a thing that is vibrant and healthy. If I had to sum up the mystery of *beorc* in a word or phrase, I would say "a good but unexpected outcome." The outcome may quite possibly be similar to what was hoped for or intended, but it will come about in an unexpected way.

There is a comforting quality to this rune. It seems to be saying that things will work out well in the end, even if current plans appear to be going astray. The birch (or poplar) is bearing no fruit, which may be discouraging, but it will reproduce nevertheless, and in the end it will be beautiful (*wlitig*). How many times have you experienced this in your life? How many times has something seemed to "go wrong," and then the outcome later proved to be very good?

The form of *beorc* is interesting in that it can be viewed as a bindrune of a double *wynn*. We will explore the *wynn* rune in a later chapter, and discuss bindrunes in the chapter Rúncræft. For now it is enough to know that *wynn* is a rune of joy and happiness, and that it looks vaguely like the letter *P*. You have already seen that the *beorc* rune resembles the letter *B*. If you were to take the letter *P*, invert it and superimpose this on the upright letter, the result would be a *B*. Likewise, if you invert *wynn* and superimpose it on an upright *wynn*, you have the shape or form of *beorc*.

$$ \text{ᚹ} + \text{ᚦ} = \text{ᛒ} $$

The form of the rune illustrates the mystery of *beorc*. Unlike Tarot and some other divination modalities, the runes have no reversed meanings. *Wynn* is a joyful rune whether upright or inverted. The shape of the *beorc* rune is a reminder that joy and contentment can arrive from different directions and manifest in different ways.

In a divination, whether or not *beorc* is a "good" rune depends on how much the querent feels a need to control the situation. The ultimate outcome will be beautiful and good, but it will not manifest in the way the querent had planned. The rune advises the querent to keep an open mind. To think outside the box. Even if one choice or path appears to be "without fruit" (*bléda léas*), it may nevertheless lead the querent to his or her goal.

Using *beorc* in rúncræft is like throwing a wild card into the mix. It can be effectively combined with *feoh* to create a prosperity talisman, but do not be surprised if the resulting prosperity comes from an unexpected direction. Use it with *gyfu* and *mann* to win new friends. Combine it with *wynn* and *dæg* for good luck. And, yes, *beorc* can also be used for a fertility charm. Whether breeding puppies or cattle, or bringing a new human being into the world, the act of reproduction always leads to unforeseen blessings. You are never sure of exactly what you will get.

In your mind's eye, envision a large, healthy birch tree. And then another, slightly smaller, and another. There are no flowers or seeds, no sign of sexual reproduction, and yet birch trees are pushing up everywhere. Each is beautiful and vibrant and whole.

The power to wound
C nervy

EOLH: Elk-Sedge

(EH-olch, ending with a glottal stop, as in *loch*)

PHONETIC VALUE: z, as in zebra

Eolh-secg eard hæfþ oftost on fenne,
weaxe on wætere, wundaþ grimme,
blóde breneð beorna gehwilcne
þe him ænigne onfeng gedéð.

The elk-sedge is native to the marsh,
it grows in the water, it can wound cruelly,
the blood of any man burns
who in any way dares to seize it.

Unlike the other botanical runes discussed in this chapter, *eolh* refers to a grassy plant rather than a tree. The sedges are a large family of plants that includes the papyrus. As with *beorc*, we cannot be certain of the exact species described in this passage of the Rune Poem, or even if the reference is to only a single species. But the passage seems to be describing a kind of sawgrass, possibly the great fen-sedge that grows throughout temperate Europe.

Most sedges thrive in wetlands where other plants do not fare as well. However, the fact that the Rune Poem emphasizes this habitat indicates a degree of significance concerning the marsh. Wetlands were mystical, sacred places for the early Germanic peoples. The marsh was a liminal space, not quite land and yet not quite water. By describing where the elk-sedge grows, the Rune Poem hints that *eolh* shares this liminal, mystical quality. This is an herb of power.

"Sawgrass" is a term describing closely related species of sedge notable for their sharp and frequently serrated leaves. These leaves can readily cut through flesh, and they present a very real threat to anyone moving through a dense growth of sawgrass. This is almost certainly the variety of sedge discussed in the Rune Poem. The power of *eolh* is the power to wound cruelly (*wundaþ grimme*). It is very likely that Anglo-Saxon druids (drýmenn) used sawgrass leaves in defensive spells. The details of how this herb was used are lost to the mists of time, however, as the majority of surviving magical herb lore has been preserved only in charms for healing or for increasing the fertility of the land.

The form of the rune *eolh* was probably intended to be a stylized representation of sawgrass. When I look at the rune myself, however, I see a person standing upright with his or her arms outstretched in a warning gesture. This is my own vision, but I do not think it is inappropriate. Like the hazard indicated by *thorn*, the danger of *eolh* can be readily avoided. Its bite is defensive, not offensive. But the power of *eolh* is an internal power. That person standing with arms outstretched in a warning gesture is you.

It is almost always a good sign when this defensive rune appears in a divination. The presence of *eolh* indicates that the querent is or has been protected in some way. It indicates safety. The wiglere interpreting the runes should keep in mind that this safety is a temporary condition. A more permanent, more stable positive condition would be indicated by a rune such as *wynn*, *dæg*, or *ethel*. Although *eolh* indicates safety, it also reveals that the querent is in a defensive position at the present time.

As you might expect, *eolh* is used in rúncræft for defensive magic. Other runes can be used for protection in specific situations, but defense is the primary function of *eolh*. Use it with *gyfu* to protect a romantic relationship or with *éoh* and *ethel* to protect your home. We will discuss magic helms in the chapter Rúncræft, but here I would like to mention that *eolh* by itself can be used to create an effective helm of protection.

I make use of the power of *eolh* whenever I plan a long drive. Not for short trips to the supermarket, but when I drive out of town. Before leaving on my journey, I mark the front, rear, and both sides of my truck with the *eolh* rune. As I do this, I visualize each rune radiating with power as I say, "*Eolh weardath me*" (EH-olch WEH-ar-dath may). If your tongue trips over the Old English, you could just say "Protect me." The point is to empower the symbol by verbalizing your desire. I believe there is a greater power in the language of the Anglo-Saxon Rune Poem—*eolh* is, after all, an Anglo-Saxon rune—but only if you can speak the words with ease and confidence. Following this brief ritual, I repeat the affirmation once again when I turn the key in the ignition.

This same formula can be used as a simple, impromptu spell whenever you feel a need for protection. Mark the shape of the rune directly in front of you. Make the primary stroke using a downward motion with your dominant hand (the right hand for most of us). Then, using both of your hands, make the upright, outward strokes in a single gesture. Say, "*Eolh weardath me*" as your hands sweep up and out in this second motion. Obviously you should never do this in view of an audience. Most people have negative reactions when they see somebody making odd gestures and muttering incomprehensible phrases. Fortunately the gesture and phrase are both so simple that it is often possible to turn away on some pretense and quickly summon the protective power of *eolh* without anyone noticing.

In your mind's eye, imagine you are standing in a marsh. This is a place of power, neither land nor open water. Thick, hard green blades of sawgrass stand in clumps. A warrior is coming toward you through the marsh. You call out for him to halt, but he pays you no heed. He continues forward. Then he stops abruptly and inhales sharply. You see the blood where the sawgrass has cut open his palm. For now, you are protected. For now, you are safe.

Review

1. What Saxon god is associated with the oak tree?

2. What is the *Lacnunga*?

3. What does the rune *thorn* tell us when it appears in a divination?

4. Why is "fertility" a questionable interpretation of the *beorc* rune?

5. Where is sawgrass found? Why is this habitat significant?

Animal Runes

The early English also had a more intimate relationship with the animal kingdom than most of us do today. Sadly, this relationship tended to be more adversarial than affectionate, and animals were often treated cruelly. This was not unique to the Anglo-Saxons. It was a common attitude in all cultures at that time, and the animals fared no better in England after the Anglo-Saxons abandoned their own gods and converted to Christianity. The value of compassion toward other species is a recent development in human history. Under the old English Common Law, animals were classified as either property (livestock) or as brute animals. The former enjoyed more legal protections than the latter, but only because they were regarded as moderately valuable property.

I do not condone or suggest a return to these barbaric ideas. There is nothing honorable or admirable about cruelty to animals. In the United States, in 1874, animal welfare laws opened the way for laws protecting children when Mary McCormack Connolly was prosecuted for beating, starving, and abusing a young girl who, according to Henry Bergh, deserved the protections accorded in the state of New York to any "animal," even though the girl was a human animal. At that time, there were no laws in New York against cruelty to children. The girl, Mary Ellen Wilson, was removed from her abusive foster home thanks to the state's animal welfare laws. Later that same year, the New York Society for the Prevention of Cruelty to Children was established. A society that is cruel to animals tends to be cruel to its own children, and vice versa. Perhaps compassion toward other species is a luxury that only modern people can enjoy. If so, let us remember that we are, indeed, modern people. We can afford compassion.

Animals were not always classified anatomically. The Anglo-Saxons classified animals according to function and habitat. The word deer (*déor*) meant any species of wild, land-dwelling herbivore. This included deer as we use the word today, but the essential quality was the animal's wild nature in contrast to that of the domesticated beast. As an adjective, *déor* meant courageous or bold, qualities the Anglo-Saxons admired in wild animals.

Fish (*fisc*) meant any water-dwelling creature. Most often these were fish as we classify them anatomically, but, as we will see later in this chapter, the beaver was considered a "river fish" because it makes its home in the water.

A worm (*wyrm*) was any lowly creature associated with the earth. It is cognate with the word *vermin*, which came into the English language through Old French. The early English had a love-hate relationship with the earth that we still hold today. On one hand, it is the earth that sustains us. On the other, the earth or soil is a place of disease. We still think of anything "soiled" as being unhealthy. The earth is also where we inter the dead. *Wyrmes* were creatures contaminated or soiled, particularly snakes, since these animals have no legs to lift them from the ground. But the word was also used for any generic reptile and even for mites or insects.

The mightiest of wyrmes was not a biological creature at all, but a spirit creature: the dragon. The dragon is a powerful and destructive spirit. Today you may occasionally hear people say that they "work with" dragons in some spiritual way. Whatever these spirits are, they are certainly not European dragons. You do not work with a European dragon for any length of time. Either you destroy it, or it destroys you, and the latter outcome is far more likely. The people who claim to work with dragons may have connected in some way with Chinese dragons, which are benevolent in nature and entirely unrelated to the great wyrmes of Europe, or they may be influenced by modern fantasy fiction, which often portrays dragons as benign creatures.

The European dragon is not a creature that a person can establish a relationship with. In the lore of England and Scandinavia, dragons are the embodiment of pure destruction. They are often but not always winged. They often but not always have legs, although the torso is more like that of a snake. The legged varieties may be quadrapedal (four legged) or bipedal (two legged). In later folk tradition, these were classified by different names—legless lindworms, bipedal wyverns, and quadrapedal dragons—but the Anglo-Saxons made no distinctions. The dragon in the epic story of Beowulf also had a venomous bite, which was Beowulf's demise. Like biological wyrmes, such as snakes, dragons are very much creatures of the earth. They not only touch the earth, they live within it, in caves and grottos.

Biological animals were sometimes given traits or qualities that defy the laws of nature. The European robin, known to the Anglo-Saxons as the *réadda*, was believed to be universally male. The bird was mated or married to the wren, which was always female. But this sexual irregularity must have been symbolic. Surely the Anglo-Saxons readily observed that robins nest with robins, and wrens with wrens, and never with the other species. The *réadda* was considered sacred to Thunor, and as a sacred bird, it still holds a special meaning even in America today. When the descendants of the Saxons eventually came to the shores of North America, they named the indigenous red-breasted thrush after the bird they were familiar with—the sacred robin. But the American robin disappeared in the autumn. Its behavior was unlike the non-migratory European robin, a bird long associated with the Yuletide. Unlike the European robin, the North American *réadda* deserted the land with the coming of winter. What a relief it was to see the sacred bird return in the spring! What a welcome symbol of divine blessing! Many North American avian species migrate south every winter, but it is the red-breasted bird sacred to red-bearded Thunor, god of strength and protection, that Americans still look for as a sign that spring has returned.

The Anglo-Saxon Rune Poem focuses on four animals that were useful in some way. All four of these are mammals. Two of the species mentioned are domestic and the other two wild. And one of these animals, sadly, is now extinct.

FEOH: Cattle

(FAY-och, ending with a glottal stop, as in *loch*)

PHONETIC VALUE: f, as in fife

Feoh byþ frofur fira gehwylcum
sceal ðeah manna gehwylc miclum hyt dælan
gif he wile for dryhtne domes hleotan.

Cattle are compensation for everyone,
though each man shall greatly share his
if he will be awarded honors from his lord.

The Old English word *feoh* has two meanings: cattle and wealth. Today these are distinct concepts, but fifteen centuries ago in England, each was the equivalent of the other. A household with even a few head of cattle was a prosperous household. Related to the aurochs—a wild European species of cattle that came to be represented by the *ur* rune—domesticated cattle provided not only milk, butter, cream, and beef, but also leather for shoes, belts, and armor and horn for combs and utensils. The manure from these cattle revitalized the fields. Land itself was a measure of wealth, but cattle were a movable form of wealth. Cattle could be traded or given away. Or stolen. Cattle raids were an early version of the bank robbery.

So this rune means, in a phrase, "movable wealth." But its mystery is deeper than this. In the Rune Poem, we are admonished to share or deal out (*dælan*) our wealth. We are to do this if we want to receive honors or praise (*domes*) from our lord. I have often seen the word *dryhtne* interpreted as "the Lord," the Biblical god, and this is possibly what the scribe intended since the runic mysteries were not recorded until the Christian era; but we need to remember that the Rune Poem was recorded at a time when everyone but the king himself had someone as his or her liege. It is just as likely, if not more so, that the term refers to one's local lord. This lord would not be impressed by a vassal who hoarded his own cattle. To maximize their value, for the community to prosper, cattle needed to be loaned out and sold or traded. The cattle needed to move.

Dickens' *A Christmas Carol* exemplifies the mystery of *feoh*. Our hearts go out to the crippled Tim Cratchit, but the most pitiful character in the story is Ebenezer Scrooge. Despite his wealth, Scrooge is miserable. His life is friendless and empty. He seems lost until three spirits convince him to share his wealth—to set it in motion. At the end we see that other people, most notably the Cratchit family, have prospered from this new generosity, but nobody has prospered as much as Scrooge himself. Loved and admired, he has finally taken his place as a valuable member of his community.

Feoh is one of the four *F* runes. Unlike the other three, however, feoh actually does represent the phonetic *F* of the Roman alphabet.

In form, two lines or cross-strokes extend out and upward from the longer vertical stroke. The rune's appearance resembles a person in profile with his arms outstretched. It looks as if this person is reaching out to receive something. Or is he giving something? It does not matter, as these are two sides of one coin. The upward cross-strokes indicate movement, in this case the movement of wealth or potential.

When *feoh* appears in a divination today, it is not likely to represent cattle unless you own or work on a ranch, which excludes most of us. Instead we need to look at this rune as a representation of wealth in motion. The latter part of this is important. A million dollars in cash stuffed into a mattress is not *feoh*, it is just paper. This rune may not mean money at all in the modern sense. It is a person's wealth—any valuable asset, tangible or not—whether this manifests as a talent, a skill, knowledge or, yes, a large bank account. All of these can only achieve their potential when set into motion.

This rune often suggests that the querent share something. What this "something" is will vary from one person to the next. Depending on the situation and the other runes near it, *feoh* can also indicate that the querent will be receiving something, but this is never a gift, which would be indicated by the rune *gyfu*. Instead the querent is receiving something earned. For the same reason, this rune does not refer to charitable acts or gifts. It is a compensation for service or goods, or what the early English people called a *feohbót* when paid in a tangible form.

In rúncraeft, *feoh* is the ultimate rune for money spells. It can be combined effectively in a bindrune with *beorc* or *wynn* for a general prosperity talisman. Use it in a charm to help in seeking employment. Combine *feoh* with *ur* and *os* if you are applying for a management-level position, or with *rád* if you want a job or career that involves travel.

However you use this rune, do not forget its inherent mystery. *Feoh* is not a get-rich-quick scheme or a windfall inheritance. It represents valuable assets that must be managed. Just as the rancher must breed his heifer, guard the growing calf, and eventually sell or butcher the animal or breed it in turn to stimulate milk production, your assets—whether these are skills or knowledge or actual money—must be stimulated in some way to grow and circulate. To move. In my experience, the most effective prosperity spells utilize this concept. It is not enough (usually) to say, "I want money." What we call money, whether it is a coin or rectangular sheet of paper or a plastic card, is just a superficial symbol for an exchange. You must know exactly what you wish to give, as well as exactly what you hope to receive in exchange.

And of course, for anyone reading this book who does own or work on a cattle ranch, *feoh* certainly can be referring, in both divination and magic, to your livestock!

In your mind's eye, envision two people transacting the sale of a heifer or steer. See the exchange of coins, but know that the animal is equally important. The exchange moves in both directions. One person offers coins, the other person offers a beast. Remember that *feoh* represents potential in motion, and that money is only one manifestation. Contemplate the form of rune itself, keeping in mind that the upward strokes indicate motion. *Feoh* speaks to us of the movement that nurtures balance and growth.

Λ

UR: Aurochs

(OOR)

PHONETIC VALUE: oo, as in boot or took

Ur byþ anmod ond oferhyrned,
felafrecne deor feohteþ mid hornum,
mære morstapa þæt is módig wuht.

The aurochs is brave and has horns above,
this very fierce animal fights with its horns,
a great wanderer of the moors, it is a proud creature.

Sometimes confused with the European bison, the aurochs was actually a wild, powerful, and temperamental breed of cattle. Aurochs were often depicted in Paleolithic cave paintings. In early Europe, to hunt and successfully kill one of these beasts was proof of a man's courage and skill. Unfortunately this very perception of the aurochs as an honorable opponent helped drive the breed to extinction. These great creatures were no longer roaming Britain by the 1200s, and the last surviving aurochs—a female—died in Poland in 1627. The Anglo-Saxons respected the aurochs both for its ferocity (*felafrecne*) and for its pride or spirit (*mód*). In this passage of the Rune Poem, we see nothing but praise for the great wanderer of the moors.

Larger than domestic cattle, the male aurochs was black and had a pale stripe running down its back. Females were a dull reddish color. Both sexes were notable for their large, forward-facing horns. These horns are significant in the Rune Poem, mentioned for their unusual position (*oferhyrned*) as well as for their role as the aurochs' natural weapons (*feohteþ mid hornum*). But what is the significance of the horn? Depictions of ceremonial helmets adorned with horns have been found in Denmark, Sweden, and England. These helmets were not worn into battle. They were probably used in religious or magical rituals. What exactly did they represent?

It is unlikely that horned helmets are related to the Pagan depictions of antlered humanoids such as the seated, antlered figure found on the Gundestrup cauldron. Antlers are not the same as horns. A fully developed antler is a dead bony growth that is shed at the end of the year. Antlers are usually only found on adult male animals, and thus are symbolic of masculine energy and sexuality. In contrast, horn is a hard protein substance covering living bone throughout the life of an animal. In some species only the male has horns, but in other animals—including the aurochs—both males and females are crowned with these growths. Horns begin to grow soon after birth and are an important means of defense. As a symbol, the horn represents sheer power regardless of sex, age, or season.

In form, the rune *ur* shows the auroch's impressive horns facing downward. From skeletal evidence we know that the horns normally faced forward. If they were drawn "up," the image would be of an aurochs staring at the sky. Facing down, they are in their power position. The beast has lowered its head and is ready, if necessary, to charge. The aurochs is in a stance that reveals its full potential.

This full potential, this strength, is indicated when *ur* appears in a divination. It usually means that the querent has the strength and courage to meet a challenge. In a single rune reading, when only one rune is drawn, *ur* could indicate that the querent needs to summon up strength or courage, which could mean that unforeseen challenges are coming. But even here the rune suggests the querent has enough personal strength to overcome these challenges.

As for its use in rúncræft, I have found *ur* to be especially effective in healing magic. It is a rune of vitality. Combine it with *eolh* or *æsc* in a bindrune for a charm to bolster the immune system, or with *éoh* for a general health charm.

But the power of *ur* is not limited to healing. Use *ur* with *wynn* and *sigel* for a potent good luck charm. Or use it with f*eoh* and *os* if you're seeking a managerial position or promotion. Entrepreneurs can use this rune with *feoh* and *gyfu* to help with success in their business dealings. Just be certain that you only use *ur* when you truly want to empower a charm or spell with unfettered vitality. The power of *ur*, like life itself, can be wild and unpredictable. When used for anything other than healing, *ur* can produce unexpected results. The aforementioned entrepreneur's business charm using *ur, feoh,* and *gyfu*, for example, might be the key to a profitable opportunity—in a city a thousand miles away.

Ur can also be used alone for self-empowerment. Use both your hands to mark the symbol before you in one gesture. Begin with the fingertips of both hands touching. Then move your left hand down sharply, while simultaneously moving your right hand out and down to form the rest of the runic character. As you do this say, "*Ic eom ur*" (eech EH-om oor), which means "I am the aurochs." As I mentioned in the last chapter, I believe using the language of the runes—Old English—is more powerful, but only if you can do so comfortably and with confidence. This simple self-empowerment spell can be enacted whenever you feel the need for renewed health, mental fortitude, or increased courage.

In your mind's eye, envision the aurochs as it prepares to charge. See the great beast lower its head, its horns pointing downward to form the shape of the *ur* rune. Feel its power and mass. *Ur* is a rune of strength.

EH: Horse

(ECH, ending with a glottal stop, as in *loch*)

<small>PHONETIC VALUE:</small> e, as in bed; a, as in bait

Eh byþ for eorlum æþelinga wynn,
hors hófum wlanc, ðær him hæleþ ymbe,
welege on wicgum, wrixlaþ spræce,
and biþ unstyllum æfre frofur.

The horse is for lords the joy of the aristocracy,
horse hooves boastful, where around the hero,
prosperous in respect to horses, it exchanges discourse,
and its restlessness is ever a help.

The horse was known throughout Europe four thousand years ago, but it was originally domesticated at least two thousand years earlier in central Asia. Being relatively expensive to maintain, the horse was a symbol of wealth and aristocratic status. A single horse can require fifteen to twenty-five pounds of forage and up to ten gallons of water every day. Thus, nobles rode on horseback while peasants usually walked.

We see this connection between the horse and its master's status in the Rune Poem. The horse is presented as a noble animal, a mount fit for a hero (*hæleþ*). It is described as a joy (*wynn*) and boastful (*wlanc*). But the horse is not a mere object or tool. It is, for the hero, an ally. A partner. The hero consults or converses (*wrixlaþ spræce*) with the horse. And then, in its role as a mount, the horse becomes a help or benefit (*frofur*) to the noble hero. The horse enables its master.

Horses were venerated among the earliest Anglo-Saxons who settled on England's shores. The hero-brothers Hengest and Horsa, who are said to have led the later Anglo-Saxon migrations, have names meaning "stallion" and "horse." There is some speculation that Hengest and Horsa may be twin horse gods or spirits who have been erroneously described as historical figures. In any event, the horse held a place of honor in Anglo-Saxon culture. The Christian missionary Augustine denounced the custom of dressing in horse costumes, which we may presume was a religious or ceremonial tradition among the Saxons.

In form, the rune *eh* resembles the Roman letter *M*. When we look upon this character, we see what the hero sees as he or she sits astride the beast. Before us we see the upright pinnae, or auricles, of the horse's ears. These pinnae can rotate to assist the horse's sense of hearing in all directions. From the hero's perspective, sitting on the horse, they look like the shape of the *eh* rune.

It is possible that *eh* represents an actual horse when it appears in a divination—if the querent happens to own a horse. Most often, though, the rune is revealing a deeper meaning. What *eh* represents is an ally that empowers the querent in some way. Today, the most literal and direct interpretation could be a reference to the querent's automobile if he or she possesses one. A car enables its owner to move faster and farther, and to carry large loads. Like the horse once was, an automobile is often a symbol of wealth or status. And so it is entirely reasonable for the wiglere interpreting the runes to consider this particular rune as a representation of the querent's car or truck. This assumes that the querent owns a personal vehicle, and that the interpretation of "car or truck" is consistent with both the question and with other runes that are drawn in the reading.

It is just as likely, however, for *eh* to indicate something else that enables or empowers the querent. This could even be another person. If *eh* represents an object, it is some kind of ally that empowers the querent. It is something he or she must have faith in. The querent must be able to exchange discourse with the object (*wrixlaþ sprǽce*) on some level. If you do not think this object could be an automobile, consider how many times you have heard people mutter words of encouragement as they turned their keys in the ignition. You are much less likely to hear anyone speaking in a similar way to a light switch or a bar of soap. These things improve the quality of life, but they do not really empower us the way some objects—such as automobiles—do.

In rúncræft, *eh* is good for summoning allies. Use it in a bin-drune with *tir* for achieving a goal. *Tir* will keep you on target, while *eh* will attract allies or help you become aware of them. Very often we do not recognize the people and tools that can help us reach our goals. You can use *eh* with *æsc* and *yr* for a charm to maximize your spiritual fortitude. The charm will not give you more of this part of your Self—known to the Saxons as *mægen*—but it will optimize what you do have.

Eh is also a rune to use for any magical working linked to your car or truck. In the previous chapter, while discussing the rune *eolh*, I described a simple runic working for protecting your ve-hicle before a long drive. By using both *eolh* and *eh,* you can ward your vehicle when you are not actually driving. There are times when we need to park our vehicles in public or semi-public loca-tions for extended periods of time, leaving them vulnerable. For this working, you'll be delineating both *eolh* and *eh*. The charm consists of two steps, one for each rune, but should be enacted so these two steps flow together smoothly.

Familiarize yourself with the characters of both *eolh* and *eh*. Face your vehicle and mark the shape of *eolh* before you. Make a sharp downward stroke with your dominant hand. Then use both of your hands to make the two outward strokes of the rune in a single gesture. As you draw this rune, firmly say, "*Eolh weardath*" (EH-olch WEH-ar-dath).

Now, for the second part, mark the shape of *eh*. Begin with your hands together, lifting them up and out for the central strokes of the rune. Then bring both hands down sharply to mark the outer strokes as you say, *"Thisne eh"* (THEES-neh ech). When performed correctly the spoken part of the charm should emerge as a single charge, *"Eolh weardath thisne eh!"*

When contemplating this rune, envision in your mind's eye a well bred, nicely proportioned horse. See the intelligence in its eyes. Imagine yourself touching the horse and then pulling yourself astride its back. This is an ally. Speak to it gently, for it is "ever a help."

IOR: Beaver

(YORE)

PHONETIC VALUE: eo, as in Creole

Ior byþ éafisc, and þéah a brúceþ,
fódres on foldan, hafaþ fægerne eard,
wætre beworpen, þær hé wynnum léofaþ.

The beaver is a river fish, and though he resides there,
he forages on land, he has a fair dwelling,
water surrounding, that place he joyfully holds dear.

What sort of animal is described by *ior*? The exact species of this "river fish" is debatable. *Ior* is sometimes translated as "eel," but nothing in this passage of the Rune Poem suggests to me the behavior or appearance of eels. The eel does not forage on land and, while it does live in both fresh and salt water, it is not a creature notable for its "fair dwelling."

More likely the Rune Poem is speaking of the beaver. This rodent was highly valued throughout Europe for its fur and scent glands, called castor sacs, which were used medicinally. The expression "river fish" may seem like an odd way to describe the beaver, but animals were historically classified according to habitat and function, rather than according to their anatomy. The word deer (*deor*) originally meant any species of wild herbivore. Thus the Rune Poem describes the aurochs—discussed earlier in this chapter—as a very fierce *deor*, even though there was nothing cervine about the animal. In the same way, the beaver was classified as a *fisc* because it made its home in the water. And it is very specifically a river fish (*éafisc*), in contrast to the eel, which is found in the sea and estuaries, as well as in rivers.

By the 1500s, due to strong and consistent demand for its fur and castor sacs, the European beaver was no longer found in England. Over the past few years, there have been attempts to reintroduce this rare animal in Gloucestershire and Lancashire. Both the European beaver and the American beaver are similar in size and behavior, but they are nevertheless different species.

As the Rune Poem says, the beaver forages on land (*fódres on foldan*) for both food and building materials. Larger trees are felled to build a dam across running water. The resulting pond is a refuge from predators, and becomes the site of the beaver's "fair dwelling" (*fægerne eard*), or lodge. Smaller trees provide food for the beaver, which subsists primarily on a diet of bark and twigs.

What the Rune Poem praises in the beaver, both in the animal's behavior and lifestyle, is its adaptability. This is an amphibious creature, living in the water and yet foraging on dry land. Not only is the beaver adaptable but so too is its environment. No animal other than man shapes its surrounding ecosystem so thoroughly. With instinctive architectural talent, the beaver creates ponds and wetlands where none existed before.

In form, the character of *ior* appears to depict an overhead view of the beaver; the central line representing the body—including head and tail—with the other strokes forming the four legs.

This same character evolved in the Younger Futhark, the Scandinavian runes, as a representation of the rune *hagol*, which suggests some connection between the two. As we will see in the next chapter, *hagol* is a rune of transformation, a concept not far removed from adaptability. The form or shape came to represent different concepts in two different runic languages. In a similar way the word *biscuit* has two meanings—similar but different—depending on whether you're speaking British English or American English.

It is the beaver's characteristic of adaptability that *ior* speaks of when it appears in a divination. In this it bears a superficial resemblance to *beorc*. Whereas the latter indicates that the outcome will unfold in an unexpected way, *ior* in a reading indicates that the querent himself must adapt somehow. Either the querent must be adaptable, or he must, like the beaver, adapt his surroundings to meet his needs. There is a need for flexibility in some aspect of the querent's life.

Ior can be effectively used in rúncræft to foster creativity, since this quality so often goes hand in hand with adaptability. Use it alone or in conjunction with *os* in a charm to deter writer's block. Combine *ior* with *ur* and *lagu* if you want to develop a new habit or break an old one. Use it with *feoh* and *wynn* if you want to break out of your current career and try something new. *Ior* is useful in any working that requires you to be adaptable or creative, so be creative in your use of it!

In your mind's eye, see the beaver in its "fair dwelling." The animal slides into the water, paddling beneath the surface toward its lodge of sticks and logs. It is equally at home on land and in water, adapting to both environments. And yet it has adapted its environment to suit its own needs by creating a large pool of safety. The beaver adapts, and simultaneously creates adaptation.

Review

1. *Feoh* is often interpreted as money or prosperity, but what is the most important quality of this rune?

2. When did the aurochs disappear from Britain?

3. Describe the differences between horns and antlers. How does this affect their symbolic meaning?

4. List three things that the *eh* rune might represent for you in a divination.

5. What quality in a beaver (or "river fish") is praised in the Anglo-Saxon Rune Poem?

Earthly Runes

The technological wonders that improve the quality of our lives also have a tendency to distance us from the natural world. We often forget how harsh and demanding the world can be. Whenever I hear people say how much they like winter, I have to wonder if the sentiment would be the same if they were deprived of artificial warmth and readily available food, and had to actually experience winter firsthand. For animals living in a temperate environment (including most of mankind throughout history), winter has always been a time of deprivation. There is nothing quaint or charming about the season for those who are fully immersed in it. There is only cold, hunger, and the threat of death.

The early, pre-Christian Saxons were thoroughly a part of the natural world. They had no electric or gas heating. No artificial lighting. No supermarket to provide foods transported from all over the world. They were truly involved with their world in a way that we can only imagine today. Survival from one year to the next was a crapshoot. Drought, fire, fungus, insects, or a shorter than usual growing season could mean starvation. The cold of winter had to be staved off for months. Stacks of firewood had to be cut or gathered. Cattle and sheep were often brought into homes to provide body warmth. And the dark of winter was equally challenging; with the fading light it became more difficult to graze livestock, and poultry ceased to lay eggs.

For travelers there were no pavements or street signs. Sojourners depended on the sun, moon, and stars as directional guides, as well as for light. Have you ever camped in the woods on a clouded night? With no flashlights or street lamps, the darkness is almost palpable.

The earthly runes of the Futhorc reflect the natural world of the early Saxons. It was a world teeming with dangers but illuminated with hope.

GEAR: Harvest

(YAE-ar)

Phonetic Value: y, as in yes

Gear biþ gumena hiht, þonne god læteþ,
hálig heofones cyning, hrúsan sellan
beorhte bléda beornum and þearfum.

The year is mankind's joy, when the god bequeaths,
ruler of the sacred sky, the earth offers
splendid crops for the well-born and the poor.

The Old English word *gear* means "year," but this passage of the Rune Poem is clearly speaking of one specific event that occurred each year in the lives of the Anglo-Saxons. Obviously food was harvested throughout the growing season, but the annual grain harvest was a cause for celebration and thanksgiving in every Anglo-Saxon community. The health, security, and prosperity of the community depended on that harvest. While *gear* may mean year, the Rune Poem does not speak to us here of the chilling cold of winter, nor of the sweet promise of spring, but of the joy and blessing of the grain harvest.

The harvested grain was either barley, rye, wheat, oats, or a combination of these. All of it was collectively referred to as *corn*, which, in Old English, simply meant seed or grain. These grains provided a significant portion of the Saxon's diet, consumed primarily in the form of breads and porridges. The harvest also provided straw, which was used as fodder, for roofing material, and in the manufacture of baskets and even furniture. A poor harvest could have an extremely negative impact on an early English community in multiple ways.

With the blessing of the god, the earth would offer up an abundant harvest that could have an equally positive impact on the community. An abundant harvest ensured plenty of food. The blessing of the god could mean surplus grain and straw to trade with neighboring villages. But who was this generous god? What deity transformed the year into "mankind's joy" (*gumena hiht*)?

At the time the Rune Poem was recorded, this passage must have been thought to reference the Biblical god. However, the wording of the poem gives us some clue as to an earlier meaning. The god in question is the king or ruler of the sky (*heofones cyning*). This sounds like an accurate description of Thunor, whose chariot causes the roll of thunder when he rides across the heavens. There is also a declaration that the god's blessing—the harvest—is intended to benefit the poor (*þearfum*) as well as the nobility, and the god Thunor is notable as a patron and defender of the common man.

The bounty of the harvest is a blessing, but it is not exactly a gift. The verb *lætan* means to bequeath, to leave alone, or to set free. Thunor can choose to prevent or allow a good harvest, but the possibility does not exist without our own effort. We must first till the soil, plant the seed, and cultivate the growing crop. The rune *gear* speaks to us of an earned reward. It represents our efforts brought to fruition.

In form, the rune is a long stroke bordered with two smaller angles. Runes were originally carved into wood and stone, and thus consisted of straight vertical, horizontal, or diagonal strokes. It does not take much imagination to see that the smaller angles, on a smooth surface, could be rounded into a circle. Viewed in this way, we see the annual cycle bisected by a longer stroke to indicate the waxing and waning halves of the year.

In the proto-Germanic Elder Futhark, the rune is marked with this form:

Here we see the waxing and waning symbolism even more clearly in a character that suggests the shape of the image representing the Taoist concept of yin and yang. I am not suggesting there is any direct relationship, but it should not surprise us if underlying universal truths manifest in similar ways within the human psyche.

These two halves, whether carved as in the Elder Futhark or as depicted in the Futhorc, also call to mind the fundamental Indo-European idea of "a gift for a gift." We give forth our effort—tilling, seeding, cultivating—and the earth gives forth new crops. We give offerings and praise to Thunor, and he in turn blesses those crops and allows them to manifest in abundance.

Gear is a rune of cycles. Its meaning in a divination can be enigmatic. When consulting the runes on someone else's behalf, unless other runes in the reading offer clarification, the wiglere should not make assumptions. Usually the presence of *gear* indicates a positive outcome. The querent will be rewarded for his or her effort. But there is no time specified for this. The reward could come a long way down the road. If so, the rune is saying "keep your chin up," which may not be what the querent wants to hear.

Furthermore, if there are no other runes giving clarification, *gear* could mean something quite nasty. If the querent has been secretly seeing another guy behind her boyfriend's back, *gear* could indicate that the boyfriend has caught on. The runes do not have upright and reversed meanings, but they certainly can have positive and negative meanings. And when *gear* is negative, it tells the querent that he is about to get what he deserves.

In rúncræft, use *gear* when you want to claim your just reward. The most obvious use is in a legal trial, so long as you are absolutely certain that you are on the right side of the law! Use this rune alone or in combination with *tir* and *ác* to get a fair decision. But *gear* does not need a judge or jury to prove its usefulness. Use it with *feoh* when you are ready to ask your boss for a raise, if you are sure you deserve the raise. If you have put in long hours on a project, whether for school or work, *gear* may help you gain the recognition you have earned. This is a rune of harvest, and that is what it brings into manifestation.

In your mind's eye, envision people harvesting a field of grain. One person is cutting the stalks with a sickle, while other people are bundling them. Notice that all are hard at work. They have an abundant harvest, but they are not getting something for nothing. In the distance, a bolt of lightning comes down from the sky, reminding you that the harvest—the result of the work these people have put in—is also a blessing of "the ruler of the sacred sky."

N

HAGOL: Hail

(HAG-ol)

PHONETIC VALUE: h, as in hat

Hagol biþ hwítost corna, hwyrft hit of heofones lyfte,
wealcaþ hit windes scúra,
weorþeþ hit tó wætere syððan.

Hail is the whitest of seeds, its circling comes from the lofty sky,
it tosses in the wind's shower,
it then becomes water afterwards.

Even today, in the most urban environments, a hailstorm is a disruption and potential danger. Hail presented an even greater threat throughout pre-Christian Europe, when men and women spent much more time in outside pursuits, and when damaged fields could mean starvation. Truly life-threatening hail is a rarity in Europe; the worst hailstorms—those most likely to form large, deadly stones—tend to occur in India, mainland China, and Bangladesh.

The Rune Poem does not emphasize or even allude to the damage caused by hail. We are told in other passages of the poem that elk-sedge "cruelly wounds," that the aurochs is "very fierce," and yet hail is described almost poetically as the "whitest of seeds" (*hwitost corna*). There was no need to mention the stinging pain these white seeds could inflict or the damage they could do to young, tender plants; hail's association with storms is evident. The hail comes from the sky and is tossed about by the wind. But the mystery of *hagol* is that it is a *corn*, meaning a grain or seed. What does this mean? Obviously the hailstone cannot be ground into meal or flour. It cannot be boiled to make a porridge. The poem uses the word *corn*, or seed, to mean a vessel for potential.

Every seed is a magical thing with the potential to transform into something else. The barley-corn bears the potential for a new barley crop. The little acorn has the potential to become a great oak tree.

None of these transformations occur until the seed falls to the earth, and the same is true for hail. While in the sky, the poem tells us, it circles and tosses. But then the seed falls and transforms, becoming water. It becomes the essential substance of life. The seed is transformed into something not only harmless, but beneficial. There is a direct relationship between precipitation and the fertility of the land. Regions with little precipitation become barren; regions with abundant precipitation are blessed with lush growth.

Hagol indicates the transformation of something unpleasant and disruptive into something beneficial. This is illustrated in the form of the rune. The two upright strokes represent the beginning and end of the transformation, with an angular stroke connecting one to the other. The angular, diagonal connection is sometimes marked as a pair of strokes instead of a single line. In the Younger Futhark—the runes that were used in Norway, Sweden, and Iceland—*hagol* took on the form that evolved into the rune *ior* of the Anglo-Saxon Futhorc. The two runes are also similar in meaning, but whereas *ior* indicates adaptability to change, *hagol* represents the change itself.

Change, like small hailstones, can be painful. Because of this, *hagol* is rarely a welcome rune when it comes up in a divination. It represents a change or disruption not of the querent's choosing. The querent should be prepared to be tossed about, metaphorically speaking. But the rune is also telling the wiglere that the ultimate outcome will be good.

In my personal experience, *hagol* usually indicates a small disruption rather than a catastrophe. Of course, at the time it occurs, a "small disruption" can seem quite imposing. An essential element of this disruption is the transformation that follows. In some way, something in the querent's life has changed. He or she may have learned a valuable lesson or forged a new relationship or profited from some other, perhaps subtle, life change, but the change—the transformation—is always there.

Because change can be painful, I rarely use *hagol* in rúncræft. Its use as an offensive, cursing rune should be obvious. Otherwise it is only useful when the rúnwita wants to create a transformation and does not care about the cost. There are times when we do have to face challenges in this way. Some examples are:

- ending an unhealthy friendship, a sour romance, or any other ongoing personal relationship
- a gay person coming out to family and friends
- any person, straight or gay, "coming out" by sharing personal feelings that may alter relationships with family and friends; Pagans who were raised in another faith, usually those raised in a monotheistic faith, often face this challenge
- changing from one career to another (not just changing jobs, but a life-altering career change)
- breaking a stubborn and enduring addiction

Hagol can be used alone when confronting any of the above challenges. There will usually be a point, a moment, when you make a resolution to move forward and endure the transformation. Using *hagol* in a simple spell, make downward motions with both hands simultaneously to mark the rune's upright strokes. Then, using your dominant hand, mark the angled stroke joining the uprights as you say *"Weortheth hit"* (WEH-oar-theth hit) in a firm voice. If you have trouble with the Old English, simply say, "It comes to pass." Notice that this is expressed in the present tense. We do not say "it will come to pass" because this places our intention at some undefined point in the future rather than here and now. The transformation will not achieve completion immediately, but it must begin immediately, so you need to express that

immediacy. This gesture and expression can be used at the conclusion of any spell intended to effect a transformation.

When trying to break an addiction, craft a charm combining
hagol with *ur* (for strength) and *éoh* (for balance).

In your mind's eye, envision a person running to get out of
a hailstorm. He protects his head with his arms as he runs. Hail
falls all around this person, countless pellets of ice pummeling the
landscape. But on the ground, the hail is already melting. Pools of
life-sustaining water form on the earth.

|

IS: Ice

(EES)

PHONETIC VALUE: ee, as in bee; or i, as in pit

Is byþ oferceald, ungemetum slidor,
glisnaþ glæshlútor, gimmum gelícost,
flór forste geworuht, fæger ansíene.

Ice is extremely cold, very slippery,
it glistens clear, like precious gems,
a floor wrought by frost, fair thing seen.

In northern European cosmology, ice and fire are the primal elements of creation. At the beginning of time, endless frost poured
from out of the north. Meanwhile endless fire raged from the
south. These two primal elements—ice and fire—came together to
form the base materials that would be molded into our universe.
And so two forces inimical to life merged to become harmless and
benign.

But these forces alone, both ice and fire, are dangerous elements.
Just as ordinary table salt is a combination of two deadly chemicals

(sodium and chlorine), the substance of the universe is a combination of two deadly forces. It goes without saying that life is threatened by extreme temperatures. Taken far enough, both fire (extreme heat) and ice (extreme cold) can eliminate all life as we know it.

The opposition of heat and cold is also a fundamental concept of the elemental theory developed in southern Europe. States of heat and cold were described poetically by philosopher-scientists as "water" (cold) and "fire" (hot). These states of energy were further defined by humidity—whether something was moist or dry—adding the elements of "earth" and "air" to this model. These elements were the postulates underlying Hippocrates' theory of humors, which served as the basis of Western medicine for centuries. We will explore this further in the Wortcunning chapter.

The Anglo-Saxon Rune Poem acknowledges the inherent danger of ice. It describes the element as extremely cold (*oferceald*). To the Anglo-Saxons, ice was the physical manifestation of cold. It was only when fields and forests died under winter's frigid breath that ice crept across the surface of ponds and encased the limbs of ash, oak, and hawthorn trees. The poem goes on to describe ice as being very slippery (*ungemetum slidor*). This slippery quality is more than a mere inconvenience even today. This past winter, while driving to a divination workshop in Pittsburgh, I was surprised when traffic came to a complete standstill on Liberty Avenue. Sheets of black ice along the street terrified motorists whose vehicles had no traction on the slick surface. Each of us was aware that we could be involved in a collision at any moment due to the ice covering the street. Fifteen centuries ago, a slick, icy surface could mean a broken leg for an ox or a horse, resulting in the loss of the valuable animal.

After reminding us of the potential danger of ice, the Rune Poem continues on to speak of its beauty. Ice is described as fair (*fæger*) and is likened in appearance to gemstones (*gimmum*). There is a reference to "a floor wrought by frost" (*flór forste geworuht*), possibly a description of the ice covering a pond or lake. Poets have long remarked on the beautiful, fairy-like landscapes often created by ice in all its forms during the northern winter.

In form, the *is* rune is a single, simple vertical stroke. The image is sharp and abrupt. For this reason we never use *is* in a bindrune. It disappears in a bindrune, much as ice disappears or melts away when cold weather recedes. The mystery of *is* can be summed up in the expression "all that glitters is not gold." In a divination, this rune warns us that all is not what it seems. What we perceive as a fair thing is, in fact, slippery and potentially dangerous. *Is* urges the querent to exercise caution.

The rune does not indicate an unavoidable catastrophe. As with *thorn*, the *is* rune speaks of dangers that can be easily avoided. The danger is visible if you look for it, only in this case it is also fair and beautiful. The querent needs to take a closer look at the situation. If you are pursuing a new romantic relationship, proceed with caution. If you are thinking about quitting your job and moving to another company, take a closer look at your prospective employer. Even if you are not aware of any changes in your immediate future, even if your life is fairly stable at the moment, poke around to see if there is a fly hiding somewhere in the ointment.

The appearance of *is* in a divination is not a cause for panic or undue concern; it is simply telling you that things are not exactly as they seem. After you see beyond the illusion, you may want to continue forward with no change in your plans. The slippery dangers hinted at by this rune may well be challenges you are willing to face once you are aware of them.

I have never used *is* in rúncræft and cannot envision any reason for doing so. It is not an influence that I would want to bring into my own life. I suppose it could be used as an aggressive, cursing rune, but I do not recommend this. For reasons discussed elsewhere in this book, I usually view cursing as a pointless waste of time, and I hope the reader is wise enough to reach this same conclusion.

When contemplating this rune, imagine in your mind's eye an icy bejeweled landscape. The ground itself seems to be "wrought by frost," while icicles hang from frozen tree boughs like sparkling gems. It is all extremely cold, and possibly dangerous, but the cold and slipperiness are masked with beauty.

ᛋ

SIGEL : Sun

(SEE-yel)

PHONETIC VALUE: s, as in sauce; or z, as in brazen

Sigel sæmannum simble biþ on hihte,
þonne híe hine fériaþ ofer fisces bæþ,
oþ híe brimhengest bringeþ tó lande.

The sun for sailors is always hoped for,
when they depart over the fishes' bath,
until their ship carries them to land.

Southern European cultures perceived the sun as masculine, but in northern Europe, this celestial orb is feminine. Germanic people called her Sunne or Sunna. Like the southern masculine solar gods, such as Helios and Ra, the goddess Sunne was depicted as riding across the sky in a cart or chariot. She was called the "glory of Elves." The Anglo-Saxons also referred to her as "heaven's gem." These kennings illustrate how the people of northern Europe adored the goddess who illuminates our Middle Earth.

The sun, of course, is necessary for our very existence, and the people of Pagan Europe were keenly aware of its importance in their lives. Sunlight affected not only the growth of their crops, but also the behavior of their livestock. Cattle cease to graze after nightfall, and egg production is determined by how many hours of light hens are exposed to. Men and women were aware, too, of Sunne's role in the earth's seasonal changes. Long, sunny days came during the warm part of the year. Great bonfires were set aflame at the summer solstice to honor the fire above.

The Rune Poem likewise commends the sun, but for a reason not given above. In the Rune Poem, the sun is praised for its use in navigation, and especially as a boon for sailors. Most early maritime travel took place within sight of the coast. But the Rune Poem is more concerned with travel that takes place "over the fishes' bath"—a poetic reference to the sea. Because their island realm was surrounded by the sea, the early English often used poetic descriptions like this when speaking of the ocean. It was called a "bath," or the "swan's road" (*swan-rad*) or "whale's way" (*hwæl-weg*).

When a ship traveled farther out to sea, sailors needed some means for determining direction. Solar navigation is the oldest and simplest form of navigation. Sunne's movement across the heavens clearly marked the east and west directions and gave some approximation of north and south. Sailors were dependent on the sun if they hoped to sail more than a few miles from the shoreline.

The rune takes the form of a ray of sunlight. The shape is angled, much like a modern representation of a lightning bolt. This is not entirely surprising when we consider that both of these— sunlight and lightning—are energy descending from the sky.

As we see from the Rune Poem, the *sigel* rune indicates guidance, and that is its meaning when it appears in a divination. It is almost always a good omen. *Sigel* tells the querent that he will receive the guidance he needs. This guidance can manifest in a variety of ways: help from a mentor, advice from a trusted friend, or a flash of personal inspiration. The querent still needs to confront his challenges—he still traverses the "fishes' bath"—but he will have the benefit of some form of guidance as he does so. In this way, *sigel* is a rune of hope. It does not guarantee a positive outcome, but it suggests that the odds will favor the querent.

Sigel has an equally positive significance when used in rúncræft. Use this rune when you want to invoke guidance and blessing. *Sigel, ur,* and *wynn* can be used together to make a charm for good luck. Use it in a bindrune with *gyfu* to help guide your way in a new, hopeful relationship. *Sigel* and *os* are a good combination for a charm if you need to make a speech, or for anyone in the teaching profession.

The *sigel* rune is imposed perpendicular to itself to form the swastika. This was long a symbol of good fortune until the Third Reich usurped and tainted it. The swastika as it was displayed in the twentieth century by the Nazi party is still burdened with the shame and horror of unspeakable atrocities, but a softer, more rounded variation of the symbol was displayed elsewhere in northern Europe, including England. This variation is known as a *fylfot*, a name that may have evolved from the Old English *féower fót*, meaning "four footed." The fylfot can be depicted exactly like a swastika, but it can also be drawn in the rounded variation like this:

I do not believe, myself, that there is anything inherently wrong with using the swastika as a good luck charm, but due to the negative associations that now shroud the swastika, I favor the rounded fylfot.

In your mind's eye, envision yourself in a large seaworthy vessel. You are on the ocean, and there is no sign of any shore. But then you see her, Sunne, the Glory of Elves, as she rises in the east. She ascends above the horizon, and the way is now clear to you.

TIR: The North Star

(TEER)

PHONETIC VALUE: t, as in tight

Tir biþ tácna sum, healdeð tréowa wel
wiþ æþelingas, á biþ on færylde,
ofer nihta genipu næfre swíceþ.

The north star is one signal, it holds faith well
with nobles, it is always on track,
throughout night's darkness it never deceives.

Just as the sun was used for navigation during the daylight hours, the people of northern Europe relied on the North Star for navigating at night. The North Star is the star that would appear directly overhead if the viewer were standing at the North Pole. It is not the brightest star in the sky, but it is the star that always appears in the north, and thus it holds faith well (*healdeð tréowa wel*). The North Star can only be used for navigation in the Northern Hemisphere, as it is not visible from the Southern Hemisphere.

In the context of the Rune Poem, the North Star is Polaris. This is the same star that we know as the North Star today, but the star that holds this title—North Star—changes from one era to the next as all of the infinite stars make their slow procession across the heavens. Five thousand years ago, the North Star was a small star now called Thuban. A thousand years from now, Polaris will be succeeded by Gamma Cephei. For all practical purposes, however, each star bearing the title of North Star can be relied on to remain "on track" (*on færylde*) for centuries.

If you live in the Northern Hemisphere, you can find Polaris by first locating the constellation of Woden's Wain, also known as

Ursa Major or the Big Dipper. A *wain* is an open wagon. Woden's Wain is always visible in the night sky, although its position changes. Once you have found the constellation, locate the two stars at the rear of the wagon, opposite the tongue. (If you are more familiar with this constellation as the Big Dipper, locate the two stars opposite the handle.) These two stars are sometimes called the Pointer Stars or the Pointers, because they point to our North Star. Visualize a line passing through these two stars up from the wagon (or dipper). Polaris is about five times farther away than the distance between the two Pointers.

Tir, or Tyr, is another name for the god who was known to the Anglo-Saxons as Tiw. I describe Tiw in more depth in *Travels Through Middle Earth: The Path of a Saxon Pagan*. Tiw is, among other things, a god of justice and order, which is why he is associated with the North Star. The characteristic that gave Polaris significance to the Anglo-Saxons was its constant reliability.

The similarity between the runes *tir* and *sigil* are immediately obvious—both the North Star and the sun were vital tools for celestial navigation. However, it would not make sense for two runes to embody the same mystery, so we must look a little deeper to identify the difference. Solar navigation is based on Sunne's journey across the sky. This movement delineates east and west. Motion is an essential element of the mystery. *Sigil* represents guidance for movement or action. In contrast to this, the North Star is useful for navigation because of its fixed position. Polaris always points due north. Thus *tir* represents guidance for order and reliability, steadiness and truth.

The *tir* rune was often carved into weapons and shields to ensure that these would remain steadfast and resolute in battle. The rune invoked the power and protection of the god Tiw. In Old English, the word *tir* can also mean fame or glory.

The form of the rune is an arrow pointing upward. As anyone with even a passing familiarity with maps knows, "up" indicates "north." The arrow is a reminder that the North Star is ever fixed in its northerly position.

The appearance of *tir* in wiglung is almost always a good sign. This rune indicates that truth will prevail. It means the triumph of justice, the restoration of order. If the querent has behaved in an honorable way, *tir* is a positive rune. It is triumphant and victorious. Under other circumstances, however, *tir* can be a most unwelcome portent. The person who has been stealing from his employer or lying to his spouse had better prepare to face the consequences when *tir* makes an appearance. Here the rune means that the querent's dishonorable acts are about to be exposed.

In rúncræft, one of the most obvious uses for *tir* is to ensure a fair trial. Work this rune into a charm with *ác* and *gear* for this purpose. *Ác* bequeaths the internal resources—the patience and temperance—to endure the trial. *Gear* creates a cycle, stating that what has been planted shall be harvested. And, finally, *tir* invokes the power of justice and order. But this charm will only ensure fairness; it is of no benefit to a wrongful party.

Use *tir* with *eh* if you want to keep focused on a goal. *Eh* provides the means of reaching the goal, while *tir* will keep you fixed on your objective. A charm incorporating these two runes would make an excellent gift for someone starting college or beginning any long-term project, assuming the other person would appreciate such a talisman.

In your mind's eye, envision the North Star glowing in the heavens, guiding you like a compass. It is ever faithful, ever sure in its position.

ᛚ

LAGU: Sea or Water

(LAH-goo)

PHONETIC VALUE: l, as in lid

Lagu biþ léodum langsum geþúht,
gif híe sculun néþan on nacan tealtum,
and híe sæyþa swiþe brégaþ,
and sé brimhengest brídles ne gíemeð.

The sea seems of endless length to people,
if they must venture on unstable ships,
and the sea waves terrify them exceedingly,
and the ship does not heed its reins.

Along with *sigel*, this is one of the two seafaring passages in the Rune Poem. In both passages, however, the sea is incidental. In the passage for *sigel*, the sea is mentioned only to illustrate the value of the sun in navigation. In this passage, too, although the sea is referred to more directly, it is secondary to the quality or stability of a ship.

The Anglo-Saxons came to England from continental Europe in ships, of course, but the sea was not as central to their own culture as it was to their Norse cousins. There are no references, for example, in Old English lore to deities such as Njorðr, Ran, or Ægir, who rule the seas of the Scandinavians. Early Anglo-Saxon ships were double-ended, having the same shape at bow and stern, and were usually rowed rather than sailed. It is these ships or boats that are the focus of this passage of the Rune Poem. The sea seems to be of endless length (*langsum geþúht*) and the waves frighten or terrify (*brégaþ*), but there is nothing inherently evil suggested here. The problem is not with the sea, but with unstable, untrustworthy ships. The problem is the ship that "does not heed its reins" (*bridles ne gíemeð*). This poetic phrase is related to the word *brimhengest*, sea-stallion, which was a kenning used by the early English to describe a ship. It is because of unstable, unreliable ships that people have cause to fear the dangers of the sea.

I have often seen this rune interpreted as indicating a journey, but the basic idea of travel is echoed in several other runes. The mystery of *lagu* is deeper than this. The Rune Poem doesn't speak directly of the journey, but rather of the potential danger of the journey. Furthermore, *lagu* tells us that we are ill prepared to confront that danger. We may have the ship—the means to traverse the waters of our lives—but that ship may not be as stable as we would hope. In this way, *lagu* often bears a resemblance to the mystery of *is*. There may be some deception or illusion if all appears well.

In form, *lagu* even resembles *is* if we were to snap the top of the latter rune and bend it down at an angle. The connection between these two runes should not come as a surprise to us. The Anglo-Saxons were aware of the relationship between ice and water. When we look at the shape of *lagu*, angled at the top, we see something broken and thus unstable. Compare also the shape of this rune with the shape of *éoh*, the yew, the rune of balance. *Éoh* is angled at both the top and bottom, creating an image of symmetry. *Lagu* only has an angle at one end, creating an image of imbalance.

When *lagu* appears in a divination, it indicates that the querent is not fully equipped to meet his challenges. He or she may or may not be aware of this. The problem could be almost anything: the querent's social support, financial resources, education, mechanical or artistic skills, transportation, emotional fortitude, physical condition, or available time. The wiglere should be aware that the exact nature of the problem will be situational, and thus should not make assumptions when consulting the runes for somebody else.

What the wiglere can safely assume is that the problem is related to some physical, social, or spiritual journey the querent has embarked upon, or is preparing for. *Lagu* is not a warning about where the querent is now. It indicates that the querent is not securely equipped to reach some destination. This does not mean that the querent should give up or turn away from the goal or destination; what the querent needs to do is check his or her preparations, evaluate resources, and correct any weaknesses that might be uncovered.

This is another of those runes of the Futhorc that has few positive uses in rúncræft. Its power is to destabilize and weaken.

In your mind's eye, envision a boat on the ocean. Tossed about by the waves, the vessel is insufficient for the journey. Water is pouring into the boat. Whether it will survive the journey is uncertain.

DÆG: Day

(DAY)

PHONETIC VALUE: d, as in deed

Dæg biþ dryhtnes sond, déore mannum,
mære metodes léoht, myrgþ and tóhiht,
éadgum and earmum, eallum bryce.

The day is the god's ambassador, beloved of men,
the great god's light, mirth and also hope,
prosperous and poor, all enjoy it.

If a contest were ever held to determine the happiest rune of the Futhorc, *dæg* would almost certainly be the winner. The Old English word *dæg* means the same as the Modern English "day"; it can mean a complete twenty-four-hour cycle, or it can mean daytime in contrast to night. In this passage of the Rune Poem, the latter meaning is obviously being used.

For the early Anglo-Saxons (and indeed all pre-Christian cultures), the day and the precious light that accompanies it were nothing less than blessings. Many activities could be continued into the night, but this used up valuable resources—oil and tallow—and it was often difficult to perform any tasks well in the flickering light of a candle or an oil lamp. The Anglo-Saxons were also keenly aware of the relationship between the length of the day and seasonal changes. Longer days came with the warmer, more fertile and productive half of the year.

Anglo-Saxon society of the time was very stratified, with distinct ranks or levels of social position. It was not entirely impossible to move up this ladder a little, but the climb was very difficult. *Dæg* did not acknowledge this hierarchy. The blessings of *dæg* were and are bequeathed equally for all to enjoy (*eallum bryce*), regardless of wealth or social position.

As mentioned elsewhere, when the Anglo-Saxon Rune Poem was recorded on paper, words like *dryhtnes* and *metodes* were assumed to refer to the Biblical god. In an earlier time, before the Anglo-Saxons—whether by choice or by force—turned away from their gods, these words would have meant an indigenous northern European deity. From the degree of praise in this passage of the poem, we might suspect that the deity in question is Thunor, who was the most popular of the Anglo-Saxon gods, but Thunor rules over the storms that brings life-giving rain. He may bring mirth and hope (*myrgþ and tóhiht*), but he is hardly a god of daylight. And the light is not the gift of just any god; it is given by the "great god" (*mære metodes*). From this we could argue that the deity is Woden himself, the leader of the Anglo-Saxon gods. But all of this is conjecture, and ultimately it does not matter because the emphasis of the poem is on the day itself, not on the deity who releases this blessing. In my own mind, I find it simpler to use the plural, letting the day be the ambassador of "the gods," and its light their blessing.

Do you remember the two upright strokes of the rune *hagol*, the rune of transformation, that represent two different states of being? The *dæg* rune has a similar pair of upright strokes, but these are connected by the angular, perpendicular strokes of the *gyfu* rune. Thus the form of *dæg* reveals a gift radiating out to bless distinctly different states of being, to bless the well off (*éadgum*) as well as those who are not so fortunate (*earmum*). The idea of this blessing being a gift is essential to understanding the deeper mystery of this rune. *Dæg* is not a payoff for work or actions. That is part of the mystery of *gear*. This rune is grace. It represents blessings given freely, regardless of what the recipients may have done or who they are.

In wiglung, the art of seeking portents, *dæg* is always a welcome rune. Its presence indicates that the querent has some divine blessing working for him or her. It is my belief that the deity bestowing this blessing varies from one querent to another and from one situation to another. If the querent has an especially close relationship with a particular deity—a god or goddess who is often known as a "patron" by contemporary Pagans—then that deity is very likely the power bestowing the blessing indicated by *dæg*. But it is also possible that this boon is coming from an unexpected direction. Whether or not the querent—or the wiglere who is interpreting the runes—will know the source of the blessing depends on a variety of factors, including how open and demonstrative the deity is.

In rúncræft, *dæg* is useful in many situations, especially those situations you do not have much control over. But even though *dæg* is a blessing of grace, do not expect this rune to undo your actions if you have proven yourself unworthy of the boon you seek. If you are looking for a job in a highly competitive career, combining *dæg* with *feoh* (and possibly other runes, depending on the nature of the work) might give you the edge you need to be noticed and chosen. If you are hoping for a raise even though you have given as little as humanly possible to your employer, *dæg* and *feoh* are probably not going to help. In this situation, you are trying to use rúncræft against your own wyrd, against the destiny that you have created through your actions, and that is not easy to do.

Dæg combined with *beorc* and *wynn* makes a strong good luck charm. Or use the rune by itself to draw "mirth and also hope" into your life.

In your mind's eye, envision people happily pursuing their daily affairs. Sunlight streams down from above. For the time being, all is well with the world.

Review

1. In northern European cosmology, what two forces came together to form the universe?

2. What does the shape of the *sigel* rune represent?

3. Describe the difference in meaning between *sigel* and *tir*. What do these two runes have in common, and how are they different?

4. What does the Anglo-Saxon Rune Poem refer to when it speaks of a sea-stallion (*brimhengest*)?

5. Describe the difference in meaning between *gear* and *dæg*.

Gift of Boons

Grace

Blessings given freely (in 2 States of Being

X Gift - dæg rune

Runes Within the Hall

The early Saxon druid served his tribe or community, and that community was centered around the mead-hall. This was where people gathered to relax and to discuss business. Oaths were sworn over drinking horns filled with mead. The mead-hall was a combination boardroom, nightclub, and recreation center. A modest mead-hall might be called a *meduærn*, while a grander structure was known as a *meduheall* or *meduseld*. In Tolkien's fictional Middle Earth, Meduseld was the name of the great hall in Rohan. In the epic poem of *Beowulf*, King Hrothgar's mead-hall is called Heorot.

The mead-hall was the site of the community *symbel*, or feast. These feasts were essential to early Saxon society. A symbel could continue for days, and included poets, musicians, and other entertainers, as well as the requisite parade of food and drink. Business deals were made and marriages arranged. Often months of preparation were devoted to hosting one symbel. The local lord and his favored guests and retainers sat at a "high table," where the best dishes and cuts of meat were served.

The house or hall where the symbel was held was a place of safety. It was a protection against rain, hail, and chill winds. It could dissuade the thief and the wild beast. The hall was where the inhíred (household) gathered at the end of the day. The runes that we will look at in this chapter reflect life in the safety of the hall. The mysteries inherent in these runes teach us how to live and prosper with our kin.

MANN: Human
(MAN)

PHONETIC VALUE: m, as in mum

Mann biþ on myrgþe his mágan léof,
sceal þéah ánre gehwilc óðrum swícan,
for þám dryhten wille dóme síne,
þæt earme flæsc eorþan betæcan.

A joyful person is beloved of his kin,
even though each one depart away,
for moreover the lord wills his fate,
the destitute flesh be delivered to the earth.

To explore the rune *mann* we must first move beyond the thoroughly modern definition of "man" as a term exclusive of "woman." Titles like policeman, fireman, and mailman have been replaced today with more egalitarian titles—police officer, fire fighter, mail carrier—but the older words were historically accurate for both males and females in these professions because "man" originally meant a person of either sex. It was a synonym for "human," a word which came to us from the Latin *humanus*.

The English language is consistently inconsistent with its vocabulary for living creatures. For many species we have only one name for the entire kind. When we want to indicate the sex of guppies, for example, we can only do this by stating that an individual fish is a male guppy or a female guppy. We have no special words to designate the sex of the fish. For other species, we have names for their entire kind, and two or more other names to indicate sex and age. We can speak of deer in general, or be more specific by calling it a buck, doe, or fawn. The sex of a horse can be identified by whether we call it a stallion or a mare. Pigs, including the "Guinea" variety, can be either boars or sows.

There are a very few creatures that we identify collectively with one word, but have another term to designate just one sex of that species. The name identifying the sex of the creature may be specific for males or females of the species. There's no reason or pattern to this, it is simply how our language evolved. For ducks we have a specific word for the male, which is called a drake. When we point out a flock of ducks, we do not have to indicate that the flock consists of both ducks and drakes. The former term includes the latter. The word *man*, or *mann*, originally fell into this category, and even today we understand that *mankind* is not in any way exclusive of females. Many centuries ago, there was a word to specifically identify a person as male. He would have been called a *wermann*, meaning a male human, in contrast to a *wifmann*, or female human. *Wermann* eventually disappeared from the English language, while *wifmann* evolved into the modern *woman*. The word *mann* without a prefix indicated the species, not the sex.

The passage of the Rune Poem describing *mann* is not especially cheery. We are presented with an image of a person who is joyful, pleasant, or perhaps sweet (*myrgþe*), and beloved by his or her kinsmen. The warmth is then swept away as we are told that they will all be separated, by death if for no other reason. There is no room for discussion. No matter how pleasant or sweet the person, no matter how beloved, he will eventually be separated from his family and tribe. When his flesh is *earme*, meaning destitute or wretched, when his body has been severed from the rest of his person, it shall return to the earth.

As sad as this may sound, the *mann* rune is drawing our attention to a fundamental aspect of our relationships with others. Whenever you bring another person into your life, whether through marriage, birth, friendship, or business, you must accept that the relationship, however long it may last, is temporary. Eventually you will separate. You will divorce or move away. If by luck nothing such as this happens, the relationship will end when either you or the other person eventually dies. This harsh, cold truth is affixed to the first line of the passage, the line telling of the pleasant man or woman beloved by kinsmen. *Mann* reminds us of how precious our relationships are. It cries out for us to appreciate our loved ones, and not take them for granted.

When we look at the form of the *mann* rune we can see two persons, represented by the upright strokes, each with his or her arm on the shoulder of the other, illustrated by the angled strokes. The image depicted by the shape of the rune is an image of camaraderie.

In a divination, *mann* calls attention to the querent's relationships with others. Exactly what the rune is trying to say, of course, depends both on the situation and on the other runes around it. It could mean that the querent will soon meet a person, or perhaps a group of people, with whom he will develop a deep and worthy relationship. It could mean that the querent needs to focus on the relationships he or she already enjoys. *Mann* is a rune of tribe and immediate community.

In rúncraeft, *mann* is useful for creating, strengthening, or sustaining community. Combine this rune with *beorc* and *gyfu* for a charm to win new friends. Or use *mann* in a bindrune with *éoh* to nurture harmony in your immediate or extended family. If you wish to use the rune in this sort of way, however, be sure to heed its message. Never forget that your loved ones are gifts that could be snatched away at any moment. Do not wait until tomorrow to show each of them how important they are to you.

When contemplating this rune, envision in your mind's eye a community of people. This could be an immediate family, an extended inhíred, or even a small town or village. These people seem happy enough as they go about their business. But among them, resting in a casket, is a corpse. Are they aware of the corpse? It must weigh on their hearts in some way. The corpse is a reminder that their time together is precious.

ᚹ

WYNN: Joy

(WEUN, the *eu* is similar to how it would
be pronounced in French, similar to the first
vowel in *burger,* without the *r*)

PHONETIC VALUE: w, as in with

Wynn brúceþ þe can wana lýt,
sáres and sorge, and him selfa hæfþ
blæd and blysse and éac burga geniht.

Joy possesses him who knows little want,
illnesses and sorrows, and himself has
prosperity and happiness and also a sufficient dwelling.

On the surface, this passage of the Rune Poem sounds fairly straight-forward. The *wynn* rune is a rune of joy and pleasure. When a runic mystery is presented in so simple a fashion, we can be certain that there is some underlying layer of meaning. We have already seen that *dæg* indicates the promise of happiness, so the mystery of *wynn* must be distinct from this in some way.

You may remember that *dæg* is described as an ambassador or messenger (*sond*) bringing light, mirth, and hope. *Dæg* is a force that can contribute to happiness. In this way, we can think of *dæg* as the cause and *wynn* as the effect. *Wynn* does not speak of what might bring joy into our lives. Instead it defines exactly what joy is. We are told that a joyful state can only exist if we are relatively free of want, illness, and sorrow. A joyful state requires a degree of prosperity, happiness, and a roof over one's head.

It may appear odd, at first, for the Rune Poem to tell us that we are not going to be very joyful if we are homeless. Why would the Rune Poem point out something so obvious? It seems as if the poem is almost challenging us to reassess our lives, to notice and acknowledge our blessings. I should mention here that the word I have translated as "prosperity" (*blæd*) does not necessarily mean "endless wealth;" it means "having enough." *Wynn* tells us that if we have enough to get by, along with a roof over our heads and reasonable health, then we should be joyful.

In form, the *wynn* rune looks much like a small flag or pennant proudly raised by the wind. Raising a flag is a triumphant and joyful act. Conversely, when we are in mourning it is customary to lower the flag. The Anglo-Saxons made use of flags or banners, which they called *fanan*, and seem to have used them much as we do today. Raising the flag is an indication of pride and, above all, ownership. This is another facet of the mystery of *wynn*, for this rune is also protective. The Old English word *burga* means a dwelling, but it implies a degree of safety or fortification. It can also refer to a castle or to a town protected by walls and towers. The dwelling only contributes to a joyful state if it is secure.

Wynn usually has a very simple, direct meaning when it appears in divination. It denotes joy. This rune indicates that the querent will have or gain all that he needs. We should keep in mind that all the querent needs is not necessarily the same as all the querent wants. Because of this, *wynn* can sometimes indicate that the querent is letting greed cloud his or her mind. Almost all of us, at one time or another, have allowed our desire for more to overshadow our appreciation for what we already have. In wiglung, *wynn* will sometimes tell the querent that he should be joyful because he already has all that he needs. More often, however, the rune is expressing itself in a future tense, reassuring the querent that his or her immediate future holds the promise of joy and delight.

In rúncræft, as you might expect, *wynn* can be used in almost any positive working. Combine this rune with *ác* and *eolh* for protection. A charm using *wynn* with *beorc* and *dæg* can attract good luck, while a bindrune crafted of *wynn* and *æsc* will guard the luck you already enjoy. *Wynn, ur,* and *sigel* are another good combination for a general good luck charm.

Wynn can also be used for more specific, defined purposes. If you want to switch to a new career or enter into a career that you have prepared yourself for, combine *wynn* in a charm with *gear* and *feoh*. Be sure that you are well prepared to handle an entry-level position in your chosen career, because *gear* is working as your "harvest" here, bringing into your life what you have earned.

If you are ready to settle down with a life partner, make a bindrune of *wynn* and *gyfu* to attract the right person. This is not a charm for romance; it is entirely possible to have barrels of romance without any long-term commitment. Conversely, you can have a solid, long-term commitment without a hint of romance, and this is desirable for business partnerships and platonic friendships. The bindrune described here can attract a suitable life partner, but it is then up to you to put some romance into the relationship, assuming that is what you want. *Gyfu* represents the commitment between the two parties, while *wynn* ensures that the arrangement will provide all you need to achieve a joyful state. The person it attracts may not be the best-looking person at your local singles' club, and he or she may not be exceptionally wealthy. Whoever it is, this person is guaranteed to come with a few flaws, but it will be a person with whom you can find happiness.

In your mind's eye, envision people in the security of a hall. This hall could be anything from a simple cottage to a palace, so long as the structure is sound. There is a table with plenty of food, and the people are well dressed. They are healthy and have "little want." This is contentment. Be aware of and grateful for your blessings.

◇

ETHEL: Home
(ETH-el)

PHONETIC VALUE: oe, as in boy or noise

Eðel byþ oferleof æghwylcum men,
gif hé mót þær rihtes and gerisena on
brúcan on bolde blædum oftost.

The home is very dear to all people,
if there they have the opportunity for justice and honesty while
enjoying prosperity in the dwelling most often.

The word *ethel* means "home" in the broadest sense. It can be a personal residence, one's native land, or an entire nation. For Americans, this word could mean the United States, but it could also refer to a local region, such as New England or the Ozarks, if either of these are your native soil. For the British, it could be the entirety of the United Kingdom, or perhaps just the Midlands. On either side of the ocean, *ethel* could mean a private estate. *Ethel* can also be a reference to the entirety of the physical world—to Middle Earth—as the land or residence of the living. The word *ethel* can mean "home" in any way we might use it in Modern English.

The Rune Poem tells us that the home—whether we are speaking of a private residence, a local region, or a nation—is a thing of value. It can be loved by or dear to all people (*oferleof æghwylcum men*) when it functions as it should. In this passage of the Rune Poem, we see that the dysfunctional household is not a modern phenomenon. The Anglo-Saxons recognized that a home must embody certain values, and in the Rune Poem these values are justice (*rihtes*) and honesty (*gerisena*).

The Old English word *rihtes* literally means "laws." What the Rune Poem tells us here is that a healthy, functional home—whether we are speaking of an individual household or an entire nation—must be governed fairly by a set of rules that everyone understands. In theory the opposite of a lawful society is an anarchy, but in practice it is more likely to be a despotism in which the rights of the people are nonexistent. In fact the Old English *rihtes* evolved into our Modern English word "rights." A home will only be dear or beloved if its people have rights and are treated justly.

The other necessary value is honesty. For a household or nation to be functional, most of its members must be honest in their dealings with each other. For the most part, we really are honest in our interactions. Humans would otherwise never have become speaking creatures. Language requires a degree of honesty, even among thieves. If we cannot presume there to be some truth in the words of others, then language has no value at all. Most of us are honest most of the time, but very few of us are honest *all* of the time, and so the Rune Poem reminds us of how important this quality is for a home to remain functional and prosperous. I do not think this can be overemphasized. In theater and cinema, dramatic performance always builds on some form of conflict. Observe any drama, whether a serious drama or a comedy, and you will see how the conflict is almost always instigated by dishonest words or a dishonest act. Dishonesty creates conflict and destroys community.

In form, the *ethel* rune is an illustration of an enclosure. It is not a circle, which has no beginning or end. We can see where the enclosure opens, at the bottom of the rune, and we can see that it is tightly shut. The household can open itself to new members, either through adoption or by birthing them. But its members are collectively enclosed and defined from the outer world. What happens within that enclosure depends on how well, if at all, the "home" embraces the values of justice and honesty.

The wiglere needs to be careful when *ethel* appears in a divination. Its definition of "home" can be situational. In this sense, it most likely refers to the qucrent's personal residence, but it could also mean his nation or even a regional subculture. For Pagans, the *ethel* rune could be a reference to their neo-tribal affiliations, to an inhíred or kindred or coven. Carefully consider the other runes in the reading when interpreting *ethel*. Even after the wiglere has identified which "home" the rune is speaking of, exactly what is it saying about the home? This, too, is situational. The rune may be telling the querent that his home, however this is defined, is a resource to rely on to help overcome his current problem. On the other hand, it could be telling him that his home is the source of that problem. Somehow, for good or ill, the home is an important factor.

This illustrates why it is necessary in the practice of wiglung to let the runes speak to you, instead of reading flat, static interpretations from the pages of a book. A really good reader will open his mind to the runes and "know" what they are saying. The runes are powerful symbols—allow yourself to harness that power.

In rúncræft, *ethel* is used for any charm or spell directed at one's personal home or tribe. Use it with *éoh* for a general charm to bless the home or tribe. This is also a good charm to help build the qualities of justice and honesty in your home. Combine both of these runes, *ethel* and *éoh*, with either *æsc* or *eolh* to protect the home or tribe.

For this rune, envision in your mind's eye a family or some other social unit, perhaps a coven or inhíred. Each person is engaged in a different activity, and yet all are obviously valued for their respective functions within the social unit. There is an overall sense of order, justice, and belonging.

CEN: Pine

(KEN)

PHONETIC VALUE: c, as in kick; or ch, as in cheat

Cen byþ cwicera gehwam cuþ on fyre,
blac ond beorhtlic byrneþ oftust
ðær hi æþelingas inne restaþ.

The pine is a tree known by all for its flame,
shining and brilliant it often burns
where the people relax inside.

This rune could arguably be grouped with the other tree runes—*ác, æsc, thorn, éoh,* and *beorc*—in the Runes of Leaf and Root chapter. Just as the Old English word *æsc* means both a spear and the ash tree that provides the wood for the spear shaft, the word *cen* can be translated as both a torch and the pine tree providing the wood for the torch. The emphasis in the Rune Poem, however, is entirely on the use of pine wood. We are told elsewhere that the ash tree is lofty and sturdy, that the birch tree bears without fruit, but nothing is said in the Rune Poem about the pine tree except that its wood burns well. In the Rune Poem, the pine is fuel. For this reason, I felt it more appropriate to group *cen* among the runes found within the halls of men.

Cen can be interpreted as meaning a torch, but the Rune Poem does not refer to it specifically in this way. A proper torch in pre-Christian England was wrapped at one end with a rag soaked with some flammable substance, often resin. Flaming pine branches could have been carried about, but these would quickly burn out. In this passage, the Rune Poem does not seem to be talking about flaming brands. The pine wood is burning where people relax or rest inside (*inne restaþ*), which implies a stationary, long-burning fire.

What we see described in the Rune Poem is a hearth fire of crackling pine logs. We know little about the people gathered around the fire, except that they are of the noble class (*æþelingas*) and they are relaxed. Their relaxed, unexcited condition will become more significant when we consider the shape of the rune itself.

In form, this rune is an upright stroke with a second stroke moving down and out from the upright. As we discussed in the chapter on tree runes, a downward stroke often indicates stability. The rune *æsc* (ash tree) has two downward strokes, and the Rune Poem tells us that stability is a primary characteristic of the *æsc* rune. The form of the *cen* rune also suggests stability, although it is not as unyielding as *æsc*. The *cen* rune indicates a more temporal stability, as embodied in the image of a household at rest.

It is interesting to note that the equivalent rune in the Elder Futhark has a distinctly different form:

<

This alternate form bears an obvious resemblance to the letter *C*, but the *cen* rune evolved into a different shape in both the Younger Futhark and the Anglo-Saxon Futhorc.

Cen indicates the presence of a peaceful, stable condition. But *cen* is not the stability itself, it is something that "often burns" there. It is something of value that can be found in the center of that stability. *Cen* can represent the home or hearth if this is your source of strength. *Cen* is that place of inspiration that burns, shining and brilliant, within each of us. It is your wód in a controlled, calm state.

In the Saxon tradition, as you learned in the first chapter, the Self is perceived as multiple parts, and one of these parts is the wód. This might be described as the fire within you. *Wód* can be translated as madness or fury, and it often can manifest this way when it burns uncontrolled, but it is also the warmth that kindles the heart of the poet. It is the flame that inspires the dancer, the scientist, and the architect. Wód is our drive to move forward with our dreams. The mystery of *cen* is this inspiration or drive as it manifests where "people relax inside." Here it is not a state of fury or disruption; instead it is a source of strength and motivation.

In a divination, *cen* reminds the querent of this source of inspiration. In general, the wiglere can interpret this rune as a positive omen, but keep in mind that the querent, if this is somebody other than yourself, may not be immediately aware of where this inspiration can be found. *Cen* can be urging the querent to seek out his or her inspiration.

In rúncræft, *cen* can be used whenever you want to add a little spark of inspiration to a situation. Use it with *gyfu* if you want to inspire romance, but not if you are only seeking a one-night fling, because *gyfu* is a rune of building commitments between people. A charm using *cen*, *dæg*, and *wynn* serves as a general blessing to promote good fortune. *Cen* accentuates or inspires the other runes around it, so you do not want to use it with runes that have even peripheral negative associations.

In your mind's eye, envision people relaxed around a hearth. A fire on the hearth burns with a bright and steady flame. The attention of the people around the hearth is not focused on the fire, but it warms them and provides sufficient light as they relax. It is the fire that allows them to pursue their leisurely activities.

✕

GYFU : Gift

(GEU-fu)

Phonetic Value: g, as in gag

Gyfu gumena byþ gleng and herenys,
wraþu and wyrþscipe and wræcna gehwam
ar and ætwist ðe byþ oþra leas.

A gift from others is an honor and praise,
a help and of worth, and for sojourners everywhere
a benefit and presence that is otherwise missing.

In all early Germanic cultures, the exchange of gifts held deep significance. Today many people demonstrate their wealth and status through conspicuous consumption. For the Anglo-Saxons and other early Germanic people, wealth and status were demonstrated through generosity. The expression "ring breaker" meant a chieftain, perhaps a king, because men of high status would break their golden armbands and give the pieces as gifts. This expression was used in the epic tale of *Beowulf*. Only a powerful person could afford to give away valuable gold in this way.

The Anglo-Saxons were well aware that there is no such thing as a gift with "no strings attached." In the Saxon tradition, and probably throughout all Indo-European cultures, the exchange of a gift creates a debt or obligation. When a chieftain gave a valuable gift, such as gold, to a follower who could not return in kind, that person then owed his loyalty to the chieftain. The same principle exists today. A smart employer rewards his best employees with bonuses and other perks to foster company loyalty. When these gifts are withheld, employees are far less likely to give anything more than minimal effort. Likewise, suitors often bestow gifts ostensibly to reflect their affection, but on a deeper level these gifts are intended to create romantic bonds.

The obligation created when a gift is exchanged is a tool for building community relationships. This dynamic takes place when even the smallest gifts—whether objects or actions—are exchanged between two people. On some level, we all understand this. Consider a person who gives a cut rose to someone he admires romantically. (I say "he," but the giver could as easily be a woman.) What was the point of this action? It is unlikely that the recipient was in dire need of a rose. The flower was probably purchased rather than grown, so the giver is not showing off his horticultural skill. There is only one reason for this exchange, and that is a desire on the part of the giver to create a deeper bond between himself and the recipient. At the moment the rose is accepted, the recipient has some level of obligation to the giver, and both parties understand that the obligation implied by this particular gift involves a degree of affection or at least friendship. Both parties also understand that the obligation in this instance is very limited. It is only a rose, after all. The Rune Poem tells us—even though we do not really need to be told—that a truly significant gift is one that is a help (*wraþu*) and of worth or value (*wyrþscipe*). It is something useful for the recipient.

Gift-giving also extends into the realm of hospitality. This was especially important in the days when there were no hotels or inns to accommodate travelers. The gift of hospitality benefited people whom I have designated "sojourners" in my translation of this passage. But the Old English word *wræcna* can also indicate people who are traveling because they have been banished from their communities. In the sixth century, there were no identification cards to check at the door, nor telephones or other rapid communications to examine a traveler's credentials. It was understood that the traveler might be an outlaw, and so appropriate precautions would be taken, but this did not negate the obligation of hospitality if there was no overt evidence of trouble. Hospitality was also another way to demonstrate wealth and status. A cottager did not have room to house a traveler, nor usually the ability to defend himself against ruffians. A chieftain could afford to give a roof and a meal to a sojourner in need.

There is no need for this custom today, but charity works in a similar way. Through charitable organizations, we offer hospitality—food, shelter, and other necessities—to strangers who have fallen on hard times. Just as the Saxon host may have at some other time sought personal shelter along the road, people who give time or money to charities today recognize that they might need similar assistance someday. While the Rune Poem describes a practice that is now obsolete, it tells us that the mystery of *gyfu* is not limited to personal gifts exchanged within the family or tribe.

The form of this rune, two strokes crossing each other, embodies the mystery of *gyfu* very well. We clearly see the concept of partnership in this shape. The strokes touch and visually form a seal or bond.

In a divination, *gyfu* often indicates an existing or imminent partnership. If the querent is a young person (under twenty years of age), this usually refers to a close personal friend or friends. If the querent is older than this, *gyfu* could indicate a marriage partner (existing or imminent), but it could also mean a business partner or close friend. It usually does not mean romance. There are other runes that can indicate a budding romantic relationship—*beorc* or *wynn* come to mind immediately—but *gyfu* more often represents a settled and mature relationship.

In rúncræft, *gyfu* can be used in any charm or shield intended to affect your partner, whether this is a partner in marriage, business, or friendship. Combine *gyfu* with *eolh* in a bindrune to protect a romantic relationship, but only if you are sure that you want this to unfold into a long-term commitment. Here the *gyfu* rune is not representing the relationship now—the romance—but rather what you intend it to become. If your marriage is going through a rough spell, as all occasionally do, use *gyfu* with *éoh* to help foster stability in the partnership. In business ventures, this rune works well with *ur* and *feoh*, because any successful business involves long-term partnerships.

If you want to use *gyfu* to help nurture a romantic relationship, you need to add the romance with other runes. *Cen*, the rune of inspiration, is good for this. *Ing* is a useful rune for introducing sensuality into the relationship, while *peorth* can promote a playful quality.

When contemplating this rune, envision in your mind's eye a gift being exchanged between two people. The exact nature of the gift is unimportant as long as it is obviously something of worth that pleases the recipient. See, if you can, beyond the superficial physical exchange. See in your mind's eye the exchange of commitment that accompanies the gift.

PEORTH: Gaming
(PAY-orth)

PHONETIC VALUE: p, as in pop

Peorþ biþ symble plega and hleahtor,
wlancum þar wigan sittaþ
on béorsele bliþe ætsamne.

Gaming is always sport and laughter,
where boastful they sit to make war
in the banquet hall cheerfully together.

The word *peorth* is often said to mean "chess piece," but I have to dispute this translation. The game of chess did not arrive in England until after the Norman Conquest. With this in mind, and in the context of the Rune Poem, it seems more likely that *peorth* can be interpreted as a reference to gaming in general.

The Saxons enjoyed a great variety of games. Most of these were dice games, or variations of a popular Germanic board game known in England as *tæfel*. Dice were usually carved from antler, although some dice made of bone or ivory have been found. They were often cubic, like modern dice, but they were just as likely to be long and rectangular. These long dice had the numbers 1 and 2 carved into the ends, with the four higher numbers on the longer sides. There are no extant rules for Saxon dice games, but it is believed that at least some were similar to modern dice games like Yahtzee®.

The variations of tæfel sometimes used dice, and very often involved wagers. A few of these board games have survived to this day. Nine-Men's-Morris is an example of a tæfel game. In some variations, such as Cyningtæfel, the two sides were unevenly matched. The playing pieces for tæfel games were made out of antler, bone, clay, glass, or stone.

The Rune Poem acknowledges the competitive nature of gaming. The people who indulge in dice games or tæfel "sit to make war" (*wigan sittaþ*). Nevertheless there is an emphasis here on the friendship, laughter, and cheer associated with gaming. The mystery of *peorth* is the mystery of play. Most of us readily recognize the importance of play in a child's development, but we are less inclined to reflect on the role of play in maintaining our vitality throughout adulthood. Play is a very human activity. Very few adult animals of other species play nearly as much as we do. One exception is the dog, who has adopted our penchant for lifelong play. For adult human beings, play almost always takes some form of gaming. Thousands of tourists fly annually to Las Vegas to play at slot machines and blackjack tables. Millions of other people gather at their local churches to play games of bingo. We adults love our board games, card games, and video games. More than

250 million Monopoly® games have been sold since its creation in the 1930s. Gaming is an almost instinctive part of human nature.

The overall tone of this passage of the Rune Poem is one of community. It describes people sitting "cheerfully together" (*blíþe ætsamne*). Today, because of the Internet and the development of artificial intelligence, solitary gaming is becoming more prevalent, but *peorth* speaks to us of a group activity enjoyed between human beings. This hints at an important function of adult play. We have already seen how the exchange of gifts creates bonds between people. This is an inherent part of the mystery of *gyfu*. Gaming— play—builds relationships in a different way. Friendships are created and reinforced through these shared experiences.

In form, the *peorth* rune suggests a cup used for throwing dice. The dice cup is on its side, indicating that the game is in progress. The dice have been cast.

How is the wiglere to interpret this rune when it comes up in a divination? I have found that *peorth* can often be a reminder of our need for play. It is easy for us to get wrapped up and imprisoned in our worries. Getting together with family and friends for a cheerful pastime can sometimes sweep away those worries and give us a fresh perspective. *Peorth* can also indicate a pleasant time ahead in the near future. But like almost all of the runes, *peorth* can have a negative interpretation in some circumstances. It could be telling the querent that he needs to stop playing around and get serious about his work.

Peorth is sometimes interpreted as "fate," since success in gaming is often determined by the luck of the dice. There is no direct reference to this in the Rune Poem, but the connection is not unreasonable. In my experience, *peorth* does occasionally indicate that events are out of the hands of the querent, although not in any disastrous way.

In rúncræft, use *peorth* whenever you want to throw a little play into your life. A charm using *peorth* with *gyfu* can help restore the magic in a marriage. Marriage is one aspect of adult life where play is often sadly neglected. An unmarried person could use *peorth* with *ing* and *mann* to create new playful, romantic connections with others. By itself, used alone as a charm, this rune fosters friendship and camaraderie.

In your mind's eye, envision several people sitting around a table playing a game. There is a sense of friendly competition and, more importantly, bonding between the players.

Review

1. What does the line in the Anglo-Saxon Rune Poem describing "destitute flesh" tell us about *mann*?

2. Describe the difference in meaning between *dæg* and *wynn*. What do these two runes have in common, and how are they different?

3. What values should be demonstrated by a worthy household?

4. Discuss the relationship of the *gyfu* rune with both love and romance. When is the use of this rune appropriate? When is it counterproductive, and why?

5. What quality do the runes *gyfu* and *peorth* have in common? How do they differ?

Runes Beyond the Hall

The early English distinguished the safety of the hall and the land immediately surrounding it from the wild *útlandes*, or "outlands." Safety, familiarity, and cultural identity were associated with physical proximity to the mead-hall. Distant lands were not necessarily evil, but they were mysterious and potentially hazardous, and the people of the outlands were certain to have outlandish (*útlendisc*) customs and behaviors.

For strangers, the lands they traveled through were the outlands. An unwary traveler could be waylaid by bandits. There was often no way for a traveler to know how he or she would be received, if there would be a meal that evening or a dry place to sleep. Most people did not travel any distance without a very good cause to do so.

Today, in our modern society, the concept of "outland" is not always directly related to physical location. The people who live near you—your neighbors—are usually not related to you. Shared values or cultural identity are coincidental. My own neighbors are all outlanders, and I do not say this in a disparaging way. I am certain that many of my own Pagan values and customs are "outlandish" from their perspective! Today most of us live among outlanders, and there is nothing wrong with this. Diversity can be a good thing for those who accept that everyone does not have to be like everybody else.

We step into the outland whenever we go to the cinema or the supermarket. Even those who have never lived outside their parents' zip codes or who have never knowingly met somebody of a different faith or sexual orientation understand and accept on some level that outlanders pass through "their" territory constantly. Nevertheless, we are all expected to observe a myriad of conventions when in public. Most of these conventions are intended to keep peace as we travel through our mutual, shared outlands. We know it is rude to stare openly at behaviors that do not directly threaten us, even if those behaviors seem strange, and most of us take care to avoid dressing or behaving in ways that are likely to offend our neighbors. Because of these conventions, there is little danger to us when we are in public among strangers. But danger was an ever-present threat to the pre-Christian Saxons whenever they ventured far from the mead-hall. The traveler entered the outland only when there was some pressing need. Travelers prepared for the journey knowing that anything could be encountered, even the gods.

NÍED: Need

(NEE-ed)

PHONETIC VALUE: n, as in no

Níed biþ nearu on bréostan,
weorþeþ hie þeah oft níþa bearnum
tó helpe and tó hæle gehwæþre,
gif hie his hlystaþ æror.

Need is oppressive on the heart,
although it often befalls this affliction of men
to help and to heal somewhat,
if it is heard beforehand.

Life was indeed hard for the Saxons in early England. Most of us today could not survive the conditions under which the Saxons struggled. The same event that opened British lands for settlement—the collapse of Rome in the fifth century—also left those lands with no law or social stability. Fighting often erupted, and the typical Englishman had only a spear and a seax to protect himself. If he was lucky, he wore a leather jerkin to help deflect an assailant's weapons.

No matter what the outcome, a skirmish could herald starvation if a village's fields and gardens were trampled in the fighting. In Saxon England, pigs roamed loose and hens roosted in the trees. Livestock would flee amidst the violence and could easily be lost forever.

Even if peace reigned throughout the year, Saxon villages often suffered from drought, late frosts, or any number of diseases that could afflict crops, animals, or people. Need was a constant companion, departing occasionally but always sure to return. It was an unavoidable evil, but the Saxons knew that need can also be a source of motivation. It is the recognition of need that drives men to accomplishment.

The mystery of *nied* is illustrated in the legends of Robin Hood. The earliest ballads mentioning this English folk hero date to the fourteenth century, but his origins predate those ballads. The earliest tales that would eventually evolve into the legends of Robin Hood were stories of the Elves, or nature spirits. Some scholars have even associated Robin Hood with the god Woden, although this connection is indirect at best. Robin Hood does have the status of a hero or demigod in English folklore, and in the earliest ballads we see him acting on the principle of *nied*. Robin Hood is described from the beginning as an outlaw and a thief, but he never robs from those suffering from poverty. Instead he robs the wealthy abbots and then gives that wealth to the destitute. He is a hero because he is motivated "to help and to heal," as the Rune Poem says.

Early chroniclers described Robin Hood in various locations and times, but legend eventually placed him in Nottinghamshire in the late twelfth century, during the reign of Richard the Lionheart. It was a time of extreme social and economic inequity. England had been under Norman rule for over a hundred years, and the Saxon commoners were broken by the high taxes demanded to fund Richard's participation in the Third Crusade. It was a time of great need; a time when a hero such as Robin Hood would stand out. It is that need which inspires the acts of Robin Hood and his men. They rob not for amusement or out of greed, but to ease the despair of the Saxon underclass.

In form, the *nied* rune is an upright stroke, crossed with a shorter angled stroke. The upright stroke is the *is* rune, the warning of potential danger. The angled stroke shows us that the danger has fallen upon us, breaking the upright in two.

Nied is never a welcome rune in a divination. It indicates some hardship or loss ahead. However, the Rune Poem also gives the querent advice as to how to meet the coming challenge. It reminds the querent that he or she can embody the spirit of the legendary Robin Hood and take steps "to help and to heal" before the hardship manifests itself. The querent need not—and should not—wait helplessly; *nied* calls for the querent to take action.

I would not use *nied* in any rúncræft of my own devising. Although need can foster positive actions, what this rune creates is not positive action but the need and despair itself. I can think of people I believe might be motivated in a positive way by the *nied* rune. I am sure you can too. But no matter how we look at it, no matter how benign our motives, this is a cursing rune. If you want to enshroud yourself with that doom, so be it, but you will have to work out the details on your own.

When contemplating this rune, envision a few people moving through the wilderness. They are exposed to the elements, and you know they are hungry. You can feel it gnawing in your gut. You can see the despair in their eyes. And yet their need drives them onward, into the outland. They move forward, taking action to help and to heal their dilemma.

ᚱ

RÁD: Ride

(RAD)

PHONETIC VALUE: r, as in roar

Rád byþ on recyde rinca gehwylcum
sefte ond swiþhwæt ðamðe sitteþ on ufan
meare mægenheardum ofer milpaþas.

The ride up to every man's hall is
comfortable and very fast for he who sits high on
a mighty horse over the miles.

Before we examine this rune it might be a good idea to review the *eh* (horse) rune that we discussed in the Animal Rune chapter. The connection between these two runes is self-evident. We saw that the *eh* rune represents an ally that somehow empowers the querent. This ally could be a motor vehicle, or it could be a horse. The ally could even be the "mighty horse" spoken of in this passage of the Rune Poem describing *rád*.

But *rád* is not the means to embark on the journey. It is the journey itself. The method of travel is unimportant. *Rád* can be a journey in a cart or wagon, or even by ship. This Old English word has the alternate meaning of "road." We can, in fact, substitute "the road" for "the ride" without changing the meaning of this passage of the Rune Poem in any substantial way. The mystery of *rád* is not embodied in an animal or any natural phenomenon. It is embodied in action.

In the Rune Poem, the mystery of this action, this journey, has two conditions or qualities. It is firstly a ride to "every man's hall" (*recyde rinca gehwylcum*). The journey's end is not some battle or a random location in the wilderness; this is a journey home. The home, of course, is symbolic and not necessarily a reference to one's physical residence. The journey leads to a spiritual home, to a place where the sojourner is meant to be.

It is the mystery of the journey home that endeared millions of people to Victor Fleming's production of *The Wizard of Oz*. This movie, released in 1939, was nominated for several Academy Awards and its eventual annual televised presentation became an American tradition for more than three decades. This popularity was not because of the movie's surface plot. Consider the story. It involves a young girl, Dorothy Gale, as its protagonist. The dramatic conflict is between her and an older neighbor, Elmira Gulch, who has a court order to have Dorothy's dog put down. Soon into the story Dorothy is knocked unconscious, and the rest of the movie relates a dream sequence that has absolutely nothing to do with her conflict with Miss Gulch. Dorothy awakens at the end of the movie, nothing has been resolved, and we can only hope that the poor dog won't be put to sleep later that day.

As an objective drama, *The Wizard of Oz* made no sense. But the mystery of *rád*, of the spiritual journey, sings out to us. Viewers understood that the story wasn't about Dorothy's dog or Elmira Gulch, it was about a girl's spiritual journey home. When Dorothy awakens, she is centered and grounded in a way she had not been before. That is what resonated with audiences in 1939, and that is why this movie is still remembered and beloved by many.

The second quality of the journey, according to the Rune Poem, is that it can be comfortable (*sefte*) and very fast (*swiþhwæt*) if the sojourner "sits high on a mighty horse." Nowhere does the Rune Poem say that the horse, the empowering ally, is requisite to make the journey. What the Rune Poem does tell us is that the road home will be much easier if sojourners have that empowering ally with them when they set forth.

In form, the *rád* rune has two "legs" and seems to be walking. Within the form or shape of this rune we see also the *wynn* rune. If you go back to that passage of the Rune Poem, you will recall that one of the requirements of *wynn*, or joy, is a sufficient dwelling (*burga geniht*). Thus we see that the journey home, the mystery of *rád*, brings us closer to a place of joy or contentment.

When *rád* makes an appearance in divination, it always indicates a journey of some kind. This could be a physical journey. *Rád* need not involve physical movement, but there is a natural connection between physical and spiritual travel. When we embark on a physical journey, we leave behind our environment, and that environment has its own spiritual presence. At the conclusion of our journey, we settle into a different spiritual presence. Thus a physical journey has the potential to instigate spiritual change within us. *Rád* does not always differentiate between the physical and spiritual aspects of the journey. At times it can represent a purely physical journey with no obvious or dramatic spiritual changes. More often, though, it speaks to us of a spiritual odyssey.

In rúncræft, *rád* is used whenever the rúnwita wants to instigate a journey. Again, the rune itself will not always distinguish between a physical or spiritual journey, so it must be used with care. A person who wants a job involving travel could make a charm combining *rád* with *feoh*. A person about to embark on a journey where he has no personal control over his transportation—as when traveling by airplane or rail—can use *rád* with *eolh* for a protective charm.

Envision in your mind's eye the journey itself. See the road before you. And the road need not be a pavement—it could be a trail, or even open water. However you have prepared, you may ride horseback, take a ship, or simply walk the road. The road and the means you traverse it may vary; what matters is the journey itself.

YR: Bow
(EUR)

PHONETIC VALUE: u, as in burger (minus the r)

Yr biþ æþelinga and eorla gehwæs
wynn and weorþmynd, biþ on wicge fæger,
fæstlíc on færelde, fyrdgeatwa sum.

A bow is for noblemen and warriors everywhere
joy and a mark of distinction, upon a fair horse,
steadfast on its course, a part of the war-gear.

It is both interesting and perplexing that the bow would find itself among the runic mysteries. The bow in question would be the iconic English longbow that came up in our discussion of the *éoh* rune. The yew tree was decimated across the English landscape to provide wood for the construction of longbows, but this was a later development in English history. The longbow only came into prominence after the Norman conquest in the eleventh century. The Normans soon turned their attention to Wales, where they suffered heavy casualties from Welsh archers. After invading Wales, the Normans conscripted Welsh archers into their own armies. By the late thirteenth century, King Edward had banned the practice of all sports other than archery on Sundays to ensure that his subjects would improve their skill with the longbow.

I present this history lesson to illustrate that the longbow did not come into common military use until after the Futhorc, the Anglo-Saxon runes, had largely fallen into disuse. But the fact that the longbow became more popular after the Norman conquest does not mean it was unknown to the Pagan and early Christian Saxons. The longbow had been in use throughout northern Europe since the Stone Age. It was not especially favored as a military weapon because, unlike the spear or seax, a longbow requires relatively extensive training. The longbow only became popular as an English military weapon after the realization that precise skill was not necessary if you could loose thousands of arrows simultaneously into an opposing army. For the longbow to be serviceable in the hands of an individual, however, that person had to be a skilled archer.

Here is where we discover the mystery of *yr*. It might be called "skill with a bow" or just "skill," rather than "bow." The bow, as war-gear (*fyrdgeatwa*), was not suitable for just anybody. Possessing a bow for this purpose would be a "joy and a mark of distinction." Among the Pagan Saxons, a person carrying a bow among his war-gear would be the exception rather than the rule. The archer had a skill that set him apart from the common man.

Our skilled archer is no ordinary peasant. He might be of noble birth, or at least of the warrior caste. He rides forth on a "fair horse" (*wicge fæger*), which indicates he is a person of means and status. He is a person who has enough free time to practice with the longbow to a point where his skill is notable. His proficiency as an archer is not simply talent, it is something he has earned.

In form, the rune is a stylized representation of a bow and arrow. The strokes are angular, of course, but we see that the bow is drawn. The arrow is presumably nocked, but is represented in a stylized way, set back from the bow itself.

In a divination, the *yr* rune indicates that the querent possesses the skills and capabilities necessary to meet whatever challenges are at hand. It is not a guarantee of success but merely an acknowledgement of the potential for success. In this way, as an omen, *yr* is an enigmatic rune. It offers no promises.

When used in rúncræft, *yr* is a rune of empowerment. Use it in any charm intended to bolster skill. Combine this rune with *eh* and *æsc* to increase your own spiritual fortitude. A teacher or public speaker can use *yr* with *os* to help facilitate communication. An athlete might benefit from a charm using *yr* (skill) along with *ur* (strength) and *tir* (steadfastness).

In your mind's eye, take up the bow. Slowly draw back the string. This bow represents your ability. Know your skill. Acknowledge it as you think of and appreciate your personal abilities. Pick one of those abilities and envision it as the bow. Hold the image in your mind. Feel and recognize your own proficiency.

ING: The Lord Ing
(ING)

PHONETIC VALUE: ng, as in thing

Ing wæs ærest mid Eastdenum gesewen secgun,
oþ hé siððan eft ofer wæg gewát, wæn æfter ran,
þus heardingas þone hæle nemdon.

Ing was first seen among the East Danes it is said,
until he later went back over the sea, his chariot following after,
thus the brave men named that hero.

The Anglo-Saxons used the word *Danes* (*Denum*) to mean Scandinavians in general. The "East Danes" (*Eastdenum*) in this passage of the Rune Poem is a reference to the Swedes and Geats. Here we have a description of the god Ing Fréa, or Lord Ing, who was known to the Swedes as Frej or Frö.

The *Ynglinga Saga*, composed in Iceland in the thirteenth century by Snorri Sturluson, confirms the Rune Poem's assertion that the god Ing—called Freyr in Iceland—was indeed first seen "among the East Danes." This god, if we believe Snorri's account, founded a great temple to the gods in Uppsala, Sweden. It is said, too, that he is an ancestor of Sweden's royal lineage.

Both Ing and his sister seem to have been less prevalent in England than they were in Norway, Iceland, and Sweden. This may be a reflection of the changing roles of these deities over time, as the Icelandic eddas and sagas were recorded hundreds of years after the English had converted to the new religion of Christianity. Certainly Ing's sister, known in Sweden as Fröja, governed functions that had once been the domain of the goddess Frigg, or Frige, in England.

Ing Fréa is a complex deity. In the *Ynglinga Saga*, he is called the God of This World. According to the *Prose Edda*, he is the Harvest God and the Wealth-Giver, the Fair and the Most Renowned. He is a bringer of peace, and yet he is called Battle-Wise and Mighty. He is the Lord of the Elves, ruling the fair realm of Elfhame.

Some people believe—or at least suspect—Ing Fréa to be the original Horned God of the Wiccan religion. There are compelling arguments both for and against this theory (which I discuss further in *Travels Through Middle Earth: The Path of a Saxon Pagan*), but ultimately there's no way to prove or disprove the idea. For many people today, Ing fulfills the archetype of the Green Man. This is related to his role as Lord of the Elves. Ing Fréa is associated with fertility—specifically with the fertility of the earth.

In recent years, Ing has become a patron deity for many more gay men than random chance would dictate. This has elicited the expected homophobic protest from some quarters that Ing/Frö/Freyr is not "gay." I do not believe that gods are limited by our own mortal desires and affections, but, if we were to debate this particular god's sexual preference, the *Poetic Edda* assures us of his legendary passionate love for the giantess Gearde. If anything, Ing Fréa may be the most heterosexual of the northern gods! That said, I see no connection between Ing's personal sexual inclination—if a god can be said to have anything like that—and his ability to be a patron or mentor for mortals with a different orientation.

The form of the *ing* rune is usually interpreted as some representation of Ing Fréa's association with the fertility of the land. I have heard the shape of this rune described as a symbol of male fertility (possibly), female fertility (unlikely), and even as a symbol of DNA (now people are just getting silly). The common denominator shared by all of these, of course, is the idea of regeneration. An image that resonates for me is that of a bound sheaf of barley. I have heard other rune sorcerers describe the glyph in this way as a symbol of Ing's connection with plant life, the harvest, and prosperity.

When *ing* appears in a divination, it usually indicates some divine intervention or connection. The deity involved might indeed be Ing Fréa, but it could just as easily be another god or goddess. For me, the appearance of the *ing* rune often does mean that Ing Fréa is intervening in my life in some way, because I have had a relationship with this god for many years. For the querent who has a closer relationship with Thunor or with Frige, the *ing* rune is more likely to indicate the intervention of one of those deities. One important thing to keep in mind is that this connection will probably be brief. The deity, whether this is Ing Fréa or some other god or goddess, will soon return or go "back over the sea" (*eft ofer wæg*). Thus the querent needs to pay attention so as not to miss the message or assistance that the deity offers.

In rúncræft, *ing* may be used to promote fertility. As we become more and more disconnected from the earth, it has become fashionable to interpret "fertility" to mean any creative endeavor, but there is a difference. The fertility spoken of by this rune is just that and nothing else; it does not mean creativity or inspiration. The creative artisan will find the *os* rune, which we will discuss next, to be more useful for his needs. Because of the historical connection between prosperity and a good harvest, the rune may indicate the former. The rune *ing* can also nurture or promote sensuality, and it is often used in that way.

Horticulturalists can combine the *ing* rune with *beorc* and *gear* for a charm to improve the fertility of their gardens. Carve or burn these runes into a strip of wood and hang this by the garden. For a would-be parent hoping to produce a child, I would recommend using *ing* with *ur*. This rune can be used in prosperity charms, and for the Saxon Pagan, the *ing* rune can also be used in any charm phrased as a prayer to Ing Fréa.

In your mind's eye, envision the god Ing manifesting before you. He is indeed the Fair God, almost painfully beautiful. Greenery surrounds him and is reflected in the depths of his eyes. He is with you, within you, and around you, the Lord of the Elves. All nature reflects his strength and beauty. The god comes to you with a message, or maybe to aid you in some way. Be ready, for he will be with you for but a moment.

OS: A God
(OSE)

PHONETIC VALUE: o, as in coat or pot

Os byþ ordfruma ælere spræce,
wisdomes wraþu ond witena frofur
and eorla gehwam eadnys ond tohiht.

The god is the creator of all language,
wisdom's foundation and consolation of sages
and every man's joy and trust.

The *os* rune is sometimes interpreted as meaning "mouth," but the Old English word for mouth is *muð*. The word *os* means "a god," and furthermore suggests a god of the Old Religion. References to Christian deity in Old English texts use words like *God* (as a proper noun) or *Fréa* (meaning "Lord"). The *oses* were the earlier gods and goddesses the Anglo-Saxons brought with them when they first settled in England. And from the context of the Rune Poem, this particular *os* was almost certainly the god Woden.

Woden had a very different relationship with the early English than he later had with the Vikings. But as with Ing, this difference may have been a change that occurred over time. The lore of the northern gods as they were perceived by the Scandinavians was recorded long after the English had turned away from those gods. Woden, in Norse lore, was known by the name Odin, and he was a war-chief preparing for a cataclysmic battle reminiscent of the Christian idea of Armageddon. This role was appropriate for the High God of the northlands at that time. The Old Religions of Europe had fallen. The Dodekatheon (Hellenic religion) was gone, the Religio Romana (Roman religion) forgotten. The Germanic gods were still honored, but only in the northernmost lands where they were making their last stand.

Centuries earlier, Woden presented a different demeanor to the Anglo-Saxons. He was the wise, hooded wizard-god. Woden ruled the wind, including the wind that issues forth from the mouths of men in the form of speech. As we see here in the Rune Poem, he was considered the source or creator of spoken language. It was Woden who inspired the words of the *scop*, or poet.

The same wind that produces speech is the æthem, or life breath, that binds the various parts of the soul to the physical body (lic). When the æthem ceases, we die, and so Woden is also a god of the dead. From the first night of winter through the Yuletide, he rides in the night in search of lost spirits. Woden, like Ing, is a complex deity. He is both warrior and wizard, both wise counsel and avenging spirit. Woden rules the heavenly realm of Osgeard, and yet wanders our own world endlessly.

The Rune Poem focuses on Woden's association with speech and language. Language, the Rune Poem tells us, is wisdom's foundation (*wisdomes wraþu*). It is what distinguishes us, perhaps more than anything else, from other animals. Almost all animals communicate with their own kind, but no other species can convey complex, abstract concepts the way we humans do. I can tell my dog Lucky to "sit," and she (most often) will quickly do so. She knows what "sit" means. But if I were to say, "Lucky, I am heating water to make a new batch of mead, and I would like you to sit quietly so I don't trip over you," she has no idea what I am saying. What she hears is, "Lucky, brog-brog-brog-brog-brog."

It is our species, and ours alone, that can pass on the wisdom of Plato and Socrates, that can share the tales of Beowulf and Oliver Twist and Tom Sawyer. It is language that allows us to preserve the past and prepare for the future.

Language is wisdom and the consolation or joy (*frofur*) of wise men. Woden's association with language and wisdom is the mystery of the rune *os*. We see this in the shape of the rune itself. Os is one of the four *F* runes, those that consist of two cross-strokes extending from a longer upright stroke. You may remember from our discussion of *ác* in the chapter on leaf and root runes that downward strokes indicate stability, upward strokes indicate mobility, and the stroke that extends down and then back up to make a *V* indicates divinity. The *os* rune has two of these latter strokes. The rune can also be viewed as a depiction of a person with his or her arms outstretched in a beckoning gesture. This might be thought of as an illustration of language as a tool for persuading or convincing others.

When *os* appears in a divination, it usually indicates communication. Often it indicates not the presence of communication, but rather a need for it. When I give offerings at my household altar and seek an omen afterward, this rune always indicates a need on my part to listen more closely to my gods. This is something that most of us often forget to do. We are quick to speak up and tell our gods what we want or need, but we very often fail to take the time to listen to what they may want or need of us. The *os* rune can also indicate a need for communication in other areas of your life. If you are having a conflict with another person—a spouse or friend or employer—the *os* rune could indicate a need to sit down and discuss your concerns.

Os is useful in rúncræft whenever you want to encourage or nurture communication. Combine *os* with *feoh* and *ur* for a charm to help you obtain or excel in a management position, because communication is essential in these careers. Use with *yr* for a general charm to facilitate communication in almost any endeavor. *Os* and *gear* can be used together to combat writer's block!

For this rune, envision in your mind's eye the god Woden standing before you, hooded and cloaked. He has only one eye. His other eye was sacrificed in his quest for the runic mysteries, and a patch now covers the wound. Woden opens his mouth and speaks to you, but his words are more than any mortal could hope to utter. His speech is palpable, flowing out from his lips like a silvery light. As you listen, your heart is filled with understanding.

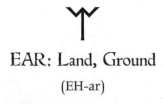

EAR: Land, Ground
(EH-ar)

PHONETIC VALUE: ao, "ay-uh"

Ear byþ egle eorla gehwilcun,
þonn fæstlice flæsc onginneþ,
hræw cólian, hrúsan ceosan blác to gebeddan;
bléda gedréosaþ, wynna gewítaþ, wera geswícaþ.

The ground is loathsome to all men,
yet certainly the body will be set upon there,
the corpse grows cold, the soil accepts its pale bedfellow;
leaves fall, pleasures depart, men cease to be.

There is something profoundly sad about the *ear* rune. It is a rune of mortality, of endings. Most of the runes of the Futhorc can have either positive or negative connotations, depending on the current situation, but it is difficult to see anything positive in the *ear* rune. It rips away the platitudes and exposes the grief we endure when confronted with death in all of its forms.

The death is not necessarily the death of a person, although the concept of physical death is central to this passage of the Rune Poem. Death is an ending, and there are many kinds of endings. A divorce is the death of a marriage. Friendships can die. Ideals, dreams, and aspirations can die. No matter how you look at it, no matter the nature of the death, *ear* is not a happy rune. The language used in this passage of the Rune Poem—cold (*cólian*), pale or bleak (*blác*), to fall or perish (*gedréosan*)—emphasizes the sense of loss and sorrow. This is not simply change. There is a distinct difference between loss and transformation, and the *ear* rune embodies the mystery of loss.

The first line in this passage may seem odd considering how our very lives are sustained by the produce of the earth. How can the ground be perceived as loathsome or hideous to men (*egle eorla*)? The Rune Poem reminds us that the same earth that sustains us also accepts death as its bedfellow. In the modern world, death is sanitized as much as possible and removed from our consciousness, but on some level we still recognize its taint and cringe from its touch. On some level, most people also equate dirt with disease. Anything "soiled" is presumed to be unhealthy. And the Rune Poem tells us why. The dead body is laid upon the earth, most often in a grave, and the soil eventually accepts or chooses it as a pale bedfellow (*ceosan blác to gebeddan*).

The shape of the rune suggests some sort of drilling tool. It may represent a device for drilling or pushing holes into the ground.

In a divination, *ear* always indicates some kind of loss. It does not necessarily mean the death of a person, but it does suggest the loss of something important or meaningful. Some systems of divination allow you to put a happy, positive "spin" on any symbol that appears. Runic wiglung does not, at least not when the *ear* rune is drawn. *Ear* is a rune of endings. The ending may not be catastrophic, but it will be a loss and will be accompanied with the sorrow that inevitably follows in the wake of a loss. We never really want to see an omen like this, but the truth is that sometimes bad things happen.

Can some good come out of this loss? Of course. The earth that embraces the corpse is the same earth that sustains the living flesh. An ending is followed by a new beginning. We can go on and on with platitudes. Yes, life will go on. Yes, the sun will rise again, and tomorrow will be another day. The *ear* rune does not deny any of this, but, conversely, none of it is related to rune's message. This rune, *ear*, acknowledges our pain and sorrow at this moment in time.

The most obvious use for *ear* in rúncræft is for cursing somebody, but I would never use the rune in this way. The magic we weave inevitably becomes part of our own wyrd, our own fortune, so why would I want employ such a cold, sorrowful rune? There simply is never any need to do so. There are runes like *thorn* and *æsc* for warding off negativity, and runes like *wynn* and *ur* to bolster your own personal strength and good fortune. One thing I have learned over the years is that successful magicians rarely waste their time and energy cursing others. Ethical issues aside, it is far more effective and productive to build yourself up than to attempt to tear somebody else down.

The *ear* rune can be an appropriate funerary symbol, because this is a time to acknowledge our pain and loss. As I have mentioned, we tend to sanitize death today and dress it up as if it were nothing more than a long holiday. This denial of loss can place an unnecessary burden on those close to the deceased whose feelings do not match the serene, almost pleasant ambience displayed by those around them. They are told that their loved one "is in a better place now." (What was wrong with the place he was in before?) Or that "he is at peace now." (Was he in turmoil up until he died?) Meanwhile people blithely ignore the deep and immeasurable pain that those closest to the deceased are enduring. I do not advise sharing this symbol with those unfamiliar with the runes at such a stressful time. They have much more important things—intense, raw emotions—to deal with. But keep the *ear* rune close to your own heart as a reminder of their pain.

When you contemplate this rune, envision people in mourning. These may be the same community of people you envisioned while contemplating the *mann* rune in the previous chapter. Those people were unaware, on a conscious level, of the death in their midst. But the people you envision now are deeply aware of a recent loss. They cry out their pain, for it is too much to hold within. The corpse is cold. The soil is ready to accept its pale bedfellow.

Review

1. How do the legends of Robin Hood reflect the mystery of the *nied* rune?

2. Describe the difference between *rád* (riding) and *eh* (horse).

3. Give two kennings or titles associated with the god Ing.

4. What is the æthem, and what is its relationship with the *os* rune?

5. In the passage of the Rune Poem describing *ear*, why is the earth or ground "loathsome to all men"?

Rúncræft

Often when people today think of runes, they immediately think of the use of runes in the practice of wiglung (augury or divination). This is indeed a valid use for the runes, and we will explore this use in a later chapter. Wiglung is a valuable skill for any wyrdworker, but, while it is a magical skill, it does not conform to the definition of *active* magic that we are using in this book. It does not directly create any change. The word *rúncræft* means "rune skill." In a broad sense, rune skill would include wiglung when runes are the means of divination (in contrast to Tarot or scrying or some other method). However, in this chapter we will be using the word *rúncræft* in reference specifically to the use of runes in active magic.

If you have been working through this book chapter by chapter, you have probably already made some use of the runes. After reading the chapter on tools, you may have carved runes into your wand or your myse to empower these tools. You may have carved runes into the hilt of your seax, or applied them to the blade using the process of Weland's Transfer. After reading about the different systems of runes, you may have made your own set of divinatory runes. As you will soon see, rune sets such as these can also be useful for active rúncræft. Let us now look at how we can use these old symbols to shape our wyrd (destiny) with spells and various charms.

The last few chapters have hinted at these uses. In the description of each rune and its mystery, I have included combinations of runes that can be used when crafting runic charms. There are even a few simple spells. Turn back to the leaf and root runes and read again the description of *eolh*, where a quick and useful protection spell is given making use of that rune. Wyrdworkers who specialize as a rúnwitan, or rune sorcerers, will eventually develop personal spells similar to this to suit their needs.

Four More Runes

I use only the twenty-nine runes described and defined in the Rune Poem, but I have not written this book to tell you how to practice my own craft. You should be aware of four other Anglo-Saxon runes: *calc*, *gár*, *cweorth,* and *stán*. Whether or not you make use of these in your practice of rúncræft and wiglung is your own choice.

I do not make use of these four runes because there is no surviving lore to explain their mysteries, or even to indicate if they had any meaning at all. It is possible that these other four runes were used only for writing. None are found in the Elder or Younger Futharks. All four evolved in the Anglo-Saxon culture to accommodate the Old English language. The only hints we have as to what they may have meant (if anything) to the early, pre-Christian people are found in the names and shapes of these runes. Therefore any interpretation or meaning you give to these runes must necessarily be drawn primarily from your own intuition. You may find descriptions of these four runes elsewhere accompanied by extensive interpretations, but you should know that the interpretations are simply the product of another person's intuition, which may or may not prove to be valid for you.

ᚳ *Calc* means "chalk" in Old English. When we look at the shape of the rune there is not much resemblance to a piece of chalk, but there is no question as to the meaning of the word itself. Related words are found in Old English referencing chalk pits and chalk ravines, as well as chalk stone (*cealcstán*). Chalk was used to make plaster or cement, and the word *calc* was also used for these materials, as well as for the raw stone.

Look again at the shape of the rune. Taking the concept of plaster into consideration, we can see the rune as a rough illustration of timbers or beams. Plaster holds the beams together where they intersect at the center of the symbol. It is possible that the mystery of *calc* involves construction or mending. It may indicate the materials necessary to initiate and complete a project. Or it may mean nothing of the sort. As I have said, to work with these four runes, you will have to rely on your own intuition.

ᚷ *Gár* means "spear." The shape of the rune is an enigma. It looks like *calc* without the central upright mark. Again, as I have said, these last four runes may have no mystic meaning. What we see in their names and shapes may be nothing more than conjecture.

If we focus on the name of the rune, a word meaning spear, we should bear in mind that *æsc* also means spear. Thus, to establish a meaning for this rune, we need to consider how it differs from *æsc*. One word emphasizes the material a spear is made from, ash wood, while the other may emphasize the shape of the spear. If we assume this to be true, then *gár* can be used for any pointed weapon: a spear, a javelin, even an arrow. The spear was the primary piercing weapon wielded by the early Saxons. The mystery of *gár* may be related to piercing or pointing, but how this applies in wiglung or in rúncræft is anybody's guess. Again, you must depend on your intuition.

ᛢ   *Cweorth* is without question the rune we know the least about. We can to look to the names of *calc, gár,* and *stán* for some understanding of the mysteries those runes may have embodied, but even the name of *cweorth* is uncertain. It is often interpreted as "fire-drill," meaning a tool used for starting a fire with friction. However, this interpretation is speculative. We do not really know what *cweorth* means, other than as the name for a runic character representing the "kw" sound or, as we are more familiar with it in Modern English, "qu."

In form, *cweorth* is similar to the *éoh* rune. This indicates a sense of balance. The opposing hooks at the upper and lower ends of the *éoh* rune are, in the *cweorth* rune, V-shaped angles that suggest divinity. If the yew (*éoh*) connects us to the earth below and the sky above, perhaps *cweorth* connects us to the divinity within the earth and the sky. Assuming *cweorth* does mean fire-drill, the mystery of this rune could also involve initiations and beginnings.

ᛗ   *Stán* is a word found throughout Old English literature. *Stán* means "stone." We may not know for certain if the early Saxons used a *cweorth* to start a fire with friction, but we do know for certain that a *fýrstán*—a fire stone, or flint—was used for starting a fire by striking a spark. We know that the early Saxons enjoyed something akin to a sauna, known as a *stánbæþ* or "stone bath," creating vapor by pouring water over hot stones. Stones could be cut from a *stánhýwet* (quarry) or gathered in a *stándenu* (rocky valley). These stones were shaped into *stánfætes* (stone vessels), used as *stánflóra* (paving stones), and for constructing *stángetimbres* (stone buildings). With more than seventy permutations, *stán* is one of the most common concepts found in Old English.

The plain, simple meaning of this name is reflected in the shape of the rune. It is a complete enclosure, suggesting solidity. It reminds us that stone is unyielding, yet reliable. If *stán* is a symbol for any mystery, its meaning almost surely includes these qualities.

Including these four runes—*calc, gár, cweorth,* and *stán*—in your work is entirely optional. I never use them. I do not believe they had any mystic significance to the early Anglo-Saxons, but I could be wrong. Next week an ancient document may turn up in an old European church or library to reveal four more passages of the Anglo-Saxon Rune Poem that have been lost until now. And even if that does not happen, you may find personal meaning in these symbols even though we know nothing of what they meant to people fifteen centuries ago.

Now you have looked at all thirty-three of the Anglo-Saxon runes—the twenty-nine that are described in the Rune Poem and four others we know very little about. The runes are your tools. How do you make use of them?

In the first chapter of this book, we discussed the difference between spirituality and magic and how these two sometimes overlap. I believe rúncræft is a place where spirituality is a very appropriate part of one's magic work. The runes—the mysteries behind the symbols—are a gift from Woden. We are told in the Hávamál that Woden (known to the Scandinavians as Odin or Odhinn) hung on the World Tree for nine days, a sacrifice to himself, in order to grasp the runic mysteries. For this reason, I always begin any significant rune work with a brief prayer:

Woden, Wise Wanderer,
Lend me the power of the runes.
Ic bidde thé nu.

The final words, pronounced "eech bidda they noo" are Old English for "I ask you now." As you can see, this prayer does not ask Woden to intervene for me or provide whatever it is I am attempting to gain. It simply acknowledges him as the master of the runes. The prayer is a way of honoring the god Woden while simultaneously centering myself for the work ahead.

If your need—the goal you are working toward—is extremely urgent, you might extend the prayer and ask Woden or another deity for help. There is nothing wrong with this, so long as you have established a relationship with the deity through devotional offerings. Just be sure that you have put something into the relationship before trying to pull something out of it. For the most part, I try to refrain from asking help from the gods unless I really need it. We have all heard the story of the boy who cried "wolf"; I do not want to ask for help so often that my pleas begin to fall on deaf ears. For most of my rune work, I use nothing more than the brief prayer given here to honor Woden.

Runic Spellcasting

Rúncræft can be worked with spells or by crafting talismans in the form of staves, bindrunes, or helms. Which approach to take depends on your need. Runic talismans are better for long-term goals, but they take time to create. When your need is immediate, a runic spell is often the better choice.

This book presents one technique for casting a runic spell, but over time the experienced rúnwita will devise other, personal techniques. Often these will incorporate other magical skills. The very word *spell*, evolved from the Old English verb meaning to speak or sing, suggests the inclusion of galdor, the magic of the spoken word.

The technique presented here includes galdor as well as some creative visualization. It consists of two parts that we can think of as the Layout and the Process. The Layout creates a focus to keep the rúnwita centered on his or her work; the Process is the active element of the spell.

Layout

For the Layout you will need your myse (working surface), your set of runes, a new red candle, and a holder for the candle. A red candle is used because red is the color of blood, and blood is a substance of power; due to the Law of Sympathy, a red candle has intrinsic power. Because of the Law of Contagion, you will want a new candle that has never been used for any other purpose. The candle need not be large; I favor small votive candles.

When we use runes to divine future possibilities—to perceive wyrd—the symbols are drawn or cast at random. Here you are going to intentionally select the runes and lay them down to declare your will. Select three runes to define your purpose. One of these should be your primary rune, representing your essential goal, and the other two should be chosen to refine this definition.

Take some time to think about what you are doing. You must identify your needs precisely in order to select the most appropriate runes for your work. Most people envision their needs in vague, imprecise terms. They will express a desire for love or money or happiness without defining exactly what they want.

Let us suppose you want a new job. This is not an unusual or unreasonable goal, but to select the appropriate runes, you need to know exactly what you are looking for. You need to know exactly what influences you want to evoke. Why do you want a new job? What do you need or want that you do not currently have? It can be helpful to sit down and make a list of all the positive and negative qualities of your current situation. You may discover that you want a new job for reasons you were not completely aware of. You may even discover that you do not really want another job at all. Our society tends to glamorize some occupations and treat others with disdain. There is no such thing as a "bad" job in any honest work. It is only bad if you are not suited for the work. Do not let social conventions dictate what you should or should not be doing.

After you have given it some thought, you may decide that the real problem with your current job is that it does not satisfy your need for human interaction. Again, the job itself is not necessarily "bad." Many people find comfort in occupations that afford privacy and seclusion. But we are assuming for the moment that you are not one of these people. You need lively social interaction throughout the day, so you choose *mann* as your primary rune. *Mann* fosters community relationships and urges us to cherish those relationships.

For your secondary runes you might choose *feoh* and *wynn*. *Feoh* is important because you want to draw the primary influence—community relationships—into your professional life in some way. These relationships will be a part of the exchange of goods or services producing an income. *Wynn* fosters happiness and, of equal importance, will help you recognize when you have achieved that goal.

Can you see how these three runes address a specific purpose? If you wanted a new job because you needed more money or less stress or a creative outlet, your choice of runes might be entirely different.

Or perhaps what you are searching for is a long-term romantic partnership. The exact same principles apply here. First, identify your needs. *Gyfu* will undoubtedly be among the runes you choose, since you are defining a permanent partnership, but what is the purpose of this partnership? What are your needs? Do you need an ally (*eh*), or are you looking for someone to ease your feeling of loneliness (*mann*)? Is it more important that your partner be athletic (*ur*) or intellectual (*os*)?

As you consider your actual needs, you may find that a spouse is not among them at this time. Social pressure can lead us to believe that we are somehow incomplete if we do not have a life partner. If you can look beyond this myth and examine your real needs, it may be that a few new friends or even a kitten might fulfill them. But let us suppose for the moment that a kitten is not enough, and that you have selected three runes defining exactly what you want to bring into your life. The spell described here will work equally well regardless of whether your purpose involves your career, romance, or something else entirely.

First, place the red candle on your myse. Now place your primary rune, whatever this may be, directly in front of the candle. The other two runes are placed to the left and right of the primary rune. Pause for a moment to contemplate each of these runes and why you have chosen them. Focus your mind on your specific desire.

Your Layout is complete.

Process

For the Process, you will need your telga (wand) and the Modern English translations for the passages in the Rune Poem that correspond to the runes you have chosen. You can find the latter in the preceding chapters of this book. Your intention is set out before you in your Layout. Now you will activate it.

Light the candle and give honor to Woden with a brief prayer.

Focus your attention on the primary, central rune. Consider again your reasons for choosing that rune and the influence you intend to evoke. For the moment, ignore the other two runes. All of your attention should be directed to the central rune.

Now read aloud the passage from the Rune Poem that defines the mystery of this primary rune. Your words should be strong and purposeful.

You may want to read the passage in its original Old English form or its Modern English translation. There are arguments for either approach. Old English is the language the Anglo-Saxons spoke, and using it creates a connection with that culture. On the other hand, when you speak in Modern English, you are emulating the Anglo-Saxons, who spoke in the language that was contemporary for their time. Ultimately the correct approach should be whichever is more empowering for you. Although I often use short Old English expressions in my spellwork, I prefer to use Modern English when reading complete passages from the Rune Poem.

After you have read the passage from the Rune Poem, take up your telga and draw the rune over the candle flame. Envision the shape of the rune as you draw it. See it crackle with power. Imagine the power of the candle rising up and flowing through the rune as you speak its name in a commanding voice.

Turn your attention to the rune to the left of your primary rune. Repeat the above steps, contemplating the mystery of this rune, reading the corresponding passage from the poem, and then drawing the rune with your wand above the candle flame.

Then turn to the last rune, the one to the right of the primary rune, and go through these steps again.

Complete the spell by extinguishing the candle flame as you say, again in a commanding voice, *"ic spellige nu"* (eech spell-ee-yeh noo). The candle should be discarded unless you intend to use it at a future time for the exact same spell. If so, be sure to label it in some way so you will remember the influences it has been imbued with. The simplest way to do this is to carve the three runes into the wax itself.

Rune Staves

Runic talismans are most often constructed in the form of staves. These are series of three or more runes chosen for their influences, just as you might choose three runes for spellcasting. Most staves (sometimes called "scripts") consist of either three or five runes. In northern magic, odd numbers are believed to be more dynamic than even numbers. The Rune Poem itself consists of twenty-nine passages, an odd number. One rune by itself is an odd number, but it is not really a script. Three or five runes are easiest to manage.

Anything longer than this can be confusing; your runic statement will work better if you keep it simple and bold.

The first thing to consider is whether your talisman is to be a permanent charm or if it is intended to have a finite effect. The spell we gave as an example for attracting a new job opportunity would be a finite effect. The spell is intended to create or attract an event. After the event occurs, the spell is done and the talisman has no further purpose. A finite talisman should be removed from the world after the desired effect has taken place. Thus, the ideal medium for a finite talisman is either paper or wood, which can be easily burned. Using our previous example of a talisman to create a new career path, the runes *mann, feoh,* and *wynn* could be marked on a sheet of parchment paper and carried in the purse or wallet as a talisman to attract a satisfying job opportunity with social interactions.

However, these same runes could be used in a permanent charm. When used in this way, their meaning shifts in subtle but important ways. The permanent charm is not intended to create an event; instead the runes are used to attract general influences. In this case, the charm would be attracting community, prosperity, and contentment. It is not directed toward a specific need. Obviously a durable medium is ideal for a permanent charm. Wood can be used, but antler, bone, or even metal are also good choices. If you choose to use metal, remember that lead is a "cursing" material. Silver or brass are more suitable for permanent charms with positive intentions.

Whether your talisman is finite or permanent, be sure to lay out your runic proclamation in a linear pattern. In our previous example, casting a spell with a set of runes, *mann* was chosen as the primary rune. It was set down, and then two secondary runes were placed to the left and right. But the primary rune was set down first, before the other two. There is no temporal order when marking rune staves, so their spatial order becomes important. To use the same runes on a stave, you would place *mann* at the beginning of the script. This would be at the left, assuming you are inscribing the runes from left to right. But runes can be inscribed in either direction. The runic proclamation of *mann-feoh-wynn* can be written both of these ways:

ᛗ ᚠ ᚹ

ᚹ ᚠ ᛗ

Keep in mind that nearly half of the runes of the Futhorc have no front or reversed position, they look identical whether inscribed forward or backward. When using only these runes, it is important that your runic statement make sense—a sense that expresses your intention—regardless of the direction you read them in.

What distinguishes the script on a charm from an ordinary runic script employed for mundane purposes? The runes *mann, feoh,* and *wynn* can be used in rúncræft, but they have no mystic meaning when a Saxon woman by the name of Mary Frances Wilder marks her initials in runes on her personal belongings to identify them. The runes are not just magical tools, they are also a functional alphabet. When using these symbols in a charm, they must be infused with power. They must be infused with your wód (inspiration). Your willa (willpower) comes into play also, but one attraction of the runes is that the symbols themselves are partially instrumental in directing raw, primal power.

Since the shape of each rune is important, they should be carefully marked out before any attempt is made to empower them. If you are creating a finite talisman with paper, the initial marking can be easily accomplished with pencil and perhaps a ruler. Do not be afraid to erase and correct any slips of the hand. At this point, you are merely delineating the form.

When crafting a wood talisman, begin by drawing the shape in pencil. Then use a wood burner to permanently mark the symbols into the wood. For bone or antler talismans, use a rotary engraving tool for this purpose. Again, you are just delineating the form, although I think it helps to keep your desired effect in mind while engraving or burning the shapes of the runes into your charm.

You can empower the talisman once you have marked the shapes of your runes and are satisfied with their order and composition. You will be doing this by coloring them while speaking a galdor. You will probably want to color your runes with red pigment, but the truth is there is no Mystic Brotherhood that will assault you for using the wrong color. I know a man who marks his runes with green and seems to have significant success, but the color red, as we discussed earlier, has an innate power of its own.

A red marker is the most practical tool when creating a finite talisman from paper. When using anything engraved—wood, antler, bone, or metal—paint may be more effective, although I have used fine-tipped red markers on antler.

While marking each rune, recite the relevant passage from the Rune Poem. This is your galdor, your verbalization, to imbue the rune with power. Further galdor can be used to empower the charm as a whole, but we will examine that in the next chapter. Further galdor is not essential or even useful if you find the technique to be awkward in any way. Always keep in mind that wyrd-working is an art, not an exact science. Only use those techniques that resonate for you.

Depending on their function, rune staves or runescripts can be kept on your person, slipped under pillows or mattresses, hung over doorways, or placed almost anywhere so long as they will remained undisturbed to do their work. I believe it is a good idea to master this skill fully before going on to work with bindrunes or helms.

Bindrunes

A completed bindrune consists of a number of runes superimposed over each other. The end result is, or should be, a unique mystic symbol. In many ways, creating a bindrune is similar to creating rune staves. The primary difference is that you are marking the runes directly on top of each other, rather than in a linear style. Whether an even or odd number of runes are employed is less important. The final outcome will be one symbol, and the number 1 has the dynamic potential the rúnwita desires.

Decide whether the bindrune is to be a permanent charm or if it will have a finite effect, and choose the appropriate medium to work with. Then, on a separate slip of paper, draw out the runes, superimposed as you intend to bind them, and consider the final form carefully. What do you see if we combine *mann, feoh,* and *wynn* in a bindrune like this?

As you can see, *wynn* disappears into *mann,* and this is perfectly all right. The fact is, *mann* consists of two *wynn* runes facing each other, and this in itself has meaning. However when we attach *feoh* on the right side of *mann,* do you see where an *eolh* rune appears in the final design? At this point we must ask ourselves if *eolh* is appropriate for our intention. Do we want the protective barrier that this rune evokes?

This is why bindrunes are tricky. Other runes can slip into the charm, and they will have their effect regardless of whether you intended them to be there. If *eolh* has slipped into your pattern, it should be welcomed and fully empowered. If you do not wish to do this, then *eolh* should not be in the final design at all.

This is also why the *is* rune is never used in a bindrune. Not intentionally, anyway. In truth, the rune (being a straight line) is found everywhere, and this is intrinsic to its mystery. *Is* tells us that things are not as they seem. Like the potential dangers it warns us of, the rune itself is hidden wherever we look.

We discussed laying out your runic proclamation in a linear, spacial order. The symbols of your bindrune will be marked in a similar way, but in a temporal order. The first symbol in your bindrune is clearly marked, and then the second symbol super-imposed over this, and so on, until all symbols in the design have been empowered. You will want to mark out or delineate the final design before you begin coloring the bindrune and empowering it with galdor.

There is no special situation or circumstance where bindrunes are more effective than rune staves, it is just another technique. In my experience the bindrune tends to have more power, but I think this is at least partially because it requires more thought to design a good symbol that says what you want and only what you want. For most purposes, rune staves are sufficient.

Helms

The multi-spoked helms tend to be more powerful than rune staves, yet easier to formulate than bindrunes. A helm, which I have also heard referred to as a shield, is a circular symbol consisting of four, six, or eight spokes radiating from a central point. At the outer end of each spoke is a rune or runes. Many examples of runic helms have survived from before the Christian era, especially in Iceland, where they are often quite ornate.

Helms are especially useful for protecting or warding. The very word *helm* suggests a sort of psychic armor.

A helm with four spokes usually creates a fifth rune, *gyfu*. For this reason, the four-spoked helm lends itself to any effect involv-ing a partnership. This can be a business partnership, and deep and lasting friendship, or a marriage. It does not matter if the spokes of the helm are drawn as an *X,* as seen in the *gyfu* rune, or if they form an upright, equal-armed cross. Just as a rune can be inscribed either forward or backward, tilting the image one way or the other does not change the meaning of the symbol. A newly formed business partnership could be protected with a runic helm such as this:

In this image you can see four *thorn* runes radiating from a central point. The primary strokes of these runes—the spokes of the helm—form a *gyfu.*

In the same way, a helm with six spokes forms a seventh rune, this time *ior,* the rune of adaptability. This creates a very different statement. Let us use six thorn runes instead of four, to create this helm:

This helm makes no comment about protecting a partnership. Instead it infers adaptability. It states that there will be protection on multiple levels. Use a six-spoked helm when you are not particular about the details but want to ensure complete coverage with whatever effect you intend to evoke. The runic helm is the exception to the "odd number rule." Helms always have an even number of spokes. Historically, eight spokes seem to have been favored, perhaps because they do not create an additional rune the way a four-spoked or six-spoked helm does.

As with other talismans, the helm should be drawn or otherwise marked carefully before it is empowered with color and galdor.

Impromptu Rúncræft

Once in a while, you may feel a need for some additional runic protection. For some reason this never happens for me when I have an extra hour or so to draw, mark, and empower a protective talisman. And while I probably have time to work a spell with my divinatory runes and a candle, either the candle or my rune sets will often be inaccessible. I can still make use of the runes in a more spontaneous fashion. Impromptu rune work can be applied to almost any purpose, but protection is one need that very often comes with a sense of urgency. Most of your other needs can wait until you have access to your proper tools and time to perform more efficacious work.

I would like to say something about protective magic before we look at the impromptu techniques here. You will not need this nearly as much as you might think. For the most part, I work protective magic when I am intentionally putting myself in an unusually vulnerable position. It makes sense to work a runic spell over my truck before embarking on a long trip, for example, but I do not do this every time I drive to the grocery store. Runic protection also makes sense for those who work with seething (trance states), as we will discuss later in this book. One thing I have learned over the past four decades, though, is that I rarely need to worry about some other wyrdworker magically attacking me. Sorcerers—the effective ones anyway—use their arts to improve their own lives and the lives of their folk. Skilled sorcerers of any merit will have one of two reactions to you. Either they (1) like you, or (2) could not care less about you. Admittedly, a sorcerer may work toward a goal that conflicts with your own, as when two people are vying for the same job or love interest. But skilled sorcerers are simply not going to waste their time actively cursing you. This is not because witches and druids are exceptionally good people (although many of us, of course, are delightful to know); it is because we are more interested in our own success and the success of our folk than we are in someone else's personal downfall.

Protective wards are relatively simple to erect and maintain. If people really are psychically attacking you, it is likely that they have not fully grasped how wyrd functions, and thus do not present very much of a threat. Elves (natural spirits) can react with hostility if insulted, but their ire is usually brief. Still, even a fool can wreak havoc for a short time, and any of us can inadvertently insult or annoy one of the Elves, so it is good to have a few techniques to sweep away temporary bursts of negativity.

I have already mentioned one of these techniques while discussing the rune *eolh* earlier. *Eolh* is a protective or defensive rune, but I think its position in the Futhorc—among the twenty-nine runes—gives it a special power of its own. It is the central symbol in the Futhorc, with fourteen runes before it and fourteen following. This gives it a sense of balance, in addition to its basic protective influence. *Eolh* can be used alone for a quick warding combining a simple galdor with an equally simple somatic gesture. The words for the galdor are *eolh weardath me* (AY-olch WAY-ar-dath may), which is Old English for "*eolh* protect me." The somatic gesture marks the three strokes of the rune. Refer back to page 108 if you do not remember what *eolh* looks like.

Stand boldly and raise your right hand. Drop your hand sharply (a movement that symbolically dissipates any hostility directed at you) as you say "*eolh*!" In your mind's eye, see a strong crackling energy follow your hand as you make the downward movement, drawing the main stroke of the rune.

Now raise both of your hands to the midpoint of this crackling line of power. With a dismissive gesture, flip your right hand up and out to the right, as you flip your left hand up and out to the left, marking the two smaller strokes of the rune. As you do this, say "*weardath mé*!" In your mind's eye, see the same crackling energy follow your two hands as you brush away any hostility that would hinder you.

Stand up and try this several times right now, until you can make the gestures and speak the words easily. There is no need to banish or unwork the rune afterward. Keep at it until you know the words and gestures.

Another technique was given to me by my friend West Hardin, who tells me he received it in a dream from the god Ing. This second technique makes use of two defensive runes, *eolh* and *thorn*. This one, too, uses both a somatic gesture and a galdor.

For the somatic gesture, touch your middle finger to your thumb. If you look directly at your hand, you will now see a rough *eolh* rune. Turn your hand sideways and you will see your finger and thumb creating the point of the *thorn* rune. When using this technique, point this outward and speak the galdor, which is simply the sound that *thorn* represents, "*th.*" I find it more effective to give this sound sharply, rather than as a drawn out lisp.

In all of these techniques—candle spells, rune staves, bindrunes, helms, and impromptu work—we have included some level of galdor. This practice, using words and sounds to shape wyrd, was an important component of early English magic. In the next chapter, we will look at how to use sound most effectively in your work.

Review

1. In Saxon belief, who discovered the runic mysteries?
2. In which direction should the runes be written: left to right or right to left?
3. What danger or difficulty does a rúnwita need to guard against when creating a bindrune?
4. Why is the *is* rune never used in a bindrune?
5. What special quality is often inherent in a four-spoked helm?

More Magic Techniques

Galdor:
The Power of Speech

The early English druids and witches understood the power inherent in sound. They called this power *galdor*, and the person who specialized in incantations and magic songs was known as a *galdre*. Much of what we know about early Anglo-Saxon magic has been preserved in verbal charms recorded by English scribes between the ninth and eleventh centuries. There were incantations for healing and animal husbandry, for childbirth and for safe travel. The numerous verbal charms that have survived reveal techniques used by the Saxon sorcerers to produce effective and resonant galdor in their magic.

Tolkien recognized the power of galdor, although I think this is more obvious in his books than in the movies they inspired at the beginning of this millennium. The first of these movies, *The Fellowship of the Ring*, dramatically showed the effect of galdor when Gandolf uttered the Black Speech of Mordor in the halls of Rivendell. Overall, however, the books themselves were more descriptive of the power of song and language. In the books, the healing and creative power of elf-song is expressed more overtly. In Tolkien's fictional Middle Earth, words have both the power to create and to destroy.

But what about the real Middle Earth, the physical plane we live in? Here, too, words have the power to create or destroy. This is the principle behind positive affirmations. When people chant, "Every day, in every way, I'm becoming better and better," they are casting a spell. As mentioned earlier, the Old English verb *spellian* means to speak or proclaim, so when we cast a spell we are casting or throwing down a proclamation.

We humans are verbal creatures. This is one of the most significant factors distinguishing us from other mammals. Much of what we call intelligence is directly related to our ability to verbalize. Language—verbalization—gives form to our thoughts. It is an act of creation. Galdor takes this act of creation to the next level. The idea or goal is to give voice to a proclamation—to cast a spell—with enough force to create ripples in the web of wyrd that connects us all.

Tina-Lisa Agresta was troubled by waking up at night with a deep sense of anxiety. After attending a galdor workshop that I presented in Pittsburgh, she designed a verbal spell of her own to help with this problem. Her spell makes use of rhyme to express her words more deeply:

Gentle slumber ... sweet repose
Night grows still as moonlight glows ...

Soft embrace of feathered bed
Warmly welcomes weary head ...

Dreams delightful come to pass
So spins the star-filled hourglass ...

A wisp of wind whispers "Awake!
Anon a new dawn awaits!"

Rhyme is perhaps the most common technique used today for creating effective galdor. Rhyme implants messages and expressions into our minds. This is why rhyme is so often used in advertising slogans. For years a successful shaving cream company lined American highways with series of signs extolling the virtues of their product, Burma-Shave. By the 1930s, these signs were using rhymed verse to attract attention and deliver their message to motorists. The Burma-Shave signs and their rhymes were an American institution until the early 1960s, when they disappeared due to the company changing hands and to the expanding use of the interstate system.

The power of rhyme can be astonishing. I can remember advertising messages that I haven't heard in forty years or more. I know how I can tell it's Mattel ("it's swell!"), and that Winston tastes good ("like a cigarette should"). You may be too young to remember these rhymes, but you can probably recall similar commercial slogans from your own childhood, or perhaps you know that Columbus sailed the ocean blue in 1492. A rhyme delivers a statement or message with such force that we remember it long after we have forgotten countless other unrhymed facts and ideas.

It should be obvious to the reader how this applies to galdor. Expressing the proclamation, or spell, in rhymed verse will give your words more force.

Rhyming your galdor requires a little advance preparation, but it is not difficult. The first thing to do is make a list of some key words suitable to your purpose. You can see that Tina-Lisa chose words relating to restful sleep: *repose, bed, awake.* After you have your list, select one of your words and go through the alphabet to find other words that rhyme with it. For *repose* Tina-Lisa may have come up with chose, close, doze, froze, glows, goes, grows, hose, knows, mows, nose, pose, prose, rose, rows, sews, shows, sows, stows, those, throws, toes, and tows. Ultimately she selected *glows.* Having a list of possible rhyming words provides a variety of material to work with.

Remember multisyllabic words too! The best way I have found to do this is to throw an extra syllable in while looking for a rhyme. The syllable does not need to make sense. I could use "ah," for example. Going through the alphabet for *repose* rhymes, I would start with nonsense words like "ahboze," discovering words such as oppose, arose, and bestows.

Tina-Lisa could have said, "Gentle slumber, sweet repose, night grows still as I lay down." That states her purpose or intention of lying down calmly. But the words fall flat. They have little power. When she rhymes, saying "Gentle slumber, sweet repose, night grows still as moonlight glows," the words take on a life of their own. It is a more powerful galdor than the first statement.

For most Saxon sorcerers, rhymed verse is an effective galdor technique. But perhaps you are one of the few who are not comfortable with rhyme. Perhaps it feels silly to you. Give it a fair try, but do not hesitate to eschew this technique if you find it counterproductive. What we are discussing are methods for creating more efficacious galdor, and you can use any of the techniques I give here alone or in combination. An experienced galdre knows the only thing that matters is whether or not the spell works!

A technique more common to the Saxons of elder days was alliteration: a sentence or verse in which many or most of the words begin with the same sound, as in "Peter Piper picked a peck of pickled peppers." Alliteration was a defining feature of Old English poetry and is often found in Old English incantations. As with rhyme, alliteration builds power through repetition. The difference is that rhyming repetition occurs at the end of a line, whereas alliteration repeats the first sound in each word. Alliteration and rhyming can be used either separately or in conjunction with one another.

Alliteration also requires some advance preparation. Again, the first thing to do is make a list of key words suitable to your purpose. Then select a key word, but instead of finding words that rhyme with it, try to find words that begin with the same sound. Go through the possible vowels (*a, e, i, o,* and *u*), using both the long and short sounds for each.

Let's take the word *repose* again and see what we can find in the way of suitable alliteration. We want words that begin with an *r* sound, but not just any word will do. The words we're looking for should have some possible meaning within an incantation.

Ray, rest, restful, real, relax, renew, review, rich, written, right, roam, rolling, rote, wrote, wrought. These are just a few possibilities. A dictionary will be extremely helpful for this, but keep in mind that some sounds can be written in more than one way. So look up words beginning with *ph* when searching for something to go with *fair*, and words beginning with *wr* when looking for something to go with *repose*.

From the list of words above, we could begin a galdor for peaceful, undisturbed sleep with something like, "Relax and rest with renewed repose." Say this aloud and notice how this alliteration, the repeated *r,* gives the words more emphasis and power.

Alliteration and rhyme can be used in combination with each other. It is not necessary to weave alliteration through the entire incantation. Alliteration may be limited to only one or two lines, whereas rhyme typically appears as a pattern throughout the verbal proclamation. We could say, "Relax and rest with renewed repose, while night grows still and moonlight glows." You can see here that both lines rhyme, but only the first line alliterates.

Although this is a good example of alliteration, it is not one I would choose for a galdor intended to induce calm, restful sleep. If you have been studying the runes, you may have already guessed why. The *r* sound is the phonetic value of the *rád* rune. *Rád,* meaning ride or road, is a rune of journeying, and that is not our intention here. We do not want either physical or mental activity. Sleep can be perceived as a sort of journey, but *rád* indicates action rather than relaxation. Our intention is to promote or induce rest. The galdor for this, as we have modified it with alliteration, may still be effective, but it would be even more effective if we evoke a more suitable runic power by alliterating with a *d* (*dæg*), *k* (*cen*), *s* (*sigil*), *t* (*tir*), or *w* (*wynn*) sound. This weaves the power of rún-cræft into your galdor to build a more powerful incantation. It is not necessary to do this, and I do not know of anyone who combines these techniques consistently, but it is something to keep in mind when you include alliteration in your incantations.

In the chapter on The Alchemy of Magic, I gave an example of a short galdor to inscribe on a sheet of lead to banish or curse the negativity felt after breaking off a relationship with somebody. The words were:

Hate and hurt held in my heart
I banish now! Be gone! Depart!

Notice the alliteration here using the *h* sound in the first line. This is the phonetic value of the *hagol* rune. The mystery of *hagol* (hail) is that of transformation. Hailstones are painful and damaging, but after falling, they transform into life-giving water. By alliterating the *h* sound we invoke the mystery of *hagol* to help create a transformation from heartache to a strong, positive state of being.

The early English also used galdor in a narrative style. By this I mean that the incantation told a story describing the desired effect. The narrative often had no more than a coincidental connection with the immediate problem. The tenth-century Nine Herbs Charm, for example, includes a brief narrative of the god Woden taking up nine "glory twigs," possibly strips of wood with runes carved into them, and throwing them at a poisonous serpent. The serpent, representing poison or disease, then shatters into nine pieces. Although this galdor did not directly address the afflicted person, its intention was to break his or her disease. The story describes the effect that the sorcerer hopes to achieve.

An effect is often more readily achieved when we direct attention away from ourselves in this way. This technique was not unique to the early English. Young lovers use the same technique today when they watch a romantic movie at the cinema or on television. Their own passions are inflamed as they observe a romantic narrative involving other, fictional people. The narrative itself may seem counterproductive, but a good romance works because it is a sort of galdor. In the movie *Love Story,* the heroine dies of cancer, nevertheless it was a good romance. The tragic death in the narrative served as a reminder to cherish our loved ones while we can.

In the same way, the details in a narrative-style galdor take second place to the overall message. Traditionally, Old English charms were designed for general situations rather than specific incidents. You may, of course, design a narrative for one finite purpose, but a skilled galdre will have an array of incantations at his or her disposal. These should reflect the needs and challenges that the galdre expects to address. Just as the Anglo-Saxons had charms for the water-elf disease, today's practitioner may have charms for influenza or asthma. Few of us now need charms to protect our cattle, but galdor to protect our cars or even bicycles can prove useful.

Traditional narrative galdor is usually written in the past or present tense, rather than the future tense. To speak of something that "will" happen (future tense) is to speculate. It has not yet happened, so you might be disappointed. A statement of something that has happened or is currently happening is more solid, as there is no speculation involved. Thus, the Nine Herbs Charm does not say that the god Woden will take up nine glory twigs and smite the serpent, it says that he has already done so. The serpent—the disease—has been shattered. It is done. There is no debate or speculation about it. Stating narrative incantations in this way commits the galdre to the work at hand. The galdre has effectively given his or her word. If the incantation fails, that word has been broken. For this reason the adept galdre will not use the narrative style for every little thing. It will be reserved for more important work. And for this reason, too, a galdre of any worth will be careful to speak truthfully as much as possible. Speaking truthfully builds the strength behind your words. Speaking truthfully strengthens your mægen, that spiritual fortitude we discussed in the first chapter of this book.

Just as you can combine alliteration and rhyme, you can also combine the narrative style with either of these techniques. One tenth-century charm against acute pain includes a narrative telling us that "the smith sat and crafted a little knife." This is a Modern English translation. In Old English the same narrative is expressed as *"sæt smith sloh seax lytel."* The words repeat a hissing *s* sound, giving us a combination of alliteration and narrative verse.

Galdor, as a magical technique, can be used all alone, and this is done so often as to be almost a cliché of witchcraft. Practitioners who specialize in galdor often utilize the Laws of Sympathy and Contagion, using colors and images to focus their spells, empowering their symbols with rhyming or alliterative incantations. But galdor is also used in conjunction with other cræftes. Look at the Old English example given here: *Sæt smith sloh seax lytel.* This is not just alliteration, the line alliterates the phonetic value of *sigil*, a rune of guidance and safety. This is an example of two skills—rúncræft and galdor—woven together to create a more powerful effect.

Galdor can be used in conjunction with rúncræft in various ways. In the example given here, the *sigil* rune is hidden in the alliterative verse. It is almost incidental, but the rune will nevertheless exert some influence. The experienced galdre will use runic sounds to his or her advantage, but it is the verbal component that is emphasized.

Your telga can be used to give more emphasis to the runic significance of your alliteration if you have included this technique as part of the galdor. Use the wand to mark the shape of the rune in the air as you recite the respective alliterated line or lines. In the previous example of Old English galdor against acute pain, the shape of the rune *sigil* could be made with three sharp gestures. As you delineate the shape of the rune, see in your mind's eye a crackling energy remaining in the wake of the tip of your wand. See the entire, complete shape of the rune hovering in the air before you. You can make the gesture with just your fingertips, if necessary, but the wand will help direct your own wód beyond your hama, or astral shield.

Conversely, just as an understanding of the runes can enhance your galdor, careful verbalization can enhance your rúncræft. We have already seen examples of this in the previous chapter, but additional and more complex galdor can be used to empower runic charms. Design a rhyming or alliterative galdor and recite this while coloring the runes. If this is distracting for you, recite your galdor after coloring the runes, using your telga to infuse each symbol with your personal power.

The Old English charms reveal that the Saxons also used galdor in conjunction with wortcunning, the use of herbs. The Nine Herbs Charm is perhaps the most notable example of this. Another Old English galdor, contemporary with the Nine Herbs Charm, is essentially a listing of nearly sixty herbs to use in formulating a "holy salve," followed by instructions for making the salve. We will explore wortcunning in the following chapter, but keep in mind that galdor can be used in almost every stage of your work with herbs. You can recite an incantation while cutting an herb, if you grow your own plants, or when preparing the herb as a potion or ointment. Still another incantation may be used when consuming the potion or applying the ointment.

I should add that you will probably use at least some galdor in your work. You may eschew runes entirely, or have no interest in wiglung, or not wish to bother with herbs, but almost all sorcerers will make use of galdor to some extent in their work. Some introspection is in order here, as you will want to use galdor that you are comfortable with. If rhyming keeps you focused and helps you remember the galdor, then use a lot of rhymes. If rhyming sounds silly to you, use alliteration and narration instead. You may revel in lengthy incantations, or you may prefer short, two-line statements. Get a feel for the galdor techniques that most empower you.

Depending on your own talents, you may find your own galdor to be more effective when expressed through song rather than the spoken word. This is a traditional technique, and one not often utilized today.

If you have been keeping a personal journal, this is a good place to record any galdor that you design. If you come up with something you really like, write it down. Do not assume that you will remember the words later. For now your personal journal is fine for recording your galdor. If you find this to be a technique you really enjoy or if you discover that you have a talent for rhyming and alliteration, you can purchase a blank book just for your incantations, a *galdorbóc*.

———————

If my use of the words *if, can,* and *may* seem ambiguous, it is because I cannot tell you how to develop your personal wiccecræft. Nothing is more intimate than your own magic. What resonates for you, as a sorcerer? You may be fascinated by the runes and the mysteries of the Rune Poem, or you may find them confusing or even boring. You may love working with herbs, or you may not. Galdor may be deeply empowering for you, but if you are uncomfortable with public speaking, then it may be more discomforting than empowering. In the final chapter of this book, we will explore how to develop a personal style of magic. The next chapters, everything leading up to the final chapter, present possibilities that you may or may not choose to adopt into that style.

Review

1. Why is rhymed verse so often a component of incantations?

2. What is alliteration, and how does it enhance galdor?

3. Why is narrative galdor expressed in the future tense less effective than galdor expressed in the past or present tense?

4. Select a general need that you or people you know are frequently challenged by. This could be health related, or connected to prosperity or community, or to any other facet of the human experience. Design a galdor of at least four lines using rhyming or alliteration, or a combination of both.

5. Select another need and design a galdor of at least eight lines expressed in a narrative style. It need not rhyme or alliterate, although you may certainly make use of either of these.

Wortcunning:
Herbs and Their Lore

The Old English *wyrtcunnung* means "plant-knowledge." The *wyrt* or *wort* can be any plant: an herb, a spice, a vegetable, or even a tree. Wortcunning is the knowledge of or skill of working with these plants.

Wortcunning is very similar to herbology. The two terms are often interchangeable, but where herbology (herbalism) tends to focus exclusively on a plant's physical properties, wortcunning also acknowledges the spirit of the plant. In the tenth-century Nine Herbs Charm, each of the plants is addressed as a sentient entity. The charm begins with the sorcerer speaking to the herb mugwort, saying, "Remember you, Mugwort, what you made known, what you set in order at the Great Announcing." The wording indicates a belief that mugwort can not only hear and understand the speaker, but that it has the ability to take action. It can proclaim or "make known." Plantain, lamb's cress, chamomile, and five other herbs are then addressed in a similar way. These plants are more than simple, organic ingredients; they are addressed as sentient and responsive allies.

Wortcunning is herb magic, but we must recognize that the Saxons made little distinction between what we would today separate into magic and mundane categories. Wortcunning is the use of plants to create an effect or a change of some kind. If an herb can soothe a cough it does not matter, from our perspective, whether or not somebody has come up with a pharmaceutical explanation for the effect. The pharmaceutical explanation, if one exists at all, is irrelevant because wortcunning uses an entirely different map of reality. There may be a pharmaceutical explanation as to why chamomile can help soothe a cough, but from a Saxon sorcerer's point of view, the effect is achieved because the spirit of chamomile comforts and relaxes the lic (physical body).

When I say "a different map of reality," what I mean is a different way of defining the world around us. For example, an acupuncturist and a cardiologist use different maps of the human body. Traditional Chinese medicine, the foundation of acupuncture, acknowledges an organ known as the triple burner. This organ is found nowhere on the cardiologist's map of the body. This does not mean that one discipline is superior to the other, or that one map is "less real." It certainly does not mean that people in China have a different anatomy! The extra organ exists because traditional Chinese medicine defines the body in a different way than anatomical medicine does. Likewise, traditional European healing has its own map and definitions.

Another difference between herbalism and wortcunning is that the former has come to focus primarily on the medicinal or remedial uses of leaves and roots. Wortcunning can and often does make use of herbs in the same way, since an herbal remedy creates an effect or change, but wortcunning concerns itself with a broader range of effects. It is as likely to be used for prosperity, love, empowerment, or protection as it is for healing. In folklore we see examples of wortcunning in stories of love potions and flying ointments. Wortcunning is used to create or nurture many different effects such as these.

Of the different wyrdworking techniques presented in this book, wortcunning requires the most in the way of equipment and ingredients. The rúnwita can get by with a set of runes, the galdre can work with no materials at all, but the sorcerer who works with herbs will need at the very least a mortar, a cauldron, a source of water and a source of heat, as well as the herbs themselves. Do not let this discourage you. You do not initially need as much equipment as you might think. Trying to acquire every possible piece of equipment at once is a mistake made by many beginners. I recommend starting out with three essential tools and build from there. These three tools are:

- Your myse, or working surface. A myse board or cloth is advisable for most wyrdworkers, as few of us can devote a permanent table surface to our work.

- A mortar and pestle. This is used for grinding and mixing herbal material.

- A cauldron, by which I mean a pot of some kind for heating water. The archaic iron cauldron is unsuitable for your work unless you routinely heat water over an open hearth.

All three of these tools have been discussed in the chapter on tools, so I will say nothing more of them here. For a source of water and a source of heat, it is assumed that you have access to a kitchen. If not, it may be difficult for you to pursue any extensive work with herbs. Fortunately this is not an issue for most people.

More essential than anything else are your herbal ingredients. Again, do not make the mistake of filling countless jars with herbs that you may never make use of. Before you purchase or plant any herb, be sure you know exactly what you intend to use it for. After we cover the most common herbs the Saxons used, we'll go over the different ways to prepare those herbs.

A word of common-sense caution: Even an experienced wyrtwita is no substitute for the advice of a qualified medical professional. If the Saxons had access to the medical technology we enjoy today, they most certainly would have made use of it!

Saxon Herbs

Witches and Saxon druids made use of many different herbs. Let us look at some of these plants and see how they can be useful in the practice of wortcunning. Most of the herbs listed here appear in one or more of the Old English charms.

Agrimony (Agrimonia eupatoria)

Highly valued by the Anglo-Saxons, the power of agrimony is found primarily in its columns of small yellow flowers. Agrimony drives away malevolent influences. The flowers can fend off the mare (a foul spirit that attacks people in their sleep) and induce a restful sleep if placed beneath the head. The simplest way to do this is to sew the flowers into a small pouch and slip this under the pillow, inside the pillow case.

When the flowers and leaves are prepared as a potion, either in an infusion or a metheglin, agrimony can drive away pernicious spirits within the body. The infused potion is said to soothe the stomach and cleanse the liver, and it can be used as a gargle to soothe a sore throat.

Sew agrimony flowers into a small cloth pouch and keep it in your pocket or wear it around your neck by a string as a protective amulet.

Alliums

This family of plants was important enough to the early English to warrant its own mention in the Alchemy of Magic chapter's recommended list of magical components. The alliums include leeks, garlic, and onions, all of which share similar fiery, protective properties. It is worthwhile to keep a leek and a couple of garlic bulbs on hand at all times. I almost always have a few on-ions stored away as well. Thanks to technological advances in food preservation, it is possible today to purchase dried onion flakes that can be reconstituted easily in water. This is a viable alterna-tive if it is inconvenient to keep fresh alliums. I prefer the fresh stalks (for leeks) and bulbs (garlic and onions), but I have used reconstituted flakes with good results.

Set out onions or garlic bulbs around the house to drive away hostile spirits.

Artemisias

This is the other family of herbs that was important enough to include in the third chapter. Wormwood, mugwort, and south-ernwood are the best known of the artemisias. The spirits within these plants have the power to drive away unhealthy things, and this includes flies and fleas as well as spirit beings. They should not be taken internally.

The artemisias are sacred to Woden, the magician-god who wanders the Seven Worlds. They promote visions and are useful for sorcerers who practice the art of seething (one method to in-duce trance states), which will be discussed in the next chapter. I often burn artemisia as an offering to Woden before beginning a divination session. Mugwort is said to be especially efficacious for this purpose.

Artemisias also have a reputation for stimulating the wód (inspi-ration) in a distinctly carnal way. Southernwood and wormwood both share this reputation. Placing some of either herb beneath a bed or just anywhere in the bedroom may arouse lust. Likewise, artemisias can be used in spells intended to nurture lust.

Betony (Betonica officinalis)

Also known as wood betony, this herb is used primarily for protective spells. The spirit of betony blocks outside influences. It was used by the Anglo-Saxons as a cure for elf-sickness because of its power to block the attacks of hostile Elves (spirits). Betony blocks dreams and visions that may disturb sleep. Negative influences may be blocked from the home by strewing the herb around doors and windows.

A potion made of betony leaves is said to be helpful in relieving headaches. Crumble the dried leaves and scatter them around the perimeter of your home to ward the interior from pernicious outside forces.

Chamomile (Chamaemelum nobile)

The power of this herb is found primarily in its small flowers. Chamomile, sometimes called Mayweed, is notable for its ability to relax the lic. The flowers are often sold in commercial preparations today intended to be infused into "teas" for relaxation. A stronger infusion can be used as a facial steam to relax muscles and soften the skin.

Chamomile also helps fortify and focus the hyge, the rational part of your being. The essential oil, while expensive, is especially good for this purpose. Sniffing the oil, as you would use smelling salts, causes the hyge to focus and to shake off distractions.

Cinquefoil (Potentilla reptans)

This herb was known to the Saxons as *fifleafe*, or "five-leaf." It was one of the ingredients in a Saxon "holy salve" and continued to retain its reputation as a general purpose herb of power well into the Middle Ages. Its power is protective and purifying. Cinquefoil can be used in any spell for protection or purification.

Carry or wear cinquefoil in a sachet to ensure a fair trial. It has a reputation for eliciting justice.

Comfrey (Symphytum officinale)

Known to the Saxons as *consolde*, comfrey is one of my favorite herbs. The comfrey plant sends down a deep taproot, and so can be difficult to transplant. Once established, however, this herb will usually thrive for many years in your garden. Folklore says comfrey protects a person while traveling. I have heard that the leaf should be worn in the shoe. Presumably a portion of a leaf is sufficient for this purpose, since comfrey leaves are enormous.

A common name for comfrey is bruisewort, which describes another of its powers. An ointment of comfrey will reduce bruises and hasten the healing of cuts and scrapes. Be sure to clean any wound thoroughly before applying the comfrey ointment. The fresh leaves can be used as a poultice for the same purpose.

Dill (Anethum graveolens)

Dill exerts a general benevolent effect. It is a tonic for the hama, the protective aura, and is thus a defensive herb. It need not be ingested for this purpose. Wearing or carrying dill seeds and leaves in a sachet will strengthen the hama and unleash this herb's protective influence.

The potion, prepared as an infusion, is useful both for soothing hiccups and for stimulating milk flow in nursing mothers.

Dock (Rumex obtusifolius)

Dock is mentioned in a tenth-century formula for curing the "water-elf disease" (*wæterælfadle*). This may be a reference to either chickenpox or measles, but we have no way of knowing for certain. In the formula, dock was to be mixed with eighteen other herbs. The complex herbal blend was then steeped in alc to produce a healing potion.

Dock root has been used medicinally, but most of the folklore that I have seen suggests using the seeds in spells to produce or increase prosperity. An infusion made of the crushed seeds can draw potential customers. The infusion is not imbibed by either the merchant or the customer, it is simply sprinkled around the merchant's shop. Most people today do not earn a living by selling wares from their own shops, but a dock seed prosperity infusion can be used in many creative ways. If you work in a corporate cubicle, wipe down your desk with the infusion. If your career involves extensive travel, sprinkle the infusion over your car.

Elecampane (Inula helenium)

This herb was known to the Saxons as *eolone*. Another common name for it is elfwort. Folklore tells us that Elves can be found living nearby wherever the elfwort grows. This is reason enough to propagate elecampane in an herb garden!

Elecampane is a tall plant with leaves growing up to eighteen inches in length. But the power of this herb is found primarily in its root. A potion prepared as a decoction can help relieve phlegmatic symptoms (chest congestion, excessive mucous, coughing). It also fortifies the myne (emotions and memories) and can be used in love potions.

Fennel (Foeniculum vulgare)

Fennel is one of the sacred plants named in the Nine Herbs Charm. Its spirit is protective on all levels. The Nine Herbs Charm tells us that "the lord" created fennel and sent it out into the Seven Worlds. At the time the Nine Herbs Charm was recorded, "the lord" was perceived as the Christian god. In an earlier age, those who followed the ways of their ancestors may have believed it was Woden who dispersed the herb throughout the Seven Worlds.

Fennel was also used in an eleventh-century spell to protect cultivated fields. It was mixed with soft soap, frankincense, salt, and some seed taken from a beggar. The mixture was then rubbed into the wood of a plowshare. As part of the spell, the beggar was given a generous payment for his contribution of seed. The spell ensured the safety of the fields throughout the following year.

Fennel can be hung over doors and windows to protect the home. Along with vervain and dill, this herb has a reputation for warding against dark magic. Because of its protective power, it is often a component in healing potions and powders.

Feverfew (Tanacetum parthenium)

As the name of this herb suggests, feverfew's power is primarily what we would today label as remedial or medicinal. From the perspective of a sorcerer, it balances and focuses the lic. The power of feverfew is found primarily in its leaves.

Sew feverfew leaves into a sachet and wear or carry this to ward off fever. Eating three to five fresh leaves every day is believed to reduce migraines. An infused potion can be taken as a mild sedative or to help relieve congestion. I have heard feverfew described as a "protective" herb, but I do not think this protection extends beyond its ability to protect and balance the lic.

Horehound (Marrubium vulgare)

The Saxons called this herb *hárhúne*, meaning "plant covered with gray hairs." Horehound's wrinkled leaves have a covering of white or gray hairs that are especially noticeable at the tips. Horehound is found in the list of ingredients for the tenth-century "holy salve." In addition to its general protective power, horehound stimulates the hyge. An infused potion is said to promote clear thinking.

The herb has a general soothing effect on the lic. Today horehound is best known as a treatment for congestion and coughs. It is often a component in commercially prepared cough lozenges. A potion prepared as a tincture or metheglin can help alleviate coughs and congestion.

Lavender (Lavandula augustifolia)

Nothing suggests the English countryside more than a row of lavender in bloom. Lavender nurtures harmony, and for this reason it is used variously in spells for love, protection, purification, and healing. The power of the herb concentrates in the blossoms.

When used in love charms, the dried lavender petals are often carried in sachets. These can be combined with rose petals or violets for a more efficacious charm.

The essential oil is now more commonly used to wield lavender's healing powers. Mix seven drops of lavender oil with a teaspoon of cold-pressed almond oil (as a carrier) and massage this into the temples to help relieve a headache. Lavender oil diluted in cold-pressed almond oil is also a good blend for use in any therapeutic massage.

Mint (Mentha spp.)

The spirit of mint cleanses and revitalizes. Mint is fun to work with just because there are literally hundreds of varieties. This includes varieties of pennyroyal, as well as endless flavors of apple, lemon, ginger, and even chocolate mint! I have found spearmint to be the easiest variety to grow. Add it to the bath for a refreshing experience. Peppermint infused as a potion can help ward against pernicious cold conditions. Rubbing fresh mint leaves on the forehead and temples is said to help relieve headaches.

Mint is associated with prosperity. The fresh leaves are best for prosperity magic. If you have your own retail business, keep a few fresh mint leaves in your cash box to attract money. Or infuse the leaves for prosperity just as you would use a dock seed infusion.

Pennyroyal (M. pulegium) should not be ingested by pregnant women.

Nettle (Urtica dioica)

Nettle is another sacred plant named in the Nine Herbs Charm. It is also known as stinging nettle because of the hairs covering the stems and leaves of the plant. These hairs have an irritant that can cause considerable discomfort, so the plant must be handled with care. Because the nettle defends itself so well with this irritant, it is a protective herb. In this way, it is similar to the sawgrass in the passage of the Rune Poem describing the mystery of the rune *eolh*. Wearing or carrying some nettle sewn up in a sachet affords protection against any curses or other negative energy directed your way.

Placing a bowl of cut nettles in a sickroom or beneath a bed is said to help drive away the malign influences causing the disease.

Wear skin protection when handling nettle plants. Wash gloves and clothes in very hot water to deactivate the nettle's sting.

Parsley (Petroselinum spp.)

Most of the lore concerning parsley comes to us from the Greeks, but we know it was valued by the Saxons (who called it *petresilige*) because of its mention in Old English charms. The Saxons used it primarily as a healing herb. Parsley has a cleansing power. An infused potion made from the leaves can be taken as a tonic for the digestive tract. The root can be prepared as a decoction to help cleanse and remove toxins from the kidneys.

Plantain (Plantago major)

Plantain, also known as waybread, is another sacred herb named in the Nine Herbs Charm. In the charm it is called the "mother of herbs" (*wyrta modor*) with the power "to withstand and to rush against." Here we see plantain as a protective herb. Carrying the root is said to protect against snakebites. This effect comes from the Law of Sympathy. Plantain's tiny flowers rise up on thin stalks, resembling small serpents rearing their heads. This appearance gives plantain another common name—snakeweed.

This is a cooling herb. The infused potion can help reduce a fever. But I have found this plant to be most efficacious when the fresh leaves are used on external rashes or insect stings. Bruise the leaves to expose the sap and hold them as a poultice against the afflicted area. I used to have several bee hives, and I found that nothing took the fire out of a bee sting faster than crushed plantain leaves.

Raspberry (Rubus idaeus)

Raspberry was known to the Saxons as *hindbrér*, or "deer bramble." It is one of the herbs listed as ingredients for the "holy salve," suggesting the early Saxons believed this herb to have healing or protective powers. Because of the raspberry's defensive thorns, I believe we can be safe in assuming it to be a protective herb not unlike the nettle, or the sawgrass of the *eolh* passage in the Rune Poem. As a protective herb, the branches can be hung over doors and windows to discourage malevolent spirits.

Of course the berries themselves are a delicious treat, and raspberries are cultivated commercially for use in many food products. Beyond this, it is the leaves that are most often used today. These can be infused as a potion to be taken by women before and during childbirth to fortify the womb.

Rosemary (Rosmarinus officinalis)

Indigenous to the Mediterranean area, rosemary was probably brought to Britain by the Romans. The herb was certainly known to the Saxons, who called it *boðen*. Rosemary has two qualities. The first of these is cleansing and purification. The needle-like leaves can be burned as an incense to purify an area before a spiritual ceremony. I often burn rosemary as I begin a *húsel* (rite of offering) to my gods. At one time, rosemary was burned in sickrooms to cleanse or purify the air. In the same way, you can burn rosemary before beginning any magic work if you have reason to believe there are negative influences in the immediate area.

In addition to its power of purification, the spirit of rosemary fortifies the myne (memory and emotional part of Self). For this reason, rosemary is used both in love spells and in workings intended to improve the memory.

Rosemary is well worth cultivating for both its beauty and scent if you live in a relatively mild climate. A tender perennial, it cannot survive harsh northern winters. It is still possible to keep rosemary if you live in a northern environment, but the plant must be brought indoors and carefully tended throughout the coldest winter months. Keep the potted plant in a cool but sunny location, water it sparingly, and take it back outside as soon as the danger of a hard freeze has passed.

Sage (Salvia officinalis)

Sage, in addition to being a popular culinary herb, promotes longevity and wisdom. Eating a bit of sage every day is said to increase a person's lifespan. Indeed, there was an ancient adage found in some form or another throughout Europe, Persia, and even China claiming that people who grew sage in their gardens could expect to live a long time. It has also been said that eating sage every day throughout the month of May would confer immortality. All of the people who said that have long since died, so I suspect it was a bit of an exaggeration.

Nevertheless, sage is an extremely useful and versatile plant. If I could have access to only one herb, it would be sage. And that is saying a lot since I am very fond of rosemary, but sage has so many uses! Crush a sage leaf and use it to clean your teeth. You will be amazed at how your teeth whiten. The fresh leaves are also excellent for stopping bleeding. Crush a few leaves and hold them to the cut. The infused potion can be taken to aid digestion, soothe a cough, reduce sweating, or help regulate menstruation. Gargle with this infusion if you have a sore throat, or make a larger quantity to use as a rinse for dark hair.

Wear or carry sage in a sachet to help promote wisdom. I have heard this is most useful for remaining connected with one's common sense. It is no accident that we call this herb "sage." It can be a strong ally during those times when you want to avoid saying or doing something foolish.

Thyme (Thymus spp.)

This popular herb is indigenous to the Mediterranean area and, like rosemary, probably came to Britain courtesy of the Romans.

Thyme nurtures courage and confidence. A potion prepared as either an infusion or a metheglin can be taken to help overcome shyness. The same potion—presumably because it confers courage—can ward off mares, the hostile spirits that disrupt a person's sleep. Folklore says that wearing or carrying fresh thyme will give you the power to see Elves.

Vervain (Verbena officinalis)

Vervain is another protection herb. English folklore states that it should be gathered at the summer solstice, but I do not know of any people who limit themselves to that one day. Despite its scientific name, vervain is not the same herb as lemon verbena (*Lippia citriodora*). Either dried or prepared as an infusion, vervain can be sprinkled about the home to drive away hostile spirits.

As a protective herb, it is also used in healing work to protect the lic. The potion has been used as a general tonic and to alleviate fevers and coughing.

Yarrow (*Achillea millefolium*)

The leaves of yarrow can be applied to small cuts to stop bleeding, and it is generally considered a healing herb, but yarrow's real power is to boost or improve the functioning of other plants. A live yarrow plant helps neighboring plants resist disease and can cause their flavors and scents to intensify. Yarrow also boosts the efficacy of other herbs when it is added potions and ointments. A simple potion of infused yarrow can alleviate cold conditions.

A few yarrow leaves mixed into a compost pile will speed decomposition.

If you do extensive work with wortcunning, these are just a few of the plants you will be using. All of the herbs we have looked at here are named in Old English charms, but I do not believe it is wise or desirable to limit oneself to these sources. Traditional wortcunning made use of whatever plants were readily available, and today most of us have access to a wide variety of herbs.

The contemporary spice cabinet holds jars of barks, seeds, and leaves that the early Saxons did not have access to. A typical spice cabinet will be stocked with herbs such as allspice and basil (for prosperity), cardamom and cinnamon (to arouse passion), and cloves (for protection and purification).

One nice thing about all of the herbs you will find in your spice cabinet is that they are safe to ingest. Long ago there were European physicians who followed a principle known as the Doctrine of Signatures. This stated that the shape and color of an herb was a "signature" indicating its use. In other words, an herb with a yellow flower was useful for kidney problems (because urine is yellow) and a plant with heart-shaped leaves was useful for heart conditions. You have probably noticed that this is essentially the Law of Sympathy applied to herbs. Unfortunately, many of their patients died because, despite the shapes of the leaves and colors of the flowers, the herbs used were often highly toxic. For infusions to sprinkle (rather than ingest) or for herbs used in sachets, the Law of Sympathy is a wonderful tool, but you should never, ever ingest an herb unless you know for certain that it is edible.

I make use of plants that grow naturally in the vicinity of my home. Some, like the purple coneflower, are indigenous to North America. Other species, like dandelion and lavender, are European imports. This is in keeping with the practices of early Saxon sorcerers, who used indigenous British herbs as well as imports like rosemary. Since this is a book about Saxon sorcery, I have not included any information here about Native American herbs, but there is no reason the aspiring sorcerer should not explore these species.

Potion

The potion, a staple of the witchy stereotype, is a medicinal or magical liquid. The early Saxons would have called this a *wyrt-drenc* and would not have bothered to make much of a distinction between medicinal and magical wyrtdrencs so long as the desired effect was achieved.

Potions can be prepared in four basic ways: infusions, decoctions, tinctures, and metheglins. Each process has its advantages and disadvantages.

The **infusion** is the simplest of these procedures. An infused potion is often referred to as a "tea," although this term can be confusing. Tea is a specific herb known scientifically as *Camellia sinensis*. Although its leaves are infused to produce a beverage, it is the herb and not the process that is "tea." Confusion can result when the term is used casually in reference to the process. If we say "yarrow tea," do we mean a blend of *Achillea millefolium* (yarrow) and *Camellia sinensis* (tea), or do we mean a simple infusion of *Achillea millefolium*?

The infusion is a process used to extract the desirable properties from leaves and blossoms. To make an infusion, place a handful of fresh herbs, or $\frac{1}{2}$ to 1 ounce dried herbs, into a large mug or bowl, using a perforated tea ball or basket to simplify straining. Put two cups of water into your cauldron and bring this to a boil. Pour the boiling water over the herbs and let this steep for anywhere from five to thirty minutes, depending on how strong an infusion you desire. Do not put the herbs themselves over direct heat or you will lose much of their power. After steeping, strain the herbal matter from the liquid.

The disadvantage of an infused potion is a short shelf life. Any of the liquid that is not used immediately should be refrigerated, and even then must be discarded after several days.

The **decoction** is similar to an infusion but is used for bark, roots, and other thick, woody parts. Chop 1 or 2 ounces of the thick herbal material and place this in your cauldron. Add two or three cups of water. Bring this to a boil, and then lower the heat and let it simmer for half an hour. If more than half the liquid evaporates as it simmers, add a little more water to make up the difference. As with an infusion, strain the herbal matter out before using the potion. This, too, needs to be refrigerated and can be kept under refrigeration for up to three days.

A **tincture** is an alcohol extraction. This has a much longer shelf life than either an infusion or decoction. The advantage of a tincture is that you can prepare it weeks before you actually need it. The disadvantage of a tincture is that you *must* prepare it weeks before you actually need it.

To prepare a tincture, begin by mixing 1 cup of water with 2 cups of a good-quality, 80-proof vodka. After this, put about 6 ounces of dried herb (or 1 pound fresh herb) into a wide-mouthed jar. Pour the water and vodka mixture over this. Cover the jar and store it in a cool, dark place for the next two weeks. Shake or swirl the jar gently every other day.

After two weeks, strain the liquid through cheesecloth to remove the herb matter. The resulting tincture can be stored for up to two years if kept away from heat and light.

It is best to extract a tincture from only one kind of herb. To create a more complex tincture, blend two or more tinctures together after completing the extraction processes separately.

Although technically a potion, a tincture is exceptionally potent. If taken internally, no more than a few drops should be ingested at a time. And of course, you should never ingest a tincture if you are not certain that the herbal component is safe and edible. Some people dilute tinctures in water, often adding a little honey to improve the flavor.

A **metheglin** is a less potent alcohol extraction, using mead rather than distilled vodka as a base. Mead is a drink made of fermented honey. The process is otherwise very similar to making a tincture. Place a good quantity of herb into a jar and cover this with mead. Use the ratio given above. Store the mixture in a cool, dark place for two weeks, shaking gently every other day. Whether you use a sweet or dry mead is your personal choice.

If you brew your own mead, you may want to experiment with adding the herbs while your mead is still fermenting. I describe the process of brewing mead in *Travels Through Middle Earth*, and there are many good mead-making books available today.

It usually is not necessary to dilute a metheglin, since it has a significantly lower concentration of alcohol than a true tincture. Nevertheless, this variety of potion is unsuitable for children or for people who have issues with alcohol.

Ointments

An ointment extracts the herbal properties into a fat. Ointments were originally made with animal fats. The Saxons used either butter or soft, fatty soap. Later herbalists used lanolin. The disadvantage of animal fats is that they go rancid. Today we have petroleum jelly (soft paraffin), a substance used in many cosmetics. Ointments made with petroleum jelly can be kept for years.

Some care must be taken when making an herbal ointment in order to avoid burning oneself. The petroleum jelly must be slowly melted in a double boiler. If you do not have a double boiler, you can put the petroleum jelly in a small pan, and place this in a larger pan holding a couple inches of water. The important thing is that you do not place a pan of petroleum jelly over direct heat.

After the petroleum jelly has melted, add your herb. About 2 ounces of dried herb works with a standard-sized jar (7–8 ounces) of petroleum jelly. Let this sit over a low heat for two hours. Watch the double boiler arrangement closely, carefully adding more water to the lower pan when necessary.

After two hours, remove the upper pan and strain your liquid ointment through cheesecloth to remove the herbal matter. Wear rubber gloves while doing this to protect your hands. The liquid ointment will be very hot and cannot be easily rinsed or wiped off if a drop spatters onto your bare hand. Pour the ointment into jars carefully but without hesitation. The ointment will begin to solidify soon after you have removed it from the heat.

Ointments extracted with petroleum jelly do not blend into the skin. They form a surface over the skin, holding the spirit or essence of the herb in contact with you. Because it blocks the pores, an ointment such as this should be spread only over a small portion of the skin. An ointment should *never* be applied to a burn under any circumstances!

Although not exactly an ointment, a **cold oil infusion** is similar in that it extracts herbal properties into a fat. To make a cold oil infusion, fill a wide-mouthed jar with your herb. These cold infusions work best when using leaves or flowers. Pack the herb into the jar fairly tightly. Then cover this completely with a cold-pressed oil. I prefer cold-pressed almond oil, as it is a light oil that accepts the spirit of the herb well. Cover the jar, put it on a sunny windowsill and leave it there for several weeks. Although you should usually try to keep your herbs away from light, which causes their essence to break down, this is one procedure where bright light facilitates the infusion. Essentially you are using light much in the way heat is used in an ordinary water infusion, or "tea."

After several weeks, strain the oil through cheesecloth to remove the herbal matter. For a stronger oil, repeat the process again using fresh herbs and covering them with your infused oil. After creating your cold oil infusion you will want to keep it away from light and heat as you would any other herbal preparation. A cold infusion can be kept for a year or more if stored properly.

————

As with everything else associated with wortcunning, exert some restraint regarding these preparations. When you first start working with herbs, you can usually rely on ordinary infused or decocted potions. If you find yourself using an herb again and again for the same purpose, you might then consider preparing a tincture or ointment.

A sorcerer who specializes in wortcunning may eventually build up a supply of various metheglins, ointments, and oils. In the final chapter, we will discuss how a wyrtwita might develop his or her cræft. When you do make herbal potions and ointments, do not hesitate to use your other arts to enhance their efficacy. Galdor may be chanted while grinding your herbs, heating water, and bottling potions. Runes can be marked over the preparations or inscribed on their containers to imbue them with specific influences. The rune *ur*, for example, is usually appropriate for enhancing herbal preparations intended to fortify or empower a person. Using your telga, mark the rune over the potion or ointment as you recite from the Rune Poem, "*The aurochs is brave and has horns above. The fierce beast fights with its horns, this great wanderer of the moors, this proud creature."* You may have noticed that I have paraphrased this slightly to give it more power as an incantation.

As a Saxon sorcerer, you should not hesitate to weave your skills together like this.

Growing Your Own

You can obtain your herbs from a number of sources. The most convenient, perhaps, is your local supermarket. From a non-culinary perspective, the selection is limited, but you will find leeks, garlic, sage, dill, fennel, parsley, rosemary, and other useful herbs in the vegetable and spice aisles. Other than leeks and garlic, you will also pay a premium price for a teeny bottle of dried herb.

If you are lucky, there may be a nearby retailer specializing in herbs. An herb shop will usually have a greater variety of herbs available for a lower cost per ounce. The proprietor probably has considerable knowledge of herbs and their uses. Even if his or her knowledge of the magical properties of herbs is limited, a proprietor of an herb shop is usually well versed in the remedial and cosmetic uses of plants. An herb shop is also a good place to acquire some of the equipment you will eventually need if you intend to make extensive use of wortcunning. If an herb shop does not carry mortars or cheesecloth or ointment jars, the proprietor or a clerk may be able to suggest where you can purchase such items.

In this day and age, there are many Internet companies offering dried herbs. Finding these can be tricky, because many of the companies offering "herbs" are marketing their own commercial preparations. Of course, there is nothing wrong with commercial preparations if they are suited to your needs. But if you just want the herbs and not the preparations, typing the words *dried bulk herb retailers* into your search engine should bring up lists of online companies offering herbs that you can use in your art.

There will be times when it is prudent to purchase your herbs from a supplier, whether your source is the supermarket, a local herb shop, or the Internet. But if it is at all possible, I strongly encourage anyone with an ardent interest in wortcunning to consider growing at least some of his or her own herbs. There are multiple benefits to this. The first is the obvious advantage of knowing exactly how fresh your herbs are. Herbs on a supermarket shelf may be months old at the time of purchase. Herb shops—whether with a storefront or on the Internet—have a stronger incentive for offering fresh product since herbs are the foundation of their business. Still, the only way to know for certain when your herbs were harvested is to grow them yourself.

Growing your own herbs will also help you connect with your "good neighbors"—the Elves who dwell unseen in the world around you. While this may appear on the surface to fall under the domain of spirituality rather than magic, it does not hurt to build good relationships with the local spirits. Many Elves concern themselves with the growth of herbs, grasses, shrubs, and trees. Sharing in this interest will attract their attention and, hopefully, their good will.

If you have no connection with them, Elves are not necessarily well meaning. I do not understand why people who understand that mortal men are not always benevolent and that animals are not inevitably harmless, believe that every spirit around them is friendly. This is not always so. As with incarnate spirits—men and women and animals—friendship and trust with the Elves must be earned. And why would anyone not want to develop friendly alliances with the spirits around us? Connecting with the local Elves by working with them in a congenial way may alleviate some problems in your life before they even arise.

Those who work a lot with wortcunning are more likely than other sorcerers to develop strong alliances with the Elves. Some of these entities are the spirits of the plants themselves. The early Saxons knew of the *wuduælfen*, or tree spirit, known to the Greeks as a dryad. Moss wives (*móswífes*) are the spirits of the bog plants that die back every year. Every plant has its own mód, its own spirit, that responds to the surrounding environment. Sorcerers who connect with these spirits find that they can be useful allies and mentors.

Digging in the soil and working with your growing plants may also draw the favor of greater spirits. Some of the Saxon gods are sovereign over horticulture and may take an interest in your activities. Thunor, known to the Scandinavians as Thor, is known for his association with thunder and the weather, but many people do not realize this is directly related to his interest in the activities and well-being of farmers. Thunor is the Great Protector, and throughout much of human history, few things needed protection more than a tribe's annual crops. It was believed at one time that Thunor's rolling thunder caused grain to ripen.

The Lord of the Elves, Ing Fréa, known to the Scandinavians as Freyr, also takes a keen interest in green growing things, both cultivated and wild. He is the same Ing described in the twenty-second passage of the Rune Poem. Ing's beloved consort, the Ettin-maid Gearde, is sovereign over gardens and cultivated fields.

Growing your own herbs is not difficult. Many herbs are amazingly easy to grow; some as easy to grow as weeds. Some, like dandelion and plantain, literally ARE weeds! If you have a sunny spot in your yard or on a patio, you can grow herbs. Annuals like basil and dill are simple to grow from seed, while perennials can provide you with years of fresh herbal material for very little work on your part.

The following plants make a nice, small *wyrtbedd* (herb bed) of traditional Saxon herbs:

- dill
- parsley
- spearmint

- sage

- mugwort

- yarrow

- comfrey

All of these plants are relatively easy to grow. Keep in mind that the comfrey will grow quite large and, with a taproot reaching down ten feet or more, it can be difficult to move once established. Be sure it has plenty of space. A rosemary bush makes a nice addition to this collection if you live in a mild climate. If your winters are cold, you can still set a pot of rosemary out in the garden, but you will need to bring it inside before the first hard freeze.

Growing your own herbs will give you an awareness of the seasonal cycles. You will gain a renewed appreciation of Sunne, the sun goddess, and the moon god Mona. You will become more attuned to the natural forces: wind, sunlight, and rain.

Even if you do not have a yard or balcony, you can still grow a few herbs on a sunny windowsill. Sage, creeping thyme, basil, spearmint, and parsley are a few of the herbs that can be successfully grown indoors if given sufficient sunlight. In my experience, indoor herbs tend to do better when grouped closely together. I do not know why; perhaps it satisfies their social needs. Whether indoors or on a patio, give your herbs the largest pots you can manage. Large pots give your plants more room to stretch their roots. They also allow for a greater margin of error. A large pot of soil is less likely to become severely over-watered, dried out, or depleted of its nutrients. That is not to say these things cannot happen in a large pot, but it takes more negligence on your part. And nobody can hover over his or her plants every hour of the day, so give both yourself and your plants some leeway and plant them in large, deep pots.

When setting up a witch's garden—whether in your yard, on a balcony, or on a windowsill—take the moon into consideration when planting seeds or setting out young plants. The god Mona governs the rhythm of life: the tides, the menstrual cycle, and the growth of plants. Seeds should be planted and young plants set out when the moon is *waxing*, growing from dark to full. The exceptions are root crops, plants whose valued gifts are tubers and roots that develop underground. Root crops should be planted in the third quarter of the moon, after it begins to diminish but before it is half dark. Very few plants used in wortcunning are of this nature, although elecampane and some of the alliums are notable exceptions.

We have looked at several traditional modalities, or cræftes, for working magic. In the next chapter we will explore the skill of knowing *when* to reweave the web of wyrd.

Review

1. Describe two uses for comfrey.

2. In the tenth century, dock was used in a charm to prevent the water-elf disease. What other, non-medicinal effect do sorcerers sometimes use it for today?

3. What is the difference between an infusion and a decoction?

4. What substances did the early Anglo-Saxons use as base materials for making ointments? What is the primary disadvantage of these substances?

5. Describe the process of creating a cold oil infusion.

Wiglung:
The Arts of Divination

Can you imagine trying to navigate an automobile or boat while blindfolded? That's a bit like us humans moving through life—we often have no idea what's coming toward us. An effective sorcerer, however, should be able to perceive the patterns shaping Middle Earth and the worlds beyond. These skills or arts are known collectively as *wiglung* (pronounced WEE-lung), a word meaning augury or soothsaying. Wiglung is often perceived as the practice of looking into the future, but it would be more correct to define wiglung as the practice of observing the influences affecting the future. Nobody can know exactly what the future holds because it is not yet set down; however, the general tides and currents can be perceived through the divinatory arts.

Over the ages, the Saxons and other cultures have devised countless ways to perceive these currents. Patterns have been found in the movements of the planets, in the entrails of butchered animals, in the rise of smoke and the fall of dice, in stones, in cards, and in dreams. Visions have been gleaned in the depths of firelight, in crystals, in mirrors, and in pools of water. The very best of these many arts, the method superior to all others, is whichever one works best for you.

In this book, we will limit our discussion to divinatory arts orig-
inating from or inspired by Saxon traditions. You could use classic astrology as a tool, and it might be no less effective than runes
or scrying or seething. But it would not be Saxon wiglung. Every
cultural tradition speaks its own language, not only in words but
also in conceptual definitions. Many people today favor an eclectic
approach to both magic and spirituality, but I believe there is wisdom in mastering one tradition rather than pasting together bits
and pieces from dozens of different cultures.

Runic Wiglung

When the subject of divination—of seeing what may come to be—
arises, the runes come into their own. In the popular imagination,
runes are almost synonymous with divination. When used in this
way, runes are a form of sortilege. This is the practice of perceiving
patterns in the web of wyrd by casting or drawing lots. Tarot is another form of sortilege, but it is based on Pythagorean mathematics
rather than Germanic mysticism.

In the chapter on Futhorc, we discussed divinatory rune sets,
and by now you may have made or purchased your own set of
runes for this purpose. Hopefully you have started to study these
symbols. When runes are used simply for sortilege and nothing
more, each symbol can seem to have a finite meaning. *Feoh* means
"wealth," *ur* means "strength" and so on. But runic wiglung can
take the practiced sorcerer much deeper than this. Each rune embodies a complex mystery that can only be mastered through con-
templation and study.

To make the most of runic wiglung, learn as much as you can
of the runic mysteries before making any attempt at divination.
Know something of the runes before you try to work with them.
When casting or laying them out, let the symbols themselves
speak to you. Do not thumb through a book to find out what an
author said about *beorc* or *dæg*. At the very most—and this should

be the exception rather than the rule—consult the relevant passage of the Rune Poem only when you are not certain of a rune's meaning. Even this should be avoided unless you simply cannot remember a thing about the rune in question. (If that is happening often, you have not studied the runes enough.) When you lay out runes and then turn to a book, you are not reading the runes, you are reading a book. Trust in your own ability, and trust in the power of the runes.

If you are using a deck of rune cards, be sure that the illustrations on the cards are faithful to the Anglo-Saxon Rune Poem. I have seen illustrations in some decks that bear no relationship to the corresponding passage of the Rune Poem. I cannot overemphasize that this ancient poem is the only extant lore we have concerning the Futhorc, and it should be your primary resource when the meaning of a rune escapes you.

Casting Runes

There are two basic approaches to consulting the runes—they can be either cast or drawn. Runes must be carved into wood, bone, or antler or painted onto stones to be cast effectively. Cardstock does not lend itself to this process. Casting is no better or worse than drawing runes, it just depends on your personal preference.

Runes are usually cast onto a square cloth. This cloth should be no larger than twenty inches on each side. Rune sorcerers who cast their divinatory runes often keep them wrapped up in the cloth when not in use. If you have a myse cloth, that could also serve as your casting cloth. Or if you prefer, a rabbit pelt or piece of soft leather can be used in place of the cloth. I own a beautiful set of bone runes, a gift that came wrapped in a white rabbit pelt for casting. You may come up with other ideas for a casting cloth. The important thing is that it provides a soft surface for the runes to fall on.

To cast the runes, take all of them up in your hands. At this point I offer a brief prayer to Woden, asking for his guidance. Then drop the runes onto the cloth, letting them fall and scatter as they will. Some of the runes will bounce beyond the edge of the cloth. Gather these up and set them aside; they are not a part of the reading. Some of the runes will be face down, obscured from your view. Set these aside also.

Now study the remaining runes on the cloth. Look for the patterns formed by these runes. Notice how they fall in clusters, lines, and crescents. Each of these patterns reveals a message.

Solitary runes in a casting—those that land by themselves with no discernible relationship to the other runes—are fairly straightforward, but remember what I have said about reading the runes rather than reading a book. Once you have a connection with the runic mysteries, a single rune lying by itself will have its own tone and inflection. *Peorth* may say one thing to you now, and then something else entirely the next time you cast. Trust your intuition.

A *cluster* of runes should be interpreted together as one collective message. There is no beginning or end, no order in which the runes are interpreted. No one rune is more important than the others in the cluster … usually. If one of the runes has a clearer, more dominant inflection, if it simply feels more important to you, then that rune is probably more important. The messages that the runes convey to you should always supersede any rules I give here.

Lines of runes should be read from one end to the other, beginning with the end closest to you. When the runes fall in this pattern, you have a linear statement indicating a series of circumstances or events. It is possible to have a cluster positioned at some point on the line. The cluster, of course, is interpreted collectively.

When runes form a *crescent*, see if the shape is encircling or "cupping" a solitary rune or a cluster. If so, interpret the runes of the crescent as outside events or situations that are influencing the solitary rune (or cluster). If the crescent is not targeting another rune or a cluster in this way, interpret it much as you would a line of runes, reading from one end to the other, beginning with the end of the crescent closest to you.

Drawing Runes

Drawing runes is simply a matter of pulling one or more runes at random and laying them out in front of you. The most elementary way to do this is to draw a single rune. This gives a very general, basic reading. Such a reading is neither long term nor specific. I draw a single rune when I want immediate guidance, or when I want a general idea of what the coming day will be like.

Single Rune

Draw a single rune each morning for some quick advice for the day. Make it a part of your morning routine. This morning I drew the rune *peorth*. At the time I did not know what that meant, but as the morning wore on I realized that I was having a hard time focusing on my writing. *Peorth* is the rune of gaming and play. The rune was telling me that I would need to pull myself away from the computer and relax for a while. If I had not consulted the runes, I probably would have remained at the keyboard, even though I was accomplishing nothing. After a bit of downtime, I am refreshed and getting more done than I would have otherwise.

A single rune drawing is also useful when you are faced with an immediate decision. It is not for long-term predictions. Draw a single rune whenever you want a simple, general idea of the pattern of your wyrd here and now.

Three Runes

Draw multiple runes—three or more—for a more detailed view of the pattern of wyrd. An easy, popular layout uses three runes positioned like this:

PAST INFLUENCE—PRESENT WYRD—FUTURE POSSIBILITY

In this layout, the first rune drawn represents your wyrd. Lay this rune directly in front of you. This is the "here and now" similar to what you would find in a single rune drawing. In fact, if you were to stop drawing runes at this point, it *would* be a single rune drawing. This rune speaks of your immediate pattern.

Draw the second rune and lay it to the left of the first. This second rune represents past influences contributing to your present condition. The rune speaks of events, words, and deeds that have led you to where you are. Although the past is behind you, this second rune is nevertheless important in understanding both your present and future. Knowing how you have come to where you are can be extremely helpful in deciding where you intend to continue on.

Finally, draw the third rune and lay it to the right of the other two. The third rune represents what may come to pass. You have free will, of course, and the opportunity to alter your future if it is not pleasing to you. The third rune does not reveal an unavoidable fate, but rather a future possibility. The rune speaks of what may come to be if your wyrd continues to unfold in its current pattern. Altering this pattern, when necessary, is the work of the Saxon sorcerer.

The Seven Worlds

The Seven Worlds layout will give a much deeper and more complete wiglung. I reserve this layout for serious concerns. Draw seven runes, laying them before you in this order:

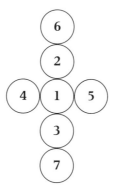

Saxon cosmology embraces the idea of seven worlds or universes. This layout places seven runes in positions corresponding to the locations of these seven worlds. Since these planes of existence—with the exception of our own Middle Earth—are extradimensional, the concepts of up and down, east and west, are poetic descriptions of their relative positions rather than actual locations.

The first rune, in the central position of Middle Earth, represents your wyrd, the pattern unfolding around you here and now. This rune tells of your current situation. It may speak of things related only in passing to your own concerns. The runes do not always tell you what you want to know, they tell you what you need to know.

The second rune, positioned in the realm of the Elves, represents factors nurturing your current situation. This rune often tells of your assets. As with the first rune, though, what this rune speaks of may be contrary to your own conscious plans. The second (Elves) rune nurtures the first (Middle Earth) rune.

The third rune, positioned in the realm of the Dwarves, represents possibilities not yet manifested. This rune tells of influences that are yet to come. If any part of this layout points to what the future holds, this is where you will find it. Dwarves bring possibilities into existence. They create. The third rune speaks of what will come to be.

The fourth rune, positioned in the "west" where the Wanic spirits dwell, represents outside creative forces. Wanic spirits are distant influences and so represent peripheral factors affecting your current situation. They can be harnessed, though, and drawn into your life more fully.

The fifth rune, positioned in the "east" where the Ettin (giants) spirits dwell, represents outside destructive forces. As with the fourth rune, this speaks of influences that can be harnessed to your advantage. We often think of a destructive force as something to avoid, but destruction is as necessary as creation. Throughout our lives, we are faced with many things that need to be destroyed—addictions, anger, sour relationships, and so on.

The sixth rune, positioned above the others, represents divine influence. This rune brings a message from the gods. It could be a general message from above, a message from your personal patron, or a message from your "higher self." It is a place of inspiration.

The seventh rune, positioned below the others, represents ancestral influence. It brings a message from the dead. The message may be from one or more blood ancestors, or perhaps from another spirit who somehow inspired you.

As you can see, the Seven Worlds layout does not give a "future prediction" as the three-rune layout does. It is more like drawing a single rune in that it describes your current situation, but the analysis is much more thorough! This is a good layout to use before making any important decision. It helps reveal not only your wyrd, but all of the influences shaping it. I do not really need a "future prediction." As a sorcerer, I intend to create my own future rather than wait passively for it to sweep over me.

––––––––––

You may practice wiglung for others as easily as for yourself, of course. In fact, I think it is actually easier to do this for others because you are not as deeply invested in the reading on a personal level. I like to have the other person draw his or her own runes (or drop them, in a casting), but this only a preference. Simply knowing as you begin that you are drawing runes for another person is enough.

Wyrd Stones

If you like the idea of practicing wiglung with rune-like symbols but do not have the interest or inclination to master the runic mysteries, I have found wyrd stones to be a very effective tool for sortilege. These are stones painted with fourteen symbols, plus one (sometimes two) additional stones to represent the querent. These stones and their symbols have been called various names. I have heard them called Witches' Runes, Dana Corby has called them the Runes of Njord, and P. M. H. Atwater refers to them as Goddess Runes. Some of the symbols are actual runes, and one appears to be an astrological symbol. I have seen the remaining symbols in Koch's *The Book of Signs* (Dover, 1955), but he unfortunately gives no sources. I call them wyrd stones.

I strongly suspect this set of symbols is Wiccan in origin. The symbols feature a heterocentric imagery reflecting the duotheist male/female construct that is fundamental to Wiccan belief. Duotheism is not found in Saxon tradition, but I believe the wyrd stones are effective enough as a divinatory tool to warrant their inclusion in this book.

The symbols are painted on small, smooth river rocks. I suppose they could be engraved or painted on other materials, but I have never seen them on anything other than stones. You will need fifteen small stones of similar size. The extra stone represents the querent, the person who is the subject of the wiglung. This stone is left unmarked. Some people use two querent stones—a spherical stone for a female querent, and an elongated stone for a male querent. This was how these divinatory stones were presented to me, and it supports my theory that the divinatory system is Wiccan in origin. The religion of Wicca divides the universe into male and female "energies." Thus it makes sense, in that context, to have two separate stones to represent these energies. But for the Saxon sorcerer, the querent stone serves only one purpose: to represent the subject of the wiglung. Since there will be only one subject for any casting, one stone serves this purpose regardless of the sex of the querent.

Do make sure all fifteen stones are roughly the same size. Flattened stones work better than spheres, which can roll a great distance when cast. The stones should also be a similar color. Choose a paint that contrasts with the stones—a dark paint for light stones, or a light paint for dark stones. Paint fourteen of the stones with these symbols:

Y   MAN, MALE

In form this symbol is identical to the rune *eolh*, but in this set of images it has an entirely different meaning. When casting wyrd stones, this symbol represents an adult male human. By "adult" I mean physically mature. It could be an adolescent, but it never represents a prepubescent boy. In the imagery used on wyrd stones, the symbol seems to be depicting a man standing upright with his arms outstretched.

The presence or influence of a man is indicated wherever this stone falls.

WOMAN, FEMALE

This symbol represents an adult female human. As with the male symbol, this could indicate an adolescent, but not an undeveloped child. Here we have one of Koch's symbols of unknown origin. It is probably intended to depict a woman in a skirt. While it is admittedly useful to know whether the wyrd stones are referencing a man or a woman, the emphasis on gender in the symbols again suggests a Wiccan origin. It would be just as useful, if not more so, to know if the person was blond or brunette, fat or thin, young or old, etc. Wyrd stones ignore these other characteristics, but alert us to the gender of whatever person the stone represents.

The presence or influence of a woman is indicated where this stone falls.

LOVE, BALANCE

Here we have something like a bindrune incorporating the previous two symbols. Man on top of woman. This image depicts love, in a rather obvious and carnal way. If we accept Wicca as the most likely origin of these symbols, then it should come as no surprise that this particular symbol indicates not just physical, heterosexual coupling, but also harmony, peace, and general warm fuzzy stuff. Traditional Wiccan rituals include the symbolic coupling of a male and female, represented by lowering the blade of a knife into the well of a cup. The meaning of this act—of the male/female union—goes well beyond the obvious benefits of species reproduction and the fertility of the soil; it is nothing less than an act of magic, creating a balance of male and female "energies," which is believed, in Wicca, to be the source of all blessings.

Wherever this stone falls, it indicates that things are going well. There is a suggestion of a state of harmony or balance.

⚙ FAMILY, TRIBE

You know what often happens after vigorous sessions of physical coupling. In this image the man is still on top of the woman, but now there are two little circles to feed, burp, and change. This image, the symbol for family, can represent children. The circles are as yet undefined, neither fully male nor female (because they are not grown). But more than this, the image represents the tribe. It is the social unit. This could be a nuclear family, but it could as easily be a family of choice, such as a coven, kindred, or grove. Whether the social unit is of blood or of choice, this symbol represents what the Saxon would call an inhíred (in-HEER-ed).

The family is usually a factor wherever this stone falls. It may also indicate a prepubescent child of either sex.

Ⲯ WAR, CONFLICT

Here we have two "man" symbols leaning in toward each other. Butting heads. No, they are not kissing—remember, the imagery on wyrd stones is entirely heterocentric. The men are fighting. This is the symbol of war. It represents conflict and aggression. The conflict is not necessarily physical in nature, but there is some struggle or confrontation involved.

This stone indicates a fight or some similar conflict.

△ HOME, TRADITIONS

Now we leave the little stick men and women and move on to other symbols. This image represents the home. On a more metaphysical level, the triangle represents creativity and the horizontal line beneath it represents grounding or centering. The home is not the same thing as the family. The family or tribe is the people. This image represents the physical sanctuary, the nest. It also represents all of the customs and traditions associated with the home.

The home is important wherever this stone falls.

 CONFUSION, DISORDER

This image is a triangle collapsing on itself. According to Koch (p. 8) it is symbolic of "disordered intellect," in contrast to the perfect triangle representing creativity or "creative intellect." This symbol indicates confusion and chaos. There is no obvious conflict here. It may indicate depression or sorrow, if this is severe enough to cause disorder.

This wyrd stone indicates a state of confusion.

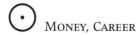 MONEY, CAREER

This image, painted on a wyrd stone, indicates money. I do not know where the connection comes from. Koch does not ascribe that meaning to the symbol. As an astrological symbol, it represents the sun. As a botanical symbol, it represents an annual (a plant that lives only one year). But on a wyrd stone, it represents money. It may also indicate a person's job or occupation, since that is where the money comes from. Atwater (38–39) claims that it can indicate the ego.

Money is indicated by this stone.

 CHALLENGES, INTERRUPTIONS

Here is the symbol for interruption. You may notice that it bears a resemblance to the *nied* rune. The upright stroke is broken or interrupted by two shorter strokes. Like *war* and *confusion*, this is a bad wyrd stone. It is a warning. There is no real conflict or confusion, but something is going to interrupt the querent's life. It usually indicates something that can be avoided if the querent is careful and anticipates the potential problem.

Where this stone falls, expect some unwanted interruption.

〈 Fire, Inspiration

We have returned to the rune-like images familiar to the Futhorc. In both the Norse and the Icelandic Rune Poem, this symbol represents a scab or sore, but the corresponding rune in the Anglo-Saxon Rune Poem represents a pine-fire. Fire is the mystery here. Among the wyrd stones, this fire is more symbolic, indicating divine inspiration rather than a physical flame. For example, the fire symbol falling adjacent to the home symbol does not mean your house is going to burn down. Its proximity emphasizes the home symbol, giving the latter more significance and power.

This stone inspires or emphasizes the importance of any other stones it falls near.

ᚹ Happiness, Contentment

Here we see the form of the *wynn* rune, and this wyrd stone conveys a similar meaning. This is a rune of comfort and contentment. Like the *love* symbol, this is a generally good image. Unlike the *love* symbol, this symbol of happiness does not necessarily indicate a state of balance or harmony. Falling adjacent to the *war* symbol could indicate a conflict that the querent has been looking forward to. Next to the *interruption* symbol, it indicates that the querent will be content overall despite the problem.

This stone indicates happiness or comfort.

✕ Gift, Reward

This symbol has the same form as the *gyfu* rune, and a similar if simpler meaning. On a wyrd stone, the symbol indicates that a gift is coming. The gift need not be something physical; it could be any kind of reward or pleasure. This could be a raise, a letter from an old friend, or an inheritance. Although the Anglo-Saxon rune indicates partnerships, the symbol does not carry the same meaning here. Partnerships are acknowledged by the *family/tribe* symbol.

This stone indicates something good is coming.

 GROWTH, POSSESSIONS

The *growth* symbol resembles the *ethel* rune, but has a different meaning. On a wyrd stone, the image represents expansion or acquisition. Like the *gift* symbol, this is a good image, but it does not represent something coming to the querent—it is something that the querent is building or nurturing himself. It can also indicate acquired possessions. Not finances, which would be represented by the *money* symbol, but personal belongings or anything the querent has collected.

This wyrd stone means growth.

 CHANGE, DEATH

The last of these symbols again resembles a rune—this time the *éoh* rune—but has its own meaning. As a wyrd stone, the image means death or transformation. It is a symbol of change. This is not a trivial change, but something memorable and profound. No change is as profound as death, but the symbol much more often indicates a some other kind of change. What sort of change depends on which stones fall adjacent to it.

Wherever it falls, this stone indicates change.

––––––––––

You may want a pouch or small box to hold your wyrd stones. Mine are kept in a sturdy denim pouch when not in use.

Wyrd stones are never drawn, they are cast collectively. I ask for Woden's guidance before casting the stones. Take the stones in both of your hands and formulate a clear question in your mind.

The stones often want to tell you something unrelated to your question, but they work best if you give them a starting point.

Drop the stones and let them fall where they may. As with casting the Futhorc runes, you should now look for patterns. In particular, look for patterns in relationship to the blank querent stone. It does not matter if a stone lands face up or face down. If you cannot see the symbol, turn the stone over so it is visible.

Look for the same patterns that you would observe when casting the Futhorc: solitary stones, clusters, lines, and crescents. But always interpret these in relationship to the querent stone. A cluster near the stone indicates an important influence. A distant cluster is only a minor, passing influence. A distant solitary stone should be ignored. It has removed itself from the configuration.

The linear statement given in a row of stones should be "read" beginning with the stone closest to the querent stone, moving outward until you come to the most distant stone.

You will find that wyrd stones are easy to master with only a little practice.

Seething

Some wyrdworkers eschew symbolic constructs altogether and practice wiglung by traveling "between the worlds." The wiglere goes into a trance state to gather information or commune with other wights (spirits).

There is nothing unnatural or even extraordinary about trance. Most people enter trance states numerous times throughout each day. We usually are not aware of this if the trance only lasts a few seconds, but occasionally we notice. When this happens we are likely to say that we "drifted off," "zoned out," or that our "minds were elsewhere."

These ordinary trance states happen by chance. In contrast, the wiglere intentionally induces trance. This process is called "seething." The Old English verb *séoðan* means to boil or cook, just as most people use the modern word seethe, but it also means to prepare or "feed" the mód (mood). Only when the mód is in the proper state can the wiglere journey beyond his physical body. To use a Freudian term, the ego is set aside during the seething.

There are different ways to induce trance, but all of them open the practitioner to outside influences. This is not as dangerous as it may sound. The hama (astral shield) continues to afford protection from malevolent wights when you enter a trance state. Otherwise we would all soon be possessed by spirits, since we naturally go in and out of brief trances throughout the day. Nevertheless, it is a good idea to set up wards or protections before inducing any prolonged state of trance. You can do this with impromptu rune work, using the *eolh* rune as described in the Rúncræft chapter. Remember that you will be using the phrase *eolh weardath mé*. Take up your seax—your ritual knife—and make a long, downward motion in front of you. See a crackling fire or light stream from the tip of the blade, hovering in the air as you say in a commanding voice, "*Eolh!*" Still visualizing this vertical line of fire, mark the two shorter strokes of the *eolh* rune, moving upward and out from the vertical line. Again visualize the crackling fire streaming from the tip of your blade. With the motion of your seax, push away any malign forces as you say, "*Weardath mé!*" The power of the rune will guard you during your work.

You may want to use a protective amulet instead of or in conjunction with this impromptu charm. If you have a talent for working with runes, craft a bindrune or helm that you can wear as a pendant during your trance work. If you find yourself drawn to wortcunning, sew protective herbs in a small pouch to wear in the same way.

After taking reasonable precautions, burn a pinch or two of dried artemisia, preferably mugwort or wormwood. This will help prepare your mód. The artemisias are sacred to the god Woden, who travels between the worlds. Burn the artemisia over a smoldering coal in a sturdy incense burner.

Find a comfortable place to sit. You want to sit in an upright position, rather than lay down, to ensure that you slip into a trance and not into an actual sleep state.

Some wigleres make use of a staff when they journey. (Construction of the staff is described in the Tools chapter.) The base of the staff is thrust firmly to the ground, and the shaft grasped with both hands. This helps the lic (body) remain centered and connected to the earth. Symbolically the staff represents the Eormensyl, the Axis Mundi that connects the Seven Worlds.

Another technique used by many wigleres is covering the head loosely with a cloth. This blocks outside distractions and symbolically sets the wiglere apart from the physical realm of Middle Earth. Those who favor the technique often have special cloaks they use for this purpose. When ready to begin the journey, the wiglere pulls the cloak over his or her own head. The cloth, however, does not need to be a cloak. Any loose cloth large enough to cover the head and shoulders of the wiglere will suffice.

Now you are sitting, some artemisia burning on a coal, perhaps with a staff held upright in your hands. Perhaps a cloak or cloth covers your head. You are prepared to begin your journey. There are different techniques you can use to induce trance, but one of the most common is to focus on your breathing. Your breath is the æthem, the force that binds the nine parts of your Self—the lic, hyge, myne, mægen, hama, wód, mód, willa, and fetch—together as one whole being. By focusing on your æthem, you can relax it and extend your perception beyond the ordinary.

Breathe in through your nose to the count of four. Then hold the breath to another count of four. Release the breath, this time through your mouth, to a count of four. Repeat this, keeping count as you breathe in, hold, and release. There is nothing special about counting to four. If this is uncomfortable for you, try changing it to a count of three or five. All that matters is that each part of the breath—inhaling, holding, and releasing—follows the same count.

After a while you should feel yourself relax and the world fade around you. At this point, be mindful of any perceptions you may have but avoid analyzing them. Some wigleres find it helpful to look for a path. This is not necessarily a visual experience, although it can be. You may sense the path in other ways, perhaps as a cold sensation, or as a scent or even just a feeling. Let yourself follow the path. Do not force anything. Allow your definition of Self, your mód, to move along the path if it will. Go no farther than you feel comfortable.

I cannot tell you what to expect after this. It is your journey, after all. Keep whatever question you have firmly in mind. Then experience what you will, and keep as much of it in mind as possible. Do not analyze any experiences you have. Later, after the seething, you can analyze all of it, but do not confuse your assessment with the actual experience.

Let us say, for example, that you see yourself passing through a meadow. As you go on your way, a striped gray cat approaches you. It may be tempting to think of the cat as a messenger sent by the goddess Fréo, to whom cats are sacred. And this is one possibility, but that is your assessment, which may or may not be on target. The cat could be something else entirely. It could be your own fetch (guardian spirit) if you do not yet know how this manifests. Or it could be someone else's fetch. It could be an elf in the guise of a cat. For that matter, it could just be a cat that has run through all nine of its lives.

Do not assume everything you meet "over there" is your good buddy. I do not understand people who think like this. I am not suggesting you be unduly concerned, but spirit entities are persons, and like any other persons, they can be good, bad, or indifferent. Exercise reasonable caution around any presence you encounter until it proves itself to be benevolent or at least neutral. If seriously threatened, which is not very likely, use your knowledge of runes and galdor to ward off the assailant.

Let me emphasize again that there is very little danger in seething. As I have said elsewhere, you simply are not that important. Unless you give a spirit entity cause to fight you, very few will exert that much effort in your direction.

To return to a fully conscious state, some wigleres like to retrace their steps. Simply go back the way you came. Alternately, use your æthem to draw your mód back. Take a deep breath, and then another, until you have pulled yourself together. You may feel disoriented after the first few times you do this. It is a good idea to eat something and have a refreshing drink to help ground you in the physical world. After you have returned and are fully grounded, feel free to analyze your experience. Since this was an exercise in wiglung, the important consideration is whether or not you received an answer to your question.

This is an effective process for inducing trance to practice wiglung, but it is not the only process. Some wigleres with musical talent may design songs and induce trance by singing galdor, while others have found that drumming helps them reach out beyond the ordinary. Saxon sorcerers develop personal styles of magic that work best for them.

Scrying

If you like the intuitive approach to wiglung but find the seething process reminds you too much of a séance, consider scrying as a wiglung art. *Scry* is a short form of the verb *descry*, meaning "to catch sight of." When scrying, the wiglere perceives visions while gazing at a reflective or flickering focal point. This can be a pool of water, a crystal shard, a crystal ball, a mirror, or a flame.

The early Saxon sorcerers almost certainly made use of scrying techniques. There are examples of scrying throughout English folklore, usually involving water in some way, and usually connected with romantic or marital inquiries. Unmarried girls knew of a scrying spell to discern who their future husbands would be.

The girl had to set a bucket of water out in the yard at midnight. On the following day, at noon, she could gaze into the bucket to see the face of the man she would marry.

There is no special trick to scrying. You either have a talent for it or you don't, and only practice will prove that talent. With practice, though, comes the inevitable personalization that a Saxon sorcerer will apply to his or her work. A friend of mine, Deana Isendun, gives a prayer and an offering—usually herbs or incense—to the gods before scrying. For her, scrying is simultaneously an act of magic and a part of her devotional practice.

Try different focal points to find what works best for you. Modern "crystal" balls are usually made of acrylic, but do not be dissuaded by this. The acrylic ball often serves as a better focal point than a sphere of true crystal, which is rarely without notice-able flaws. If you want to work with true crystal, try scrying with a large quartz shard. Or try a true crystal ball, but be forewarned that these are expensive.

Any mirror can be used for scrying, but wigleres who special-ize in this art frequently prefer special scrying mirrors. A scrying mirror is a piece of glass painted black on one side. This creates a smooth, reflective surface without the distractions captured in an ordinary mirror. A frame for the scrying mirror will help protect it from breakage.

Maria Stoy, the spiritual leader of an ecumenical Pagan group in western Pennsylvania, uses nothing more than a bowl of water for scrying. She believes that the water, "because it travels through the worlds from underground to the surface to the sky and back again," gathers and contains the knowledge she is scrying for. She says that the surface of the water becomes "a window" for her. Maria explains:

Once I am focused and calm, I imagine or allow the water in my bowl to become sacred waters, connected to all worlds. I keep my focus on the water, casting my attention down into the

waters, allowing my mind and spirit to be receptive of mes-
sages I may receive. I tend to see images floating from the bot-
tom of the bowl to the top and then dissipating. Some folks see
a mist gather on the water that forms images.

When I feel the message has been received I take a moment
to try and organize what I have seen into a coherent thought or
message. Sometimes the meaning is obvious, sometimes it takes
a while.

Fire, too, can be used as a focus for scrying. Deana uses fire as
her focus. "I can scry in as little as a candle flame," she says, "but
it is easier with a larger fire, such as a campfire."

Whatever focus you decide on, sit comfortably if you can and
gaze into it. Let the visions come to you naturally. It may take
some time before you see anything, and you may not see anything
at all the first few times you attempt this. People who use a bowl
of water or a scrying mirror often speak of it "clouding over" before visions appear. This, of course, is their subjective perception,
but if you experience this you can take it as a sign that you are
beginning to master the art of scrying. Deana explains:

I stare into the fire until the flames begin to make patterns and
images. As I recognize the images, I begin to interpret what
those images mean. If I am having difficulty "seeing" any
patterns or images, I usually put more offerings into the fire. I
have also found that closing my eyes for a few moments helps
clear my vision if I am having any difficulty. When I reopen
my eyes, the vision is often much clearer.

Deana also believes, and I concur, that it is better to practice
this art alone before attempting it in the presence of other people.
Even a few people can be a distraction, and the first thing a person
must do while scrying is try to block out all outside distractions.
Maria warns, "Scrying can be a much more subjective method of

seership than using runes or another 'closed' symbol set. For me it works really well in personal practice."

Do not be concerned, though, if you have little or no talent for scrying. Consulting the runes, casting wyrd stones, seething, and scrying are all very different approaches to wiglung, and each is suited for people with different ways of functioning. Few people are going to be proficient with all of these modalities. Equally few will be unable to master even one of them. If the runes work best for you, stay with runic wiglung. If you enter a trance state at the drop of a hat, seething may be a better approach. The very best modality is the one that works for you.

Review

1. What is sortilege?

2. What are the two basic approaches to consulting the runes?

3. Although wyrd stones can be a useful tool for the Saxon sorcerer, what is their probable origin?

4. Why do some wigleres cover their heads with cloaks or cloths while seething?

5. Name three focal points that can be used as tools for scrying.

Blood to Blood:
Health Magic

By this point you should have a basic working knowledge of rún-cræft, galdor, and wortcunning. If you are unsure of how your work should proceed, you can utilize divinatory runes, wyrd stones, or the arts of seething or scrying to perceive influences shaping the future. Let us now explore the application of these skills on issues that the majority of us are likely to be confronted with at some time or another.

A common issue that everyone faces is his or her own state of health. Throughout much of our lives, this is something we tend to take for granted. Like every other part of your Self, your lic is an intelligent and responsive entity. Your heart beats with no conscious instruction from your mód. Your lungs take in fresh air and release carbon dioxide as needed. When the lic is compromised, you do not need to issue commands to release antibodies, or send out marching orders to your leucocytes. The lic itself handles all of that for you. For many of us, myself included, health only becomes a concern when things go wrong.

But things do go wrong from time to time, no matter your age or general condition. And the skills you have learned can often

277

help set things straight. Note that I said "help." You should always see a physician if you suspect anything may be seriously wrong with you. What follows in this chapter is intended to assist the healing process, not take the place of medical attention.

When the sorcerer's concern is healing, wortcunning comes into its own. This is so much so that many people today identify wortcunning solely with herbal "teas" and remedies. What most of these people do not know is that much of our Western herbal lore is based on an elemental theory developed by early Greek scientists. Four of the elements are the same basic building blocks recognized by many Pagans today—earth, water, air, and fire—but they have specific qualities that few people are aware of.

The Saxons turned from their gods before Western elemental theory became widespread in northern Europe, but there is no reason to believe their conversion caused them to accept the theory any earlier or more readily than they would have otherwise. Elemental theory is not related to any particular spirituality. It became widely popular throughout the Western world simply because it worked. Hippocrates' own theories of restorative healing, based on the four elements known in his time, were the basis of traditional European medicine for centuries.

Each element is essentially a description of two qualities: temperature and humidity. Elemental theory postulates that everything in the universe is either hot or cool, and either moist or dry, in varying degrees. Water describes the combined condition of coolness and moisture; earth, the condition of coolness and dryness; air, the condition of warmth and moisture; and fire, the condition of warmth and dryness. Since these conditions can and do change, the elements are constantly transforming into one another. Thus, water transforms into earth if it loses its moisture. On the other hand, it will transform into air if it begins to warm up. Hippocrates, the Greek physician who became known as the Father of Medicine, took this further with his theory of humors. Humors are essentially the same four elements as they relate to the human body. They are perceived as four "body fluids" known as black bile (earth), phlegm (water), blood (air), and yellow bile (fire).

Traditional European medicine strove to achieve a state of health by balancing the body's four humors. Disease was accepted as an imbalance of one or more humors. Diet, massage, exercise, and herbs were used to restore the balance. Hippocrates' teachings were more successful than anything else at that time in history, and over the next millennium, his ideas spread across Europe.

Some of this Hippocratic lore survives even today in our language. We understand almost instinctively what a person means if he or she says, "I've caught a cold." All of us who grew up in English-speaking families understand what a pernicious cold condition is. Most colds are phlegmatic in nature, cold and moist, and thus related to the element of water. Balancing this is a matter of warming and drying the body. In Hippocratic medicine, herbs associated with air and fire would be used to help accomplish this.

In practice, of course, Hippocratic medicine was far more complex than I have described here. Foods and herbs were not just hot or cold, moist or dry; there were varying degrees of each of these qualities. One earth herb might be cooler or drier than another earth herb. Every influence in a person's life was taken into consideration. The person's diet and lifestyle, his or her emotional state, and even the season of the year factored into an evaluation of that person's condition.

It might be argued that herbal remedies are not magic, but the Saxon sorcerer does not make this distinction. Wortcunning can be used for many different effects, and healing is but one of them. Nevertheless, healing is a widely popular effect today among people who work with herbs, and there are countless books about herbal remedies available for those interested in pursuing the subject in depth. I especially recommend Ody's *The Complete Medicinal Herbal*.

A sorcerer's remedies will often be magic by anybody's definition. When I carve the *ur* rune into a piece of wood and place it in a small red pouch with a garlic clove and dill seeds, it is difficult to describe my remedy as anything other than magic. The dill seeds are to fortify the hama, and the garlic is to ward off pernicious wights, but I don't intend the garlic or the dill to be ingested as a medicine (not that it would hurt anybody if they did). The pouch, put together to ward against colds, is intended to be carried or worn.

A Wortcunning First-Aid Kit

No matter what effect a practitioner is attempting to achieve through wortcunning—healing, protection, prosperity, etc.—some advance preparation is usually needed. This is especially important when using herbs for remedial effects. If you want to use herbs in this way, keep your essential materials together in one place. Nobody afflicted with a headache or upset stomach wants to rummage around for herbs and the equipment to prepare them. All of this should be kept together in one convenient area. Think of it as your wortcunning first-aid kit.

The herbs should be prepared for convenience as much as possible. Ointments, infused oils, and tinctures should be prepared in advance. If your kit contains any dried herbs intended for infusions, a tea ball should be included with them.

The exact contents of your kit will depend on your personal needs and the needs of other members of your household. Here are a few suggestions:

- comfrey ointment for cuts and abrasions; clean the wound thoroughly before applying the ointment
- marigold ointment for athlete's foot and similar fungal infections; by "marigold" I mean the herb *Calendula officinalis*, not the garden variety of marigold

- lemon balm oil for insect bites
- dried peppermint to infuse as a potion for indigestion
- dried lavender blossoms to infuse as a potion for headaches
- dried chamomile blossoms to settle the nerves
- tea ball
- cotton swabs
- tweezers
- tea tree essential oil for use as a natural antiseptic

Keep the contents together in one container, and keep the container in a place where you can quickly find it. The location should be dark and cool to extend the longevity of the herbs and herbal preparations. A bathroom cabinet is ideal.

Examine your herbs and herbal preparations periodically to make sure they are still reasonably potent. If stored in a cool, dark place, the dried herbs in your kit should easily last a year. Tinctures and ointments will remain potent much longer.

Hama Lácnung

Wortcunning is not the only art available to the Saxon sorcerer for use in healing work. *Hama lácnung* is a technique for relaxing a person's hama, which in turn causes every part of the Self to relax and become receptive to healing.

This technique is related to the age-old practice of "laying on hands," but hama lácnung involves no connection with the subject's lic. There is no direct, physical touch. Instead the practitioner touches and manipulates the subject's hama, the astral body surrounding and protecting that person. Today the hama is sometimes given names like biomagnetic field or energy field. Hama lácnung uses principles common to Pranic healing, Reiki, acupressure, and other modalities of energy healing.

To practice hama lácnung, the subject should be seated or laying down. Meanwhile the practitioner should be calm and relaxed. A short prayer can help the practitioner become spiritually centered. The practitioner reaches out with both hands, bringing them within two or three inches of the subject's head. With slow motions, the practitioner moves his hands downward, stroking the hama, keeping palms and fingers within a couple of inches of the subject's skin. The stroking movements should be long and smooth, but not hesitant. At no time does the practitioner physically touch the subject.

The practitioner moves downward, stroking lower portions of the hama over the neck, chest, arms, and abdomen. Then lower still, over the thighs and legs, until eventually coming to the feet.

While stroking the subject's hama, the practitioner may feel areas of warmth or coolness, or a tingling sensation. When this occurs, the practitioner should remain at that area, giving additional attention to that region of the hama. The practitioner can then continue downward; after reaching the feet, he or she should return to any "problem" areas to ensure that the anomalies have been drawn away. The locations of the anomalies in the hama may be entirely unrelated to the location of a physical complaint in the subject's lic. The practitioner may go over the subject's hama several times, until the work feels complete.

Keep in mind that hama lácnung does not directly address a physical complaint. Its purpose is to relax the hama, which helps facilitate the healing process in a general way.

Healing Runes

The runes of the Futhorc can be powerful healing tools. There are various approaches to this, but first let us look at some specific runes useful for various healing needs. Again I need to credit my friend West Hardin for some of this, and thank him for sharing the results of his own rune work with me.

ᚠ *Feoh* can help fortify the blood in a rune working. This makes absolutely no sense if you have fallen into the trap of assigning a simple, finite interpretation to each of the runes, because this rune is usually interpreted as "money." But when we look at the deeper meaning of the rune, we see that it is interpreted as money only because money is a flow or exchange of potential. *Feoh* nurtures a continuous flow, which is essential for our blood to ensure a state of health.

ᛉ Use the rune *eolh* to alleviate skin conditions. The skin is the protective covering of the lic, and is rejuvenated by the protective influence of *eolh*. The rune can also be used to repair the hama if you have reason to believe that part of the Self has been compromised in any way. As a general protection rune, this symbol can be used for almost any healing work.

ᚱ Not all disease is purely physical in nature. *Rád* is useful for work in combating addiction. From the perspective of the rúnwita, it does not matter if the addiction is physical or psychological. *Rád* is the rune of journeying. It creates movement and, more importantly, the movement is toward a place of contentment. It is a journey home. Thus, this rune is useful to help leave an addiction and move on to more wholesome, productive behaviors.

ᚺ *Hagol* is useful for work intended to improve the digestion. It is the rune of transformation, and digestion is the process of transforming food into the components necessary for sustaining and rebuilding the lic. Consider the description of *hagol* in the Rune Poem. How "its circling comes from the lofty sky," as food passes downward into the digestive tract, and how "it then becomes water afterward." Hailstorms are a blatantly destructive force, but then digestion itself is essentially the destruction or transformation of food matter into energy.

ᚺ Glandular disorders may be helped with the influence of *sigel*. The rune of the sun is a rune of navigation and guidance. The early Anglo-Saxons did not understand how glands regulate bodily processes, but this does not matter. It is the function it-self—body guidance or regulation—that matters. The *sigel* rune promotes guidance. Use this rune, too, to help delay the progression of dementia.

ᛜ *Ing* is the rune to use to stimulate or nurture the sexual or-gans. The god Ing, represented by this rune, is sovereign over sexual pleasure. In the eleventh century, the historian Adam of Bremen describes the god's statue at Uppsala as having a large erect penis. He went on to say that Fricco (another name for Ing) was a god of peace and "sensual delight." The *ing* rune can be used to benefit the sexual organs of men and women equally.

Note that sexual pleasure is not the same thing as fertility. There is no single rune indicating fertility, but *ing* can be combined with other runes such as *beorc* and *gear* to nurture this effect.

———

The runes mentioned here can be used alone to affect specific aspects of the lic. But most of the other runes are also useful for healing work when used in appropriate combinations. As with all rúncræft, the first step is to familiarize yourself with the runes and the mysteries they embody.

One approach to healing is to create runic charms for the ill to carry on his or her person. A permanent health charm can be crafted from wood, bone, or antler. I prefer cardstock or even paper for a charm to induce a finite effect, because the charm can be readily disposed of by burning after it has served its purpose. However, for most of my own runic healing work, I apply the runes directly to the body.

Healing runes can also be applied directly to the body. Paint the rune or runes over the area they are intended to affect. Use a non-toxic, water-based red paint. While painting the rune onto the skin (or immediately afterward if this is too complicated to do at the same time), recite the relevant passage from the Rune Poem. If painting a bindrune, paint each symbol completely, one over the other, to achieve the final form.

If the rune or runes will be on a visible part of your body, do this in the evening, when you do not plan to go out in public. Since you are using a water-based paint, it will shower off the following morning, leaving at most a slight discoloration.

Bringing It All Together

The first thing to do is determine whether the problem requires the attention of a physician. If there is any question in your mind, err on the side of caution.

There is rarely any need for scrying when it comes to healing work. Either you are sick or you are not. However, if you receive any indication through a wiglung that your health may soon become compromised, you can work some general proactive healing magic. Whether taking precautions about potential challenges or addressing a current issue, decide what modalities will work best for you. You may use a single technique or combine as many as you like. We know from the Old English healing charms that wortcunning and galdor were frequently used in conjunction with each other.

The amount of work needed should correspond to the severity of the complaint. There is no reason to work through hours of chanting and rune carving for a mild headache when a simple betony potion will do the trick.

Several years ago, a lump formed on my thyroid. I needed a biopsy, and the only way to ensure a reliable result was to have half of the thyroid gland removed. Healing work was done, and I obviously survived the experience. Let us look at this and consider my options.

A physician was already aware of the problem. In fact, it was my physician who discovered the lump in the first place, so that issue was already settled. Any healing work would be done to support the unavoidable surgery; it was not a replacement for medical care.

Wortcunning offered little in this situation. I could have brewed a potion for my nerves, or perhaps as a general tonic, but I did not. For myself and my situation at that time, other techniques were more appropriate. I chose rúncræft as the primary modality for the healing work. Fortunately I am blessed with other wyrdworkers in my life who were able and willing to help with this.

A few minutes of hama lácnung prepared me to receive the healing influence of the runes. I laid down on a massage table, which kept me elevated. One person recited a short narrative galdor.

Runes were then painted in red on my throat, directly over the thyroid gland. One person painted each rune while others helping with the work recited the relevant passages from the Rune Poem. This wove into a group chant by the time the final rune was applied. From a subjective perspective, I felt as though I was rising above the table. I had a sensation of floating. I was on a lake, or so it seemed, and the sun was streaming down. (*Sigel* was one of the runes used, since it assists glandular functions.) The wyrdworkers chanted lines from an eleventh-century healing charm, "Bone to bone, blood to blood." They chanted this over and over, sealing the power of the runes painted on my neck. And those runes remained on my neck throughout the night until I washed them off the following morning before going to the hospital.

If the subject had been a person other than myself or if my condition had been a different challenge, another approach may have been more appropriate. A successful sorcerer must always be flexible in his or her work.

Review

1. What is the first thing to consider before proceding with any healing work?
2. An "element" is a description of what two qualities?
3. What is the purpose achieved by hama lácnung?
4. What rune or runes would you select to help soothe an upset stomach? Is there an herbal potion you could use in conjunction with this?
5. What two cræftes are often used together in Old English healing charms?

Heart to Heart: Love Magic

When we are healthy and whole, our thoughts likely turn to winning the affection of another person. This is necessarily a generalization, of course, but it holds true for the majority of us. The onset of puberty opens a wondrous new world that quickens the pulse and warms the blood. Romantic love is the subject of the majority of song lyrics that have been written and performed. In the music, we seek love, we gain love, we lose love. In the motion picture industry, love stories will often be inserted into scripts for the sole purpose of ensuring that films will appeal to the widest audience possible. Love is humanity's common denominator. Love inspires us, frightens us, entertains us, enrages us, comforts us, flusters us, and heals us.

Love is a word like *magic* in that it can mean many different things to many different people. We use the word *love* to describe almost any positive response we have to the stimuli around us. You may love mashed potatoes, but not in the same way you love puppies, and neither of these in the same way you love your boyfriend or girlfriend (hopefully). In this chapter, we are using the word *love* to mean a positive response related in some way to sexual attraction.

For the moment, let us put aside any love we may have for ice cream, picnics, or the Steelers, and focus instead on sex.

Even this more narrow definition leaves us with a boggling array of feelings, needs, and opinions. For one person, sex is the goal. For another, sex is a tool for bonding two people together. Yet another person may perceive sex to be just one part of a healthy relationship. None of these definitions are incorrect; they simply reflect the needs of different individuals. The important thing is that you be painfully honest with yourself. Understand exactly what it is you need and want, because the person or people who can best satisfy your needs are those who have the same needs themselves.

Love magic, regardless of your needs and regardless of what cræftes you use, should always be worked to enhance yourself, not to entangle or coerce others. When I say *you* and *your*, I mean whoever the subject is—this principle applies equally to love magic worked on behalf of others. This is not only a matter of ethics. Yes, it would be unethical to coerce the affection of another person, but that is beside the point. There is a very selfish reason why coercive magic should be avoided: you want people to desire you of their own accord, not because you have cast a spell.

It might be argued that coercive magic can produce a satisfactory effect if all you are looking for is a one-night stand, but why on earth would you waste that much energy on one person for no more than a few hours' pleasure? If that specific person really matters so much, then something more is going on. You do not really want just one night with him or her. Again, know yourself and be honest with yourself.

No matter your needs, coercive sorcery will almost always prove to be a disappointment. Coercive sorcery includes any spell directed at a specific person. Unfortunately most "love magic," contemporary and traditional, takes this coercive approach. No matter how many tricks and traps we can find in folklore, the fact is that coercive magic rarely works in the way the sorcerer hopes. Trying to coerce love is a little like pulling on a pumpkin vine in the hope of making it grow faster. Instead of getting a positive response, you are much more likely to kill the vine.

Magic in folklore is typically coercive because most people simply react to the world around them instead of taking positive actions to create what they want and need. Why does Tom want to cast a love spell on Jennifer? Because he is reacting to his own infatuation. This sort of spell—which is nothing less than a form of magical stalking—probably will not work. Even if it does work, Tom will never know if Jennifer genuinely desires him. At the time he may not care, he may think the only thing that matters is that she be with him, but eventually the question will begin to gnaw at him.

If Tom is a sorcerer with any degree of wisdom, he will take a different approach. He will design a spell or charm to attract the right person to him. While he will be open to the possibility that this may be Jennifer, he will recognize that she may have another path to follow. And if this is true, then he will be happy for her, because real love places the other person's needs before your own. Tom's magic will be directed to the world at large, seeking a woman who can fully return his love. He knows that his true need is for a woman who can return feelings similar to those he has for Jennifer.

Honestly assess your needs, but do not carry this to an extreme. Know what the true deal breakers are for you. If sex is your end goal, there really are not many deal breakers. You are not going to be with the other person long enough for it to matter whether he or she wants children, enjoys the outdoors, or dislikes sushi. But if you are looking for any kind of lasting relationship, you will have further needs that must be met. You will also have likes and dislikes that are not as essential, but should be taken into consideration. Knowing what your actual needs are will carry you a long way along the path to finding a long-term partner.

I recently overheard a man complaining about how difficult it was to find such a partner. His requirements were that the prospective partner be "decent" and "normal." The prospective partner could not be into "hyper-socializing" or "herding pets," had to be lean, and couldn't have any tattoos or piercings. No over achievers or social climbers. Is it any wonder this person was single? Whenever I hear a person say that he or she is looking for a "normal" person, what I hear is, "I am looking for someone who has absolutely no interesting qualities that differ in any way from my own." Everyone has his or her own quirks. If you are looking for a person without anything like that, somebody without any habits or characteristics that make them distinct and interesting, you might be better off with a Cabbage Patch doll. And if a tattoo is going to come between you and a loving relationship, perhaps you really would be happier staying single.

That is all right, too. One of our cultural myths is that nobody can be truly happy unless he or she is partnered with somebody else. Love can be beautiful, but it can also be extremely inconvenient. Sharing your life with another person entails constant compromise, and for some people, this is a miserable way to live. Again, be honest with yourself and know your own needs. If you do not want to take on the burden of another person, do not let social conventions mislead you into believing you need this to be complete and happy.

On the other hand, if you do want to take on that burden, know what it is that you absolutely need from the other person. For me, my partner must be Pagan. My spirituality is an essential part of me, and it is imperative that my partner share in this aspect of my existence. My partner must also perceive sex to be one small facet in the broader spectrum of a loving relationship. For myself, sex is not a tool for bonding with another person; it is a part of my relationship, but it is not the defining feature. As another need, my partner must understand and appreciate that I have always lived with dogs, that I share a bond with them, and that my lifestyle would be incomplete without a dog at my side.

Those are a few of my needs. Almost everything else, though, really falls into the "wants" category, and wants are not the same thing as true needs. My partner does not have to fulfill all of my wants. That's why the gods put seven billion other people on the planet. I can find other people to fulfill some of my wants, some wants I can fulfill alone, and there are still other wants that I am willing to forfeit in exchange for a loving, long-term relationship. I know what my wants are, and I can distinguish between these and the real deal breakers.

While you are assessing yourself, extend this further and acknowledge realistically what you have to offer in exchange for what you want and need out of another person. What do you have to give? Look at yourself objectively. As a first step, do this literally. Stand alone in front a full length mirror in private, take off your clothes, and look at yourself. This is what you have to offer. The initial thing you will notice, almost certainly, is that you do not look like a model or movie star. So right away you can cross off models and movie stars from your list of potential life partners.

People will tell you that looks do not matter, that the important thing is who you are inside, but the fact is that looks do matter, very much, when it comes to attracting a love interest. Most people looking for partners are looking for others who appear healthy and whole, and who are roughly in the same age bracket as themselves. These traits are initially assessed primarily by observing the other person's appearance.

Looking at yourself in the mirror, consider what you can change to improve what you have to offer. Please notice how I worded this. Anorexia is not an improvement. On the other hand, if you are sixty pounds overweight, you are not in a healthy condition. If you are not sure what a healthy weight range is for your sex, age, and height, ask your physician. Likewise, if you have no muscle tone, an exercise program can improve what you have to offer. The healthier your appearance, the more desirable you will be to others. This does not mean people are just shallow—it is only natural for a person to prefer somebody fit and healthy for a long-term relationship. We want our partners to be full participants in life for as long as possible. Whether it is exercising, eating a more healthy diet, or giving up cigarettes, anything you do to improve your health will also improve your desirability. As a side effect, you will live longer and feel better.

Some of our physical appearance, of course, is purely genetic. Consider these immutable features also, and how you can present them in the best way. Choose your clothing with an eye for how it will emphasize your good features and draw attention away from less favorable areas. Here again, people will tell you that this does not matter, but it does. Your clothing need not be expensive or especially fashionable to enhance your appearance. If you are thinking that you do not care about your clothing or appearance, then why should anyone else find you attractive? Because of your personality? Your sincerity? Nobody can see your personality or sincerity. If you want people to respond to these qualities, you first need to attract their attention. Inner beauty is important, certainly, but it is buried beneath your outer appearance.

A runic charm for a long-term partnership should include the *gyfu* rune. The "gift" rune encourages social bonds of any kind, and here we are discussing love as a social bond associated with sexual attraction. If sex is your end goal, this is not the rune to use. *Gyfu* has nothing to do with sex. But if you are seeking something more permanent, *gyfu* is the relationship rune.

Consider the mystery embodied in this rune. The Rune Poem speaks of the gift as being "an honor and praise, a help and of worth." What you present to prospective partners should honor and praise those people. Your words and actions should make the other person feel important. Furthermore, you should ask yourself how you can help the other person. Rather than asking what you can get out of the relationship, ask what you can give. Ask yourself what worth you give to the relationship. If you feel you have nothing to give, why should this other person be interested in pursuing a relationship with you?

If you are using the *gyfu* rune—that is, if you are seeking a more lasting relationship—nightclubs, bars, and Internet dating sites are not always your best venues. You may fare better at gatherings of people who share your own needs and interests. Place your deal breakers at the top of your list whenever possible. From my own deal breakers that I have mentioned, it would make sense for me to become involved with Pagan organizations, since it is very important to me that my life partner be Pagan. And that is in fact what I did. I might also have joined a local dog obedience club, or volunteered with an animal welfare organization.

If you are not looking for a long-term commitment, you can still use rúncræft, just avoid the *gyfu* rune. Instead make a charm using *ur* for vitality, *ing* for sensuality, and/or *æsc* because it is "stiff in its trunk," to quote the Rune Poem. Craft this as a permanent charm, using wood, bone, or antler. Wear it as a pendant, or carry it in a pocket or purse. Before going out (or going online to visit an Internet dating site), clasp the charm firmly in your hand and say:

Lustful longing in my loin,
Awaken now the flesh conjoined.

The galdor combines alliteration and rhyming. Of course, you may wish to design a galdor more specific to your own needs.

Love Potion

This potion is for the person hoping to find a long-term partner. The potion itself is a very simple infusion. You will need dried rose petals, one ordinary tea bag, and a steeping pot (a ceramic pot with a handle and spout). Put some water in your cauldron and bring it to a boil. While waiting for this, place the steeping pot on your myse. Put the tea bag and a handful of rose petals in the steeping pot. When the water has come to a boil, pour this into the steeping pot and let the herbs steep for at least fifteen minutes. Remove the tea bag and strain out the petals, pouring the infused potion into a cup.

You may wish to pray to the goddess Frige at this time if you have developed any relationship with her. Frige is Woden's wife, and is sovereign over marriages. I do not believe, however, that it is appropriate to come before a god or goddess asking for favors if you have not yet given anything first. If you have never given Frige an offering or praise, be sure to give something to her before you ask for help with your spell. You could burn a scented candle in her honor, or pour a libation of a good wine or mead.

Brew and drink your potion every night for seven nights in succession. Begin on the night when the moon is in its first quarter. This is when the moon is growing from dark to full, at the point when the moon is half full. (Any almanac can give you the exact date.) At nine o'clock in the evening, sip the potion slowly and in silence. After you have finished the potion, say *"ic spellige nu."*

Repeat this six more evenings, seven in all. You should do this at the same time every evening. Nine o'clock is a good time that works for most people, but it could as easily be sunset, or midnight, or whatever fits your schedule best.

On the seventh night or on the night immediately following, *but no later than the night of the full moon*, go out somewhere you can meet people. Keep in mind that magic does not shatter reality, it only enhances the possibilities. If you want to meet that special someone, you have to go out and find him or her. Ideally you should go out where people sharing interests similar to your own are meeting. If this is not possible, go to a club. You can go out with friends if you like, but do not become so caught up in your clique that you forget your purpose. Be attentive to the possibility of new relationships.

Continue this regimen each month until you attain your goal.

Love Oil

This can be used by anyone, regardless of whether you are seeking a permanent relationship or if you are more interested in short-term connections. Love oil attracts people to you. Where things go from there is up to you. If you are drinking love potions, love oil can also be worn when you go out.

This is a basic cold oil infusion. Although timing is not strictly necessary, you might want to prepare and set your infusion on a Friday, or Frigesdæg, if you are hoping for a permanent relationship. This day is sacred to the goddess Frige, who is sovereign over marriages. The infusion must be prepared before sunset, however, as this hour marks the end of Frigesdæg and the beginning of Sæterniht in the Saxon week.

Fill a wide-mouthed jar with a mix of cinnamon bark and fresh rosemary branches. Cover the bark and branches completely with cold-pressed almond oil. Then cover the jar and set it on a sunny windowsill for several weeks. Swirl the jar every few days, but be sure that the herbs remain fully covered with oil.

After three weeks, strain the oil through cheesecloth to remove the herb matter. Love oil should be stored in a cool, dark place.

Dab a small amount of the oil on the nape of your neck and on your wrists whenever you go out on a date or to a place where you are liable to encounter a love interest. Cinnamon is a hot herb that nurtures sexual arousal. Rosemary fortifies the myne, the part of the Self that holds memories and emotions. Together the essences of these herbs will make you more memorable, in a romantic way. Use only a very little, though—the scent should not be obvious or distracting.

Some people find that cinnamon can irritate their skin, so test a very small amount of love oil on the inside of your arm before putting much on. This is rarely a problem when using a cold oil infusion.

Bringing It All Together

Before you look for love, always be sure you know exactly what it is you are looking for. Know your needs. Also know your wants, and understand how these differ from your needs.

As with any other work, you can combine techniques as you please. Let us consider how we can work with different techniques to help somebody find love. In practice this "somebody" could be you or someone you know.

Our hypothetical somebody will be a man we will call Bob. He is in his late twenties and is looking for a long-term relationship. Bob is a heterosexual male. He teaches high school English. In his spare time, he enjoys oil painting and reading. He has a French bulldog.

The first thing we are going to do is define Bob's needs. We want him to be aware of these so he does not waste time pursuing doomed relationships. First, we know that he needs a woman. Sexual orientation is almost always a need rather than a want! Bob is heterosexual, so another man is not an acceptable option. Even people who identify as bisexual usually lean one way or another; this should be considered a need for a long-term relationship.

Bob has no intention of giving up his French bulldog, so "must like dogs" is also a need. And he wants to be a father someday. This, too, is non-negotiable.

He has a preference for redheads, however, he recognizes that the color of a woman's hair is not necessary for his long-term happiness. This is a want, but he is leaving himself open to any woman who can fulfill his true needs. He would also like a woman who shares his interest in painting, but this is another want.

To ensure the greatest chance of success, we should encourage Bob to get involved with groups of people who share interests similar to his own. He might consider joining a book club, since he is an English teacher and enjoys reading. He could also join a breed-specific French bulldog club, if there is one in his area, or perhaps a dog obedience club. Because of his oil painting hobby, Bob could sign up for art classes or join an art club.

Bob is in reasonably good health. He is not an athlete, but he is not overweight or in bad shape. We are not going to worry about improving his physical appearance.

We will use wortcunning primarily, but to help things along, we can make him a runic charm. We will use *gyfu*, *gear*, and *ethel* to make a runic statement, "the gift brings the harvest of the home." What Bob has to offer, his gift or worth, will be rewarded with a family. We will carefully mark the runes, in red, on card-stock and have Bob carry this in his wallet. It is a finite charm, intended to create one specific effect, so we want Bob to be able to dispose of it readily after it has served its purpose.

Equipped with his runic charm, Bob will now begin brewing a love potion each month. On the night the moon enters the first quarter, and for six nights after that, he will brew a cup of the potion and sip it at nine o'clock in the evening. At the end of each seven-night session, Bob will go out someplace where he can meet with other people. If possible this will be with his dog club, or his art class, or his book club. If not, he will go out to a club or bar. He will continue this practice until he finds the woman who can fulfill his needs, and whose needs he can fulfill in return.

Because marriage is Bob's goal, Bob will burn the runic charm to dispose of it after his wedding day.

Review

1. Why is coercive love magic ultimately ineffective?
2. When is it appropriate to use the rune *gyfu* in a love charm?
3. What influence does the rune *æsc* contribute to a love charm? Can you think of a situation where this rune has no purpose in a love charm?

4. Why is Friday before the hour of sunset often the best time to set up infusions of love oil? In what circumstance is it *not* an especially auspicious time to set up a love oil infusion?

5. What purpose does rosemary serve in an infused love oil?

Rags to Riches:
Prosperity Magic

Those of us who live in America in the twenty-first century are extremely fortunate. The overwhelming majority of us live better than any other people at any other time in history. We do not worry whether we will have anything to eat tomorrow, or the next day, or the following winter. Most of us own some form of transportation, a luxury achieved only by the aristocracy in many earlier societies. We have clothing, warm shelter, and entertainment. We enjoy a level of comfort that medieval barons could only dream of. Compared to the people of almost any other era, the majority of us are, in a word, rich.

Nevertheless, most of us also want more. Or at least we claim to want more. There is rarely much passion behind our words. Prosperity is just not all that sexy and, because of this, prosperity magic can be more difficult than love magic. Love can become almost an obsession. Few people feel the same depth of passion for money that they feel for romantic companionship.

The secret to prosperity is really not a secret at all. Wealthy people know that hard work by itself is not the path to success. Those who have started at the bottom and climbed to the top are very open about their "secrets." I was fortunate in the late 1970s to come into the employment of Mr. and Mrs. Robert Waid. Forty years earlier, the Waids had been struggling through the Great Depression. Determined to build a better life for themselves and their children, they mortgaged everything they owned and opened a small restaurant in Kansas City. Eventually, nurtured with a lot of work and dedication, Waid's Restaurant grew into a small chain. When I began working for the Waids in 1977, they had recently sold their restaurant chain and were millionaires. Mr. Waid never bragged about his money, but you could hear the pride in his voice whenever he talked about other men whom he had helped rise to success. He took me under his wing and shared many of his secrets with me. Mr. Waid would give me books to read and albums to listen to, and he would interrogate me to make sure I was reading and listening, and none of this was anywhere in my job description. I resented the extra work a little until I realized where he was going with it. Both he and his wife were always available to counsel and advise me, not only for work-related issues, but also in my personal life.

None of the secrets they shared with me were new, novel, or covert in any way. The secrets to prosperity have been public knowledge for a long time. In the 1930s, a man named Napoleon Hill wrote a book called *Think and Grow Rich* that outlines these secrets in a clear and concise sequence. The book is still in print, is listed in this book's bibliography, and is a volume you should purchase and read if personal prosperity is high on your list of priorities.

For most people, though, prosperity is not very high on that list, and this is itself one of the secrets that has been shared openly with the public for countless years. You need to develop a deep and sincere desire for prosperity if you hope to achieve it. Desire alone is not enough, of course; you cannot just wish for wealth and have it fall into your lap. But without desire, your efforts will be halfhearted and unfulfilled.

Most people do not really understand what prosperity is. They confuse the physical form of money with the essence of prosperity. Coins and bills and checks are not prosperity, they are merely the symbols representing this concept. The secret of prosperity, the nature of its essence, is the mystery embodied in the *feoh* rune.

Feoh means "cattle" but, in early English society, cattle were a measure of a family's wealth, so much so that *feoh* also means "money." There are more than twenty Old English words with *feoh* as their root that refer to some sort of financial concept. By contrast, there are only three or four words with *feoh* as their root that refer specifically to cattle. The Rune Poem tells us this:

Each man shall greatly share his (cattle)
if he will be awarded honors from his lord.

Cattle must be shared if they are to have value. Modern cattle are specialized as beef or dairy breeds, but the cattle of the Anglo-Saxons were multi-purpose. These cattle were shared or exchanged as a means of building prosperity. A bull was shared when put to stud on someone else's cow. The resulting calf was shared when sold. A young heifer might have been kept for milk, but some were slaughtered for beef. Young males were either sold and slaughtered for beef, or castrated and trained as draft animals. Only a lucky few males were left as intact bulls. All of this sharing and exchanging created wealth for the community. Cattle provided beef, milk, butter, cheese, leather, horn, and manure. When shared and nurtured, cattle were a primary source of prosperity.

Superficially, prosperity seems like a very different concept now, but the most significant change is in our own perception. Today we may count dollars and cents instead of cattle, but the basic principles of prosperity remain the same. Cattle standing idly in a field were not prosperity. It was their productivity that generated wealth. Likewise, today, all of our paper and coins and electronic transfers are merely symbols of productivity. Some exchange must go on to build prosperity.

Money is an abstract concept with little meaning in itself. We can and should continue to use monetary symbols, but they must be used with precision. Here is where many traditional money spells fall apart. There is no use in working magic for "more money," because the expression has no substance. As soon as you pick a penny up from the sidewalk you have "more money" than you did a moment before. "A lot of money" is no less vague. How much is a lot? Ten dollars is a lot of money compared to a nickel.

To work prosperity magic and achieve any degree of success, you must define a precise goal. This goal can be expressed however you desire so long as it is not vague or subjective in any way. Having an income of X dollars per year is a specific goal. Having "enough money to be comfortable" is not.

Your goal also has to be believable. If you do not believe it can be achieved, any magic you attempt is almost guaranteed to fail. If you are working the magic for someone else, your subject must fully believe he or she can reach the stated goal. If your ultimate goal is not believable, you can often change this by breaking it down into parts. Working prosperity magic can be much like climbing a flight of stairs—leaping to the top may be impossible, but taking each step one at a time is fairly easy.

As an example, let us imagine a woman who has a talent for art. It does not matter what kind of art. She has decided that her goal is to become a professional artist earning X dollars or more each year from the sale of her work. (I am saying "X dollars" because the real value of money fluctuates constantly. If I were to give a dollar amount, no matter what the figure, this book would be as outdated as the Jitterbug in just a few years.) Our hypothetical artist looks at this goal and realizes it is not believable. She can easily *imagine* herself with an income of X dollars from art sales, but it is a fantasy, not something she really believes in. She can, however, break this dream down into realistic portions. Her first goal could be to become a professional artist. To sell something. Anything. As she takes this step, she is not going to worry about the long-term goal. She can glance up at the top of the stair-case once in a while, but, understanding the secrets of prosperity magic, she will focus on the immediate step before her.

Her second step, after she has sold one or two pieces of art, might be to set up her own business. At this point, it will prob-ably be more of a hobby business. Our professional artist will not be quitting her day job. Again, her only concern is reaching the next goal. The goal is realistic. She can believe in it and achieve it.

By breaking down a larger goal into manageable steps in this way, you can create smaller goals leading toward prosperity. You do not need to be an entrepreneur to put these principles into ac-tion. Not everyone wants to go into business for himself or herself. The same concepts apply in a corporate setting. Set small, reason-able goals leading toward the larger picture. You are not likely to walk in from the street and immediately assume a high-level posi-tion in any company unless you have already held a similar posi-tion elsewhere. To get a senior position, you will need a plan con-sisting of a series of steps, each building on the last. Focus on the next step of your climb rather than worry about why you are not already at the top of the stairs.

Each step must be as precise and defined as your ultimate goal. It is not enough to say, "I want to be making more money six months from now than I am today." As I have said, "more money" is too vague a concept. Exactly how much more, and is that before or after taxes?

These steps—achieving small, believable goals over and over—reveal another secret of prosperity. The most successful prosper-ity magic involves repetition and persistence. Repetition builds the momentum of your magic. And persistence is an absolute necessity. You cannot turn away from your goal when you stumble. Be pre-pared for this, because you will indeed stumble somewhere along the way. Stumbling is part of the process. It is only a failure if you allow it to be.

Runes of Prosperity

The rúnwita will immediately think of *feoh* as a rune to use for prosperity magic. It is difficult to imagine a runic spell involving money that would not include this symbol. *Feoh* embodies the mystery of wealth, teaching us that the exchange of energy (work) and resources (goods) is the foundation of prosperity.

Another important prosperity rune is *gyfu*, the "gift" rune. It relates to *feoh* in that it further reveals the creative, constructive power built through an exchange of energy or resources. The Rune Poem tells us:

A gift from others is an honor and praise,
a help and of worth.

True prosperity is not measured by how much you own, but by how much you can afford to give. This is a subtle but important distinction. A miser is not prosperous, no matter how much he or she possesses. Charles Dickens showed us this in *A Christmas Carol*, where Ebenezer Scrooge lived as poorly as a pauper despite his resources. There can be no prosperity unless energy and resources are shared, and there can be no sharing without giving.

The place of *gyfu* in prosperity magic is more apparent when your goal includes a business partnership, but the fact is that almost every work relationship is a partnership in some way. If you can internalize this, you are much more likely to prosper in whatever job you apply yourself. Sadly, the mystery of *gyfu* goes unnoticed by many people today who only look for what they can get from their occupations and have little concern for what they might give. It does not matter how menial you think your occupation is, give it all you can. If you do not treat your work as important, then why should anyone else believe your work—and by extrapolation, your own worth—is important?

Sigel and *tir* are both useful as runes that can help guide you toward your goal. Although these are both runes of guidance, each has its own unique nature. *Sigel* is better if you are trying to achieve something other than what you already have. Once you have reached your goal, *tir* is more appropriate to help stay the course. Going back to our hypothetical example of the woman who wants to become a professional artist, *sigel* would be the rune to use as she begins her quest. Just as the sun—the Glory of Elves—travels across the heavens, *sigel* guides us from one point to another. After the artist achieves her dream, selling enough art-work to be self-sufficient and perhaps owning a gallery or online store, then *tir* becomes more useful in rune magic. *Tir* is stead-fast, keeping us focused on our destination. Our hypothetical art-ist is still on a journey, of course, but now she has reached a point where there is no question as to how she will arrive. There is little if any need to change course or alter plans. The artist has achieved her primary goal and now needs to simply stay on track.

Speaking of journeys, *rád* has its place in prosperity magic as a rune that can help you "move" your situation toward something more desirable. The Rune Poem tells of a journey to your hall, or home. It carries you to your destination. The Rune Poem further reminds us that the journey is "very fast for he who sits high on a mighty horse." The rune has a message: you will achieve your goal more quickly if you have an ally or allies. That ally could be another person (taking us back to the *gyfu* rune), or it could be something abstract, like education or a financial loan.

Wynn works well in prosperity charms because it teaches us that enough is sufficient enough. The *wynn* rune is interpreted as joy, but it has this meaning because it defines precisely what joy is. Our hypothetical artist may have dreams of selling her works for millions of dollars, but this is not realistic and, further, it is more than she needs to achieve success. *Wynn* will help keep you focused on true success. I recently spoke at length with a man who has a senior executive corporate position earning a healthy six-figure income. He is very close to achieving success and pros-perity because he knows, now, that he does not enjoy or want the stress of a senior executive position. His prosperity goal is to find a position with less stress that still provides an income sufficient to his needs. Or, to quote the Rune Poem, an income that will ensure he "knows little want." *Wynn* reminds us that more is not necessarily better.

Creating a Prosperity Cycle

Remember the secret of repetition and persistence? You can make a runic charm or cast a spell for a raise or for a new job at any time of year, but for long-term success, you should create a prosperity cycle. This is a series of spells intended to shape your wyrd in a way that will help draw prosperity and abundance to you. We are speaking of reasonable prosperity and abundance, not something unbelievable. It takes a lot of energy to achieve great wealth, and most of us are just not that devoted to the task, but neither should you accept chronic deprivation as your due.

For the early Anglo-Saxons, cattle and wealth were inextricably connected. They were aware of their dependence on the earth and its cycles. We are now more removed from this relationship, but our wealth is no less dependent on the earth. You may work at a computer keyboard each day, and the goods you purchase—your food, your clothing, your car, and your home—may be raised, built, and packaged by people you have never known, but the raw materials ultimately come from the earth. For this reason—to harness that primal flow of energy—Saxon sorcerers plan their prosperity cycles in harmony with earth's seasonal cycles.

I have had good results timing prosperity rituals with Ewemeolc (early February), May Day (May 1), Lammas (early August), and Hallows (late October or early November). This sets up a plan for a prosperity spell every three months, which is enough time to let your work mature before you follow it with another spell. These four seasonal workings present one annual prosperity cycle.

Ewemeolc, in early February, is the time for planning. It is a seasonal holiday originally observed when the new spring lambs were born, but is now usually celebrated on February 1 or 2. The Saxons called this month Solmonath, because it was the month when sol-cakes were offered to the earth. *Sol* is Old English for "mud," and the cakes, which were likely more similar to coarse breads, were ploughed into the barren, muddy fields as offerings.

For your prosperity cycle, this is the time to define a reasonable and believable goal for the coming year. Do not grasp for something beyond your reach. You may ultimately see gains beyond your defined goal, but the goal itself is something you will be committing yourself to. Using runes, herbs, and galdor, design a prosperity spell to bring this defined goal into your life. Remember that you are creating an exchange of some kind. Define not only what you envision receiving, but also what you intend to give.

May Day celebrates the beginning of summer. By now you have planted the seeds of prosperity and should be seeing some result, however minor. The first of May is a time to assess your progress. What if you have already achieved your annual goal? That is great! It is still early enough in the year to put in a second "crop," so move on to the next step. Commit yourself to a new goal.

It is more likely that you have some way to go before achieving your annual goal. Repeat the spell you worked at Ewemeolc. This is the repetition you need. You are continuing to build momentum.

The next phase in your prosperity cycle will come at Lammas. Like Ewemeolc, this is a seasonal holiday. Lammas celebrates not the first grain harvest, which would come in June, but the first bread. It was observed in early August after the grain had been cut, sheaved, dried, threshed, and ground into flour. The ninth-century Anglo-Saxon Chronicle called this holy tide "the feast of first fruits."

Again you should assess your progress, but by now your own first fruits in your cycle of prosperity should be evident. You have only three more months to attain the goal that you set for yourself at Ewemeolc. If there is any question about this, ask yourself why. Have you followed all of the principles given here? Was your goal both specific and realistic? Have you nurtured a strong desire to achieve that goal? Are you giving all you can to create the necessary exchange of energy? What must you still do to attain success in this year's cycle?

If everything is going well and you can see reasonable progress toward your goal, this is a time to give thanks. An offering to your gods is appropriate. Or you might thank someone who has helped you get as far as you have come, whether this is an employer, a co-worker, or a friend. If you are married or partnered, thank your spouse also. Expressing gratitude is an important part of your prosperity cycle. By expressing gratitude, you are investing energy into the cycle again.

Hallows is your final harvest. By this time, if not before, you should have attained your goal. If you did not meet your goal by the end of October, make no excuses. Acknowledge this, and learn from the experience as well as you can.

Now the cycle is complete. Even if you did not meet your goal, give thanks for any progress you did achieve, no matter how small. This is the time of year to preserve what you have reaped. Your prosperity spell should have a thankful tone, but this time it should reaffirm the magic you have worked and ensure that your gains are stable and secure.

For the next three months you have no new goal to achieve. Your task now is to become accustomed to the step you have taken and to consider what goal you will set for yourself the following Ewemeolc.

Desire, repetition, and persistence are your keys to success with prosperity magic.

Bringing It All Together

Our artist friend is a Saxon wyrdworker, and she is going to create a cycle of prosperity to lead toward her ultimate goal. Let us see how she might approach this.

For some time now she has dreamed of quitting her job and earning a living with her paintings. In her imagination, she can see herself sipping champagne as her latest collection of paintings is unveiled to an admiring crowd of wealthy art patrons. It is a lovely vision, but the first thing she does is pull her head out of the clouds and look at her dream realistically. She knows that she can live comfortably enough if her art will bring her X dollars a year. That cannot be her goal for the coming cycle of prosperity, though. No matter how vivid her imagination, she knows in her heart that it is not going to happen. The goal is not believable. What she can believe in, though, is the idea of selling a painting during the coming year. That is going to be her goal.

On the first or second night of February, she plans a spell involving a small charm that she will keep with her until she achieves her goal. She gathers a few things: some red cloth and thread, a needle, a red candle, a small holder for the candle, a few small amber beads, and three camel hair artist's brushes. She also sets out an incense burner and a floral incense. All of these are placed on her myse.

Our artist first offers a prayer and burns a little incense to honor the goddess Fréo. She does not need to do this, but Fréo is sovereign over both beauty and wealth, and our artist has given offerings to this goddess in the past. She is not asking for Fréo to work a miracle for her; the work will be her own effort, but she would like the blessing and support of the goddess.

Fréo's brother, the god Ing, can also be responsive to prayers while working prosperity magic. Ing is called Fégjafa, meaning the Wealth-Giver, in the *Prose Edda*. But the blessings of these deities, or any others, should only be sought if you already have a relationship with them. If you have never given them honor pre-viously, do not expect them to honor your request. It is possible they might, but rather unlikely.

After giving her prayer and offering of incense to Fréo, our art-ist lights the red candle. She meditates for a few minutes, defining in her mind what she hopes to achieve during the coming cycle of prosperity. Her commitment is to sell one painting. This she can do. She reminds herself that it does not matter, now, how much the painting sells for. It does not matter, now, if she sells no more than one. A single sale will be a success.

Now she takes the cloth and thread and begins to sew a small pouch. As she sews, she recites this galdor over and over:

Colors cultured cast on canvas
Craft a calling for my own
Kernels gold and candle bold
My work be true, my work be known.

The kernels gold are the small amber beads. Amber attracts pros-perity; they are the tears of Fréo. The artist places these beads in the pouch. Then she breaks off the handles from the three artist's brushes and puts the small heads of the brushes in the pouch with the amber beads. Here she is calling on the Laws of Contagion and Sympathy. The bristles will lay next to the amber beads, acquiring their power of attracting prosperity through the Law of Contagion. This power will in turn be transferred, through the Law of Sympathy, to the brushes our artist actually uses in her paintings.

With this first spell, the artist has set her prosperity cycle in motion. Now she needs to give it something to affect. There are many things she could do at this point. She might enroll in an art class to improve and explore her painting techniques. If she has a few works that she is proud of, she could look into setting up a website offering prints for sale. She could also search for inexpen-sive venues, such as sidewalk art festivals, where she can try to sell her work.

Three months pass and the artist has not sold anything, but she has made a few friends in the local art community. She is still carrying her charm bag. Now, for May Day, she wants to engage the repetitive process by making another charm. This time she will use runes.

The artist recognizes that the galdor she designed three months earlier alliterates a "k" sound. This is the phonetic value of the *cen* rune, which evokes the flame of inspiration. Looking at the passage from the Rune Poem, our artist decides that *cen* aptly describes the inspiration behind her painting.

To this she adds the runes *sigel*, for guidance, and *feoh*, for the obvious reason of attracting prosperity. These three runes will be marked in that order, presenting a linear statement to say "my inspiration shall be guided toward material compensation." This will not be a permanent charm. She intends it to have a finite effect, to help her make the one sale she needs to complete her prosperity commitment. For this reason she decides to paint the runes, in red, on a small, flat piece of wood that she can burn after the charm has taken effect. She drills or punches a hole in one end of the wood so it can be tied to her charm bag.

She rewords her galdor slightly this time, as there are no "kernels gold" in this new work. Most of the galdor remains the same. In particular, she retains the first two lines because they carry the alliterated "k" sound of the *cen* rune. Now as she paints the runes, she chants:

Colors cultured cast on canvas
Craft a calling for my own
Runes inspire my heart's desire
My work be true, my work be known.

Our artist has no reason for concern, as this is only May Day. But she assesses her progress and how it might improve. She has been looking into artists' venues, and has become more aware of the fact that supply and demand are working against her. Selling an original painting can be difficult. She begins to imagine alternative ways to market her work. She has registered as a vendor at a sidewalk art fair, however, and she will wait and see if she has any success there. To help things along she will brew a prosperity infusion with crushed dill seeds. At the art fair, she will sprinkle the infusion on the sidewalk around her displayed paintings.

There is no way to say what will happen next, but we can be reasonably sure our artist will make her first sale before Hallows. She may go much further than that, which would be wonderful, but the cycle of prosperity has worked as soon as she reaches her goal of selling one piece of art. At that point, depending on the time of year, she could set a new goal or begin to make plans for the next cycle. Step by step, she will make her way toward her dream.

Desire, repetition, and persistence.

———————

Over the years I have worked with other sorcerers using this prosperity cycle. It can be done as either a solitary or group working. I once went through this cycle with a woman who was dissatisfied with her career. She wanted to find a successful position in the field of alternative healing. We used the principles I have given here and worked our spells at Ewemeolc, May Day, and Lammas. That was as far as we could go with it together. By the end of the summer, my friend had been offered a position in another state. I was sorry to see her go, but happy to know she had found—had created—her heart's desire.

Review

1. What important quality do you need to work effective prosperity spells?

2. How does the mystery of the *gyfu* rune apply to prosperity magic?

3. What is the best time of year to begin a cycle of prosperity spells? Why?

4. Why are expressions of gratitude important for prosperity work?

5. What two Anglo-Saxon deities are particularly associated with wealth and prosperity?

Conclusion:
The Druid and the Witch

In pre-Christian England, there were two categories of wyrdworking: wiccecræft and drýcræft. A witch—in Old English, a *wicca* or *wicce*—was simply a wyrdworker, any person skilled in shaping the forces of wyrd. The witch's reputation and fortune depended largely on luck. As long as things were going well, the witch might enjoy the appreciation and admiration of his or her neighbors; however, a drought, the death of a child, or even something trivial like a broken heart could place the witch in a precarious position.

The Saxon druid (*drýmann* or *drýicge*) had a higher status, and thus more security. These people could be thought of as "professional witches." The druid served his or her community under the patronage of a local *thegn*, or even under the king himself. Beyond this, the primary difference between drýcræft and wiccecræft appears to have been the level of training. The witch may have known no more than a few simple spells and a bit of herb lore, whereas the druid probably served an internship to learn the skills necessary to his or her profession. We can surmise that the Saxon druids bore some resemblance to Celtic druids, as the Old English word *drýmann* is cognate with the Brythonic *drouiz*, the

Manx *druaightagh,* and the Irish *drui.* Serving largely illiterate communities, the Saxon druids were teachers and historians, as well as sorcerers.

For the Saxon sorcerer today, the key difference between a witch and a druid is that the latter serves his or her community and is recognized for this service. In other words, "druid" is a functional title. If you serve no community, you may indeed be a skilled witch, but you are not a Saxon druid.

Service alone is not enough. I do not believe a title like this is something you should assume for yourself. It should be given to you by others in recognition of the work you have done. It is a reputation, not a crown. If you assume the title of druid, you then need to defend that title, which can be an awkward burden. The acknowledgement should come from someone else. It might be a mentor who names you *drýmann* or *drýicge* in recognition of your skill. Or if you are self-taught, it might be your fellow híredmenn, the folk of your extended family or tribe, who acknowledge your ability. When others acknowledge you as a druid, you do not need to defend the title yourself.

Here I am talking about traditional Saxon druids. There are some Neo-Pagan religious organizations today—Ár nDraíocht Féin (ADF), for example—in which all members are referred to as "druids." Within these organizations it is understood that all of the members are not necessarily accomplished as sorcerers, although some members may be. And within organizations such as this, the word is not being used as a title that might be challenged. For ADF members, being a druid simply means that you are an ADF member, nothing more or less.

Outside of these organizations, however, I believe you should only describe yourself as a druid if you have been acknowledged as such by your community. Even then the title has authority only as far as others choose to recognize it. You may not even want this acknowledgement and responsibility. You may be entirely content shaping your own wyrd, and possibly the wyrd of your immediate family members, and going no further than that. You may be content as a witch with no druidic aspirations at all, but whether witch or druid, you will undoubtedly develop a personal style of sorcery suited to your own interests and talents. Now that you have read about various Saxon cræftes, you may already have an idea of how your own style will unfold.

The Rúnwita

The path of the rune sorcerer requires study and meditation. You will need to master all twenty-nine runes described in the Anglo-Saxon Rune Poem. You may also be interested in studying the other four runes—*calc, gár, cweorth,* and *stán*—but this is your personal choice. You should be able to give a basic interpretation of each rune without glancing at a book.

You may be, and should be, accomplished in the art of runic wiglere, but a true rúnwita is also skilled with active rune magic. Some basic equipment you will want to acquire includes:

- a set of divinatory runes; you can begin with the Elder Futhark, but eventually you should have a complete set of all twenty-nine (or thirty-three) runes of the Futhorc
- solid material for crafting runic charms—this can be wood, bone, or antler, or an assortment of all these
- a tool for carving or engraving runes into the aforementioned material; a wood burner works best for wood, while a rotary drill is good for bone or antler
- red paint or dye for coloring the runes
- cardstock (or paper) and red marking pens to make quick, finite charms

Rúncræft combines very well with both wiglere and galdor. Studying either of these skills will improve your rune work.

Although these arts are not especially dangerous, I believe it is always better to err on the side of caution, and so I recommend the aspiring rúnwita wear or carry a protective runic charm. This can be as simple as the *eolh* rune, or it may be a more elaborate series of runes or even a bindrune.

The Galdre

At first glance, the skill of galdor might seem one of the easiest paths to take. No equipment is required, and the sorcerer does not need to study Rune Poems or herbs to master his or her cræft. But the path of the galdre, the wyrdworker who uses song and chants, can be more challenging than any other. For this reason, it is most often used in conjunction with some other cræft. It can be difficult to shape wyrd using only your voice unless you have a special talent for this.

If you are drawn to galdor as your primary style of wyrdworking, you probably have a better than average vocal talent. You may be a *scop* (pronounced "shope"), an entertainer, either by profession or as a hobby. You do not need much equipment to pursue this discipline, but you will want to have incantations for a variety of needs. In fact, you may want to keep a galdorbóc, or book of incantations, to collect all of your chants in one place.

The sorcerer who primarily uses runes or worts will usually chant as he or she works, but sorcerers who focus on galdorcræft are just as likely to use song. Giving tunes to your lyrics can endow them with greater power. The tunes need not be original, and you can recycle your favorites over and over if you wish. The contemporary Pagan community has a history of filking songs (giving new lyrics to traditional tunes) in this way.

As an alternative style, you can recite your galdor as a poem or prose while playing a musical background accompaniment on a guitar or dulcimer. This may work better if singing makes you feel self-conscious, but it requires some ability with a musical instrument.

The Wyrtwíta

Requiring as much study as rúncræft, wortcunning also demands more in equipment and supplies than any other discipline. Nevertheless, many sorcerers are attracted to the magic inherent in herbs and roots. You should know the uses of (and have on hand) a variety of herbs. Consider planting your own witch's garden.

Healing magic comes almost naturally to wyrtwitan, but a sorcerer skilled with wortcunning should have a wider range than just healing. Some of the basic materials you will need include:

- a couple of books devoted specifically to herbology, at least one of these outlining magic uses for herbs
- a mortar and pestle
- a cauldron or pot for heating water
- strainers (teaballs and cheesecloth)
- an assortment of wide-mouthed jars
- a double boiler for making ointments
- a good variety of herbs with a range of magical properties
- red cloth, thread, and needles for sewing herb pouches
- vodka and/or mead for making tincture potions
- petroleum jelly for making ointments
- cold-pressed almond oil for cold infused oils

As the Old English charms indicate, wortcunning combines very well with galdor. This is a good secondary skill to develop. A set of chants to use while brewing your potions will enhance your work.

You might want to sew several protective herbs in a pouch and carry this as a charm. Or brew a protective infusion that can be sprinkled in your immediate vicinity should you feel threatened in any way.

The Wiglere

Although the focus of this book has been on active magic, with wiglere (divination) as only a tool for guidance, there are some people who find they have an exceptional talent for soothsaying. If this is your strength, then it makes sense that you develop it to the best of your ability. However, do not assume you are destined to be a wiglere just because you have had some visions or insights; such a talent is not unusual among sorcerers. Explore some active magic skills and see if your repertoire is wider than you imagine at first.

If not, then hone your skill as a wiglere. Learn different methods for approaching this art. A good wiglere may have a talent for seething, but it is nice to have runes or a set of wyrd stones as a backup system for when you have hiked all over the Seven Worlds without getting your answer.

The equipment or tools you use will depend on what methods you develop for your own practice of wiglung. Some things to consider:

- a set of divinatory runes, preferably including all twenty-nine runes of the Futhorc
- a set of wyrd stones
- a staff and cloak (or cloth) for seething
- a large, clear crystal or a scrying mirror

There are possibilities not mentioned here because they are based on non-Saxon concepts. Tarot, which developed from Pythagorean mathematics, is one such system. Astrology, based on southern Mediterranean constellations, is another. This does not mean they are in any way inferior for divination, only that they are beyond the scope of this book.

A protective charm of some kind is especially useful for the wiglere who practices extensive seething or scrying. The charm can be herbal or runic in nature, or the wiglere may choose to carry a small thunderstone (quartz crystal). These crystals are sacred to Thunor and are infused with his protective force. It was once believed that they were delivered into the earth when lightning struck.

––––––

I advise focusing on one or, at most, two of the modalities we have discussed. You have undoubtedly heard the expression "jack of all trades, master of none." You are unlikely to become very good at any of these disciplines if you try to work with all of them at the same time. You can always branch out later after you have mastered your first skill.

Conversely, it helps if you know at least a little about these various disciplines. What I am suggesting is that you become both the jack of all trades *and* a master of one or two skills. At least a passing familiarity with all of these arts will enhance your work as you follow the path of a Saxon sorcerer.

The Runes—
Their Names, Meanings,
and Phonetic Values

ᚠ	*feoh*	cattle	f, fife
ᚢ	*ur*	aurochs	o͞o, boot (long) oo, took (short)
ᚦ	*thorn*	hawthorn	th, thin *th*, them
ᛟ	*os*	a god	ō, coat (long) ŏ, pot (short)
ᚱ	*rád*	ride	r, roar
ᚲ	*cen*	pine	k, kick ch, cheat
ᚷ	*gyfu*	gift	g, gag
ᚹ	*wynn*	joy	w, with
ᚻ	*hagol*	hail	h, hat
ᚾ	*nied*	need	n, no
ᛁ	*is*	ice	ē, bee (long) ĭ, pit (short)

ᛄ	*gear*	harvest	y, yes (consonant)
ᛇ	*éoh*	yew	ī, as in pine
ᛈ	*peorth*	gaming	p, pop
ᛉ	*eolh*	elk-sedge	z, zebra (z to begin or end a word)
ᛋ	*sigil*	sun	s, sauce z, brazen (z mid-word)
ᛏ	*tir*	north star	t, tight
ᛒ	*beorc*	birch	b, bib
ᛖ	*eh*	horse	ĕ, pet (short) ā, paid (long)
ᛗ	*mann*	man	m, mum
ᛚ	*lagu*	sea, water	l, lid
ᛝ	*ing*	lord Ing	ng, thing
ᛞ	*dæg*	day	d, deed
ᛟ	*ethel*	home	o͞e, noise (diphthong)
ᚪ	*ác*	oak	ä, father
ᚫ	*æsc*	ash	ă, pat
ᚣ	*yr*	bow	œ, burger minus the *r* (y as a vowel)
ᛡ	*ior*	beaver	e͞o, Creole (diphthong)
ᛠ	*ear*	land, ground	ā ŭ, ay-uh (diphthong)
ᛣ	*calc*	chalk	k, kick
ᚸ	*gár*	spear	g, game
ᛢ	*cweorth*	(unknown)	kw, quote
ᛥ	*stán*	stone	st, sting

Appendix B

Wyrdstones— Their Names and Meanings

ᛉ	man	The presence or influence of an adult male
ᛘ	woman	The presence or influence of an adult woman
ᛞ	love	Harmony, balance
ᛤ	family	The family or tribe; alternately, a child of either sex
ᛉ	war	Conflict, struggle
△	home	Traditions, the homestead
ᚼ	disorder	A state of confusion
⊙	money	Career, monetary gain
⊥	disruption	Interruption of plans
‹	fire	Emphasizes the importance of nearby stones
ᚦ	joy	Contentment, comfort
✕	gift	An unexpected boon

ᛟ	possessions	Growth, acquisition
ᛇ	transformation	Change

Appendix C

How to Write with Runes

Writing with runes is both complicated and simple. It is complicated because Old English may be old, but it is nevertheless English, and is as insane as our modern variation when it comes to spelling and pronunciation. At the same time, it is simple because there were so few standardized rules when the Futhorc runes were used for writing. It is difficult to really get it "wrong" very often.

The most important principle to keep in mind is that you are writing phonetically. Consider the sound you are making, not the exact letter from the Roman alphabet. For example, if you were to write *east* it is tempting to write *eh, ác, sigel, tir*, substituting runes for letters of the alphabet. But *ea* is always a diphthong in Old English, sounding something like "ay-ah." The *is* rune would be a better vowel choice, and *stán*—giving the "st" sound—would be a more economical way to end the word.

Vowels

As in Modern English, most of the runic vowels have both long and short forms. The difference in pronunciation is more akin to regional dialects; they do not render the writing indecipherable. Consider the modern word *been*. Some people pronounce this with a long *e*, and others pronounce it as a short *i*, but we all understand what is said. The following vowel sounds are arranged in Modern English alphabetical order.

ᚪ The *æsc* rune makes an *a* sound as in *ash* or *track*.

ᚫ As a long vowel, *ác* makes the sound of *a* (ah) as in *father*. The short vowel sounds like the *u* (uh) as in *buddy*.

ᛖ The long vowel *eh* is our modern English long *a*, as in *gate*. As a short vowel, this gives the modern English short *e* (eh), as in *bed*.

ᚣ The exact pronunciation of this rune is debatable, but it has been postulated that it represents an "ah-ee" sound, as in *pie* or *try*.

ᛁ *Is* gives a long vowel sound like the modern English long *e*, as in *feed*. The short vowel is like a modern short *i*, as in *fit*.

ᚩ The long vowel sound of *os* is like the modern English long *o*, as in *coat*. The short vowel is like the modern short *o*, as in *pot* or *cot*.

ᛟ I have given the phonetic value for *ethel* elsewhere as "oh-ee," as in *noise* or *boy*, however I am not entirely convinced this is correct. I have seen this and no other alternative given in many sources. The reason I question the phonetic value is because it is rarely found anywhere in Old English literature. It seems odd to me that a diphthong worthy of its own rune would have disappeared almost entirely from the language when the Roman alphabet was adopted. I personally believe this was a variant of the consonantal "th." After the adoption of a Roman alphabet, Old English script retained several unique symbols, including one known as *eth*, which gave a "th" sound and was written as Ð (capitalized) and ð (small form).

ᚢ As a long vowel, *ur* makes the "ooh" sound we hear in *food*. As a short vowel, it becomes the sound we hear in *took*.

ᚣ *Yr* does not have any equivalent sound in Modern English. It most closely resembles the "eu" sound in some French words. I have heard it described as sounding like the first vowel in the word *burger* if you drop the *r*. You will not be using this rune for writing unless transcribing Old English words like *fyrn* (meaning ancient) or *myne* (that part of the Self that includes memories and emotions).

ᛡ The *ior* rune is a diphthong pronounced as a Modern English long *e* gliding into a long *o* sound, as in *Creole*.

ᛠ This rune, *ear*, is pronounced as a Modern English long *a* gliding into an "uh" sound.

Consonants

Many of the consonants of the Futhorc are used and pronounced like their Modern English equivalents, but there are—as one might expect with any variant of English—numerous exceptions. These are arranged in Modern English alphabetical order. Any letters that are not discussed are obvious equivalents.

ᚠ In Old English, *feoh* was pronounced like the modern *f* when it came at the beginning or end of a word, and usually like the modern *v* in the middle of a word. Two *feoh* runes together in the middle of a word always make an "f" sound. Use *feoh* for "f," and double it when the sound comes in the middle of a word.

ᚸ Use the *gár* rune whenever you want a hard "g," as in *game*, *get*, or *girl*.

ᚻ *Hagol* is usually pronounced just as we pronounce the modern *h*. At the end of a word, and when doubled, this rune indicates the "ch" in the Scottish word *loch*. But unless you are going to write *loch*, you can pretty much ignore this. What you should not ignore is that *hagol* comes before *wynn* when making the sound we now indicate as *wh*. Just as it sounds. I have no idea why (pronounced "hwigh") or when (pronounced "hwen") we decided to reverse the letters in the spelling of the words.

ᚳᚷ or ᚳᚳ There is no letter *j* in the Futhorc. In the middle or end of a word use a *cen* followed by a *gyfu* to indicate a "j" sound. At the beginning of a word, use the double *cen*.

ᚲ Our modern letter *c* can indicate two sounds, "k" and "s." In the same way, the *cen* rune indicates two different phonetic sounds, in this case "k" and "ch." If it precedes an *eh*, or either precedes or follows an *is*, this rune usually makes a "ch" sound. If it precedes any other vowel or a consonant, it makes a "k" sound. Doubling the rune changes this to a "ch" regardless of the following consonant or vowel, as in Old English words like *wicca* (witch) and *feccan* (to fetch).

For the most part, you can substitute this rune for the letter *c*. In words like *china* and *children,* the rune by itself indicates the "ch" sound. If you want a "ch" in front of any vowel other than *e* or *i*—as in words like *charge* or *chore*—use a double *cen*.

ᛜ This single rune makes the sound we write as *ng*. Be careful when you use this rune. Although we write *finger* in Modern English, the *n* and *g* in the middle do not make a true "ng" sound. In *finger* the *g* is hard (fin-ger). For a word such as this, use *nied* and *gar*. Contrast the pronunciation with the word *singer*, where we do hear the clear "ng" sound (sing-er).

ᛢ *Cweorth* indicates a "kw" sound, which we now usually write as *qu*. There was no *q* in Old English. You can also indicate the "kw" by writing *cen* followed by *wynn*, but *cweorth* shortens the sound to a single rune, which can be a great time saver if you are carving an inscription into stone.

ᛋ At the beginning or end of a word, *sigel* makes a sound like the modern *s*. In the middle of a word it makes the sound of a voiced *z*. To make an *s* in the middle of a word such as *essay*, use a double *sigel*.

ᚻᚲ I should mention here that the "sh" sound is made with a *sigel* followed by *cen*. This combination of consonants can also very rarely indicate a "sk" sound. The "sk" sound is only found in Old English words related to foreign cultures, as in the word *Scottaland* (Scotland). There is no rule for the different phonetic values; they must be determined by the context of the writing.

ᚦ *Thorn* represents the sound "th." This combination of letters represents two sounds in Modern English, the voiced "th" in words like *thin* and the unvoiced "th" in words like *them*. The good news is that *thorn* is used in the same way. In the early English variety of the Roman alphabet, a script known as the Insular Hand, the "th" sound was indicated by two letters: þ (pronounced *thorn*) and ð (pronounced *eth*). The letter *thorn* is just a smoother, rounded version of the runic *thorn*, whereas *eth*, as I have mentioned, may be a version of the *ethel* rune. Both of these letters were used interchangeably, sometimes by the same scribe in the same document. I realize that does not make sense, but then when did English ever make much sense?

ᚠ There really is no rune that represents a true modern *v*. Use a single *feoh* when the *v* comes in the middle of the word. In Old English, the *v* sound is never found at the beginning of a word. Of course, if you are using runes to write in Modern English, this is a huge stumbling block when you come to words like *very, visit,* or *voice*. I handle this by using the *wynn* rune, which gives my runic writing a Slavic tone, like Ensign Chekov's dialect in the original *Star Trek* television series, but it is nevertheless understandable.

ᛟ *Gear* should always be followed with an *eh* or an *is*, and indicates a consonantal *y*. To create a *y* sound followed by any other vowel, use *gyfu* and *eh*, and then continue with your word. For example, the word *yard* would be written (using Roman letters) as *geard*, which is in fact exactly how the word was spelled by the earliest English scribes. Again, this will impose a distinct archaic dialect in your writing, but the runes were not intended to accommodate twenty-first-century speech.

ᛉ or ᛦ Use *eolh* when you want a *z* at the beginning or end of a word. *Z* sounds in the middle of a word are represented by a *sigil*.

————————

All of these rules may seem intimidating at first, but do not let them scare you. Nobody is going to laugh if you use the wrong vowel, or if you forget and use *tir* and *hagol* rather than a *thorn* to make a "th" sound. You want your runic writing to be comprehensible, but, beyond that, it does not matter much if you make a few mistakes. Very few of the early Saxons could read or write at all, and here you are writing with runes! Have fun, and be proud of your accomplishment.

Glossary

Æthem ("A-thum"): The breath of life that unites the nine parts of the Self.

Cræft: An art or skill. Often used as a suffix, as in drýcræft (druid's skill) or wiccecræft (witch's skill). The plural is *cræftes* ("CRAFT-es").

Drýcræft ("DRU-craft"): The skills of the Saxon druid.

Drýmann ("DRU-man"): A Saxon druid. The feminine form is *drýicge* ("DRU-ee-jeh"). The drýmann or drýicge is a sorcerer whose contributions to his or her community are recognized in some way.

Elf: A discarnate or disembodied spirit. This includes any pure spiritual being, including dwarves and ancestral spirits. In a more specific sense, *elf* refers to a nature spirit, or land wight.

Fetch: A part of the Self that might be thought of as one's guardian spirit. The fetch usually takes on the appearance of an animal.

Futhorc ("FOO-thork"): The English runes, thirty-three total, but only twenty-nine with extant lore describing their mysteries.

Galdor ("GALL-dor"): Sound or voice magic. Galdorcræft is the skill of singing or chanting to create magical effects.

Galdorbóc ("GALL-dor-boke"): A sorcerer's book of incantations.

Galdre ("GALL-dreh"): A sorcerer adept at working spells with galdor. Sometimes pronounced *galdere* ("GALL-deh-reh").

Hama ("HAHM-ah"): An astral part of your Self shielding you from hostile forces. The plural is *haman*. Also the name of the spirit who stands guard at the gates to the realm of the gods.

Hyge ("HU-yeh"): The part of your Self that thinks rationally and objectively. The plural is *hygas*.

Infusion: A drink prepared by steeping herbs in hot water, often for use as a potion.

Inhíred ("in-HEAR-ed"): A Saxon family or tribe. This is the term I use, but other words—mót, hearth, kindred, and so on—are sometimes used. The structure (or lack thereof) can vary greatly from one group to another. The Saxon tradition strongly encourages group participation. The plural is *inhírdas*.

Lic ("leech"): The physical part of the Self. Your body. The plural is *lices* ("LEECH-es").

Mare ("MAR-eh"): A spirit that harms or harasses people in their sleep. The plural is *maran*.

Mægen: A part of the Self that might be thought of as one's spiritual strength or fortitude. Pronounced like the word *Mayan*, the plural is *mægenes*.

Mead: A drink similar to wine, but made of honey.

Metheglin: A mead flavored or enhanced in some way with herbs, often for use as a potion.

Middle Earth: Our own world, the physical world. So-called because of its central location between the other worlds or planes of existence.

Mód ("mode"): A part of the Self that maintains one's self identity. This word evolved into the Modern English word *mood*, meaning a state of mind or emotion. The plural is *módes* ("MODE-es").

Myne ("MU-neh"): The part of the Self that includes our memories and emotions.

Myse ("MU-zeh"): The sorcerer's table or working surface.

Os ("ose"): A Saxon god or goddess.

Rúncræft ("ROON-craft"): The art or skill of using runes, particularly those of the Futhorc, for divination and magic.

Rúnwita ("ROON-wee-tah"): A sorcerer adept at rune magic.

Scop ("shope"): The Saxon equivalent of a bard. A person who entertains with songs or poetry.

Scry: To seek visions by gazing into a reflective or flickering focal point.

Seax ("SAY-ax"): Depending on your point of view, either a very large knife or a very small sword. The seax was the Saxon's personal weapon and general purpose tool. Because of the iron in the blade, a sorcerer will often make use of a dagger like this to disperse or redirect outside forces.

Seething: The art of entering an intentional trance state. From the Old English word *séoðan*, meaning "to prepare the mind."

Symbel: A feast. The Saxon symbel is often accompanied with oratory, boasts, and oathing.

Telga: A wand, used to project one's own power through the hama.

Tincture: An alcohol extraction, often for use as a potion. Metheglin is one example of a tincture.

Wéofod ("WAY-o-fode"): Literally, "the place where the image of deity stands." A spiritual altar, the wéofod can also serve as your myse, if you wish.

Wicca ("WEE-chah"): A Saxon witch. The feminine form is *wicce* ("WEE-cheh"). Unlike the druids, witches usually worked alone for the benefit of themselves and those closest to them. This does not mean their magic was any less positive than that of a druid. The plural is *wiccan* ("WEE-chan").

Wiccecræft ("WEE-cheh-craft"): The skills of the Saxon witch.

Wight: Any spirit, incarnate or discarnate, including Elves, gods, ghosts, animals, plants, and human beings.

Wiglere ("WEE-leh-reh"): A sorcerer adept at divination. A soothsayer.

Wiglung ("WEE-lung"): Augery or soothsaying. The arts of divination.

Willa: The part of your Self that motivates you. Your willpower. Determination and desire. The plural is *willan*.

Wód ("wode"): The part of your Self that inspires you. By itself, untamed, wód is madness. This is fury and frenzy, but it becomes a source of power when harnessed.

Wortcunning: Knowledge of herb lore, and the practice that ensues when this knowledge is put to use.

Wyrd ("weurd"): Often defined loosely as "fate," wyrd is the process in which the future unfolds. Since all things are connected, wyrd is sometimes viewed as a vast, infinite web expressing this connectivity.

Wyrtwita ("WEURT-wee-tah"): A sorcerer adept at herb magic.

Bibliography

Albertsson, Alaric. *Travels Through Middle Earth: The Path of a Saxon Pagan*. Woodbury, MN: Llewellyn, 2009.

Aswynn, Freya. *Leaves of Yggdrasil*. St. Paul, MN: Llewellyn, 1990.

Atwater, P. M. H. *Goddess Runes*. New York: Avon Books, 1996.

Bates, Brian. *The Way of Wyrd*. San Francisco: Harper and Row, 1983.

Beyerl, Paul. *The Master Book of Herbalism*. Custer, WA: Phoenix, 1984.

Blain, Jenny. *Nine Worlds of Seid-Magic: Ecstasy and Neo-Shamanism in Northern European Paganism*. London and New York: Routledge, 2002.

Bremness, Lesley. *The Complete Book of Herbs*. New York: Viking Studio Books, 1988.

Buckland, Raymond. *Practical Candleburning Rituals*. St. Paul, MN: Llewellyn, 1970.

Cooper, Jason D. *Using the Runes*. Wellingborough: Aquarian Press, 1987.

Cunningham, Scott. *Cunningham's Encyclopedia of Magical Herbs*. St. Paul, MN: Llewellyn, 1985.

Dugan, Ellen. *Herb Magic for Beginners: Down-to-Earth Enchantments*. Woodbury, MN: Llewellyn, 2006.

Flowers, Stephen. *The Galdrabók: An Icelandic Grimoire*. York Beach, ME: Samuel Weiser, 1989.

Fries, Jan. *Helrunar, A Manual of Rune Magick*. Oxford, UK: Mandrake of Oxford, 2002.

Griffiths, Bill. *Aspects of Anglo-Saxon Magic*. Norfolk, UK: Anglo-Saxon Books, 1996.

Gundarsson, Kveldulf. *Elves, Wights and Trolls*. New York: Avon Books, 1996.

———. *Teutonic Magic*. St. Paul, MN: Llewellyn, 1994.

Hill, Napoleon. *Think and Grow Rich*. New York: Ballantine Books, 1987.

Huebner, Louise. *Power Through Witchcraft*. New York: Bantam Books, 1971.

Hutton, Ronald. *The Pagan Religions of the Ancient British Isles: Their Nature and Legacy*. Malden, MA: Blackwell, 1991.

Koch, Rudolf. *The Book of Signs*. New York: Dover, 1955.

Ody, Penelope. *The Complete Medicinal Herbal*. New York: Dorling Kindersley, 1993.

Osborn, Marijane, and Stella Longland. *Rune Games*. London: Routledge & Kegan Paul, 1982.

Owen, Gale R. *Rites and Religions of the Anglo-Saxons*. London: David & Charles, 1981.

Paxson, Diana L. *Taking Up the Runes*. York Beach, ME: Weiser Books, 2005.

Pennick, Nigel. *Complete Illustrated Guide to Runes*. London: Harper Collins, 2002.

———. *Practical Magic in the Northern Tradition*. Leicestershire, UK: Thoth, 1989.

Rose, Jeanne. *Herbs & Things*. New York: Grosset & Dunlap, 1972.

Runic John. *The Book of Seiðr: The Native English and Northern European Shamanic Tradition*. Somerset: Capall Bann, 2004.

Simpson, Jacqueline, and Steve Roud. *A Dictionary of English Folklore*. Oxford, UK: Oxford University Press, 2000.

Thorsson, Edred. *At the Well of Wyrd: A Handbook of Runic Divination*. York Beach, ME: Samuel Weiser, 1988.

———. *Futhark: A Handbook of Rune Magic*. York Beach, ME: Samuel Weiser, 1984.

———. *Northern Magic: Rune Mysteries and Shamanism*. St. Paul, MN: Llewellyn, 1992.

———. *Runelore: A Handbook of Esoteric Runology*. York Beach, ME: Samuel Weiser, 1987.

Tyson, Donald. *Rune Magic*. St. Paul, MN: Llewellyn, 1988.

Willis, Tony. *The Runic Workbook*. Wellingborough, UK: Aquarian Press, 1986.

Index